S0-BSO-511

They Were
SAN FRANCISCANS

They Were
SAN FRANCISCANS

By

Miriam Allen deFord

ILLUSTRATED

Essay Index Reprint Series

BOOKS FOR LIBRARIES PRESS
FREEPORT, NEW YORK

INTERNATIONAL STANDARD BOOK NUMBER:

0-8369-1914-9

LIBRARY OF CONGRESS CATALOG CARD NUMBER:

70-117781

PRINTED IN THE UNITED STATES OF AMERICA

Table of Contents

List of Illustrations

They Were
SAN FRANCISCANS

Introduction

I T HAS BEEN said that if a traveler were taken
blindfolded into an airplane and let down in a
strange city anywhere in America, it would be impossible for him to say in what particular place he had
found himself.

But there are still a few American cities of which that
libel—or, if you prefer, that tribute to our standardiza-
tion — cannot be uttered. Certainly if our putative
traveler cast his blindfold aside at Times Square, he
could not doubt that he was in New York; or if on Pennsylvania Avenue that he was in Washington; or if on
Canal Street that he was in New Orleans. I think also
he might instantly recognize Boston from Tremont
Street, Chicago from Michigan Avenue, Baltimore from
Charles Street, or Honolulu from Fort Street.

And most of all, if his journey had ended at Powell
and Market Streets, he would be aware at once that he
must be in San Francisco. In the first place, the hill
before him would be so steep, and the air so brisk even
in summer, that he would know he could not have
alighted on the prairie. Then the flower stand on the
sidewalk, the wooden turntable on which the cable cars
were being pushed around to start their upward journey,

and finally, as he boarded one of those cable cars and journeyed upward, the view of the two great bridges, across the bay and across the Golden Gate, would tell him that by good luck he had landed in the city of St. Francis.

Cities are marked in two ways—by their topography, and by their population. The contour of San Francisco is dramatic and exciting—the beautiful landlocked bay, the score of steep hills, the isolation at the tip of a narrow peninsula with the Pacific Ocean washing its western shore. Its climate is stimulating, its air is electric, and the fog enmeshes its tall buildings in romance.

And the people of San Francisco are bred in a tradition of romance, of adventure, of a slightly synthetic glamour that has turned a legend into a myth. Here is the city that grew up overnight from the sleepy Spanish pueblo of Yerba Buena to the roaring metropolis of the argonauts of '49. Gold and the railroad and a mighty harbor —these were the trinity that made of San Francisco "The City" all up and down the Coast. Drab as modern life may be, one need only scratch the Rotary Club and the Chamber of Commerce to find beneath their skin the heady, highhanded, openhearted, and just a bit tipsy San Francisco of the '49ers.

Added to this tradition is the heterogeneous population attracted by a great seaport. Look at a newspaper story, from just before World War II, buried in the shipping news: "The south end of the Embarcadero looked like an international general store. There was leaf tobacco from Havana; olive oil, antipasto, rice, vermouth, and cuttlefish bones from Genoa, and one trunk from Port Said; mopheads, candy, shoe polish, slippers, codfish, and wine barrels from Boston and New York; and 350 cases of cashews from Colombo." The item is a parable. Here is the largest Chinatown of the Occident, next door to an Italian city of respectable size; here is every people of Europe, from Basque sheepherders on vacation to Russian Molokans who for nearly sixty years have led on Potrero Heights their austere, heretical lives: and all inextricably part of a great industrial metropolis, the banking center of the Pacific Coast—some of whose mightiest industrial figures were descended from Irish saloonkeepers who struck it rich in the Mother Lode or the Comstock. It is a city which still cherishes its pet lunatics; presents unabashed the hideous jigsaw architecture of the eighties next door to the streamlined functional architecture of tomorrow; builds engineering marvels to astonish the world and neglects to keep its streets clean; cheerfully squabbles over one of the worst traffic setups in the world and turns out *en masse* in whiskers and sombreros at the first opportunity for a popular fiesta.

Polyglot, impetuous, hedonistic; rich today and poor tomorrow; undaunted by fire or earthquake; easygoing, with a wink for corruption and a tolerance for the demands of labor until a hidden streak of violence brings sudden brutal suppression: Prince Hal hobnobbing with Falstaff, though with the dignity of kingship plainly in the offing—that was the San Francisco which drew the fascinated Bret Harte and Mark Twain, Stevenson and Kipling; and inherently it is the same San Francisco today. It has grown up, of course; the gayety has become less juvenile. The city has ended its long adolescence. Today it wears its vine leaves with a difference. But it has not forgotten its youth.

From such a city riches of biography may be mined. Many claims have already been staked out and filed upon. To give only a few modern instances, in one year there were three biographies of Ambrose Bierce. The "Big Four" of the Central (later Southern) Pacific Railroad have had their recent definitive biographer; W. C. Ralston, the pioneer banker, has had two. Even "Emperor Norton," prototype of San Francisco's darling eccentrics, has twice in a year been presented between covers. Many of San Francisco's great belonged to the world, and the world has written their stories. A few of them have been so important to humanity at large that no survey of our history could overlook mention of them. Others are known to every San Franciscan, perhaps to every Californian, but their names are unfamiliar elsewhere. Some of these deserve a wider acquaintance—they were authentic personalities, part of the juice and vigor of the American scene. They belong to history even though history has not acknowledged them.

And there are a few, to be discovered by the curious researcher, whose lives, though private, stand out from the herd. They too have earned recognition—perhaps only as lessons in the variability of our human stock, perhaps as memorable parts of the multicolored fabric that is San Francisco.

Not all my subjects, then, were famous; and not all of them were models of virtue and achievement. There is a place for the failure as well as for the success, for the delinquent (though none of them was exactly that) as well as for the moral example.

I have had two criteria only for inclusion of a man or woman among these biographical studies. First, he must have lived long enough in San Francisco to have been identified with it, to have been thought of as a San Franciscan. Robert Frost (to instance a living contemporary) was born in San Francisco, but he left it at the age of ten, and never returned; he could no more be thought of as a San Franciscan than Poe could be thought of as a Bostonian. Isadora Duncan was a native of San Francisco, too, and spent there and in Oakland all of her childhood and early girlhood; but the part of her life which makes her of public interest was all lived elsewhere. Many of the people in this book were adults before they ever saw the Golden Gate—that was inevitable with the '49ers. James Lick was middle-aged, almost elderly, when he came to San Francisco; but from that time on he was inextricably a part of the city, both before and after his death. And many of these people died far from "the City"—notably Henry George, who collapsed during his second campaign for the mayoralty of New York. But it was in San Francisco that he conceived the idea of the Single Tax, and wrote *Progress and Poverty*, without which he would no more have run for the office later adorned by Fiorello LaGuardia than would any other printer and minor editor. On the other hand, a few of these names— Lillie Hitchcock Coit, George Sterling, Fremont Older, for example — are so much a part of San Francisco (though no one of these was a native) that their whole lives might have been altered had chance sent them somewhere else in their most impressionable years.

For the sake of clarity, I have limited the word "San Franciscan" to mean exactly that. There is a metropolitan Bay Area, extending roughly from San Rafael or even Santa Rosa on the north, to Hayward on the east, and San Jose on the south, which has San Francisco as its focus, just as northern New Jersey and southern Connecticut depend on New York. Large cities like Oakland, Berkeley, and San Jose are included in it. These people read San Francisco newspapers, listen to San Francisco stations on the radio, though they have papers and radio stations of their own as well; and without derogation of their own status may be considered semisuburban. Every weekday scores of thousands of them pour into San Francisco for their daily work, returning at evening to their homes—unless they stay to see a movie that has not yet come to their neighborhood theaters. A similar situation in southern California has produced the sprawling phenomenon of metropolitan Los Angeles, a congeries of once independent towns. Around San Francisco, county lines, as well as an absence of the agglomerative spirit, have prevented this consolidation. If it had been effected, metropolitan San Francisco would still be almost the size of the city to the south. But in this book I have omitted even celebrated men and women who happened to be identified with, say, Oakland or Berkeley instead of with San Francisco proper (though a few of my subjects spent a small part of their years in one of these outlying cities).

That, for instance, is why there is no chapter on Jack London—that and the fact that two full biographies of Jack London have recently appeared.

For this same latter reason, that the public has only lately been presented with full information, I have omitted detailed consideration of such men as Bierce and Ralston. What I have tried to find are people about whom biographies have never been written, or whose biographies are old and out of date, untouched by the psychological interest which the modern reader has learned to look for. And I have, of course, treated only of persons who are dead, and whose feelings can no longer be hurt by a frank if friendly analysis of their personalities and careers.

My other criterion has been interest. The people, good or bad, famous or humble, who were *different* have been the ones I have hunted for and, I hope, found. I have not included any actual lunatics, of whom San Francisco has had its plentiful share, though a few of my subjects may be described as extreme eccentrics— as unusual people are likely to seem to their workaday neighbors. Dr. Louis Bisch tells us to be glad we're neurotic. It is the neurotics, the eccentrics, the centrifugal temperaments, that give color to life. In a city itself centrifugal and colorful, they have a better chance than elsewhere to leave their impress on the community.

But one can be colorful without being eccentric. I am conducting not a peepshow, but a diorama, the picture of a city in terms of its inhabitants. Some of the spectacle is missing. I searched for, without finding, an outstanding Chinese, not a leader from the days of tong wars, but a vivid personality in his own right. Perhaps the San Francisco Chinese have been too busy, until the present generation, making their peaceable livings and achieving their modest prosperity in an alien world. And the best known among the Italians, our second largest national group, are still alive. Occupations as well as racial elements are missing. Our scientists for the most part function in Berkeley or Palo Alto, at the University of California or Stanford; Dr. William Wallace Campbell came to his lamentable death in San Francisco, but his active career was associated always with Berkeley or Mount Hamilton. The only scientist who came into my net, George Davidson, enters into the story of James Lick, where some account of this astronomer's unusual career is given. Neither have I a painter or sculptor, though they have flourished always in San Francisco, for the excellent reason that outstanding men like William Keith or Arthur Putnam led hard-working but not very exciting lives. There have been great religious spokesmen in the city, but the essence of leadership in orthodox religion is conformity with the norm in external affairs. The really great among religious leaders are of course obvious exceptions to this; but so far San Francisco has produced no saint and no mighty heretic. Perhaps we can claim Padre Junipero Serra, that great wayfarer, as a San Franciscan, for he started the whole thing in 1776 when he established the Mission Dolores. But the establishment did not involve residence, and San Franciscans really have no more right to Serra than have San Diegans or Santa Barbarans.

In other words, this is by no means a complete survey.

It is merely a sampler, a series of biographical sketches held together by the slender but strong thread of identification with a place, of the connection of its subjects with a city which they loved, and which in many cases loved them.

It remains to say something about a number of other people who were San Franciscans too, and interesting San Franciscans, but who have no chapter of their own because not enough is known about their lives, because too much has been written about them already and a brief mention is sufficient, because their residence in San Francisco was too short to justify more than a word or two in regard to them, or, in a few cases, because their careers as a whole were not overwhelmingly interesting, and yet a bright spot shines here and there that deserves to be captured. As I write this, for example, Carl Dondero has just died at ninety-six. Who remembers Carl Dondero? And yet he came to San Francisco from Italy in 1857, and it was in his print shop near Portsmouth Square that The San Francisco *Chronicle* was first set up. He also founded an Italian daily, *La Voce del Popolo*, which lived for many years. In his own lifetime, between the farm near Genoa where he was a boy, and Genoa Street in Oakland where he died, he spanned all the lifetime, and more, of San Francisco itself.

Who knows the life of Jerry Thomas, author of *The Bon Vivants' Companion,* the famous bartender who invented the Martini and the Blue Blazer? Who, outside of San Francisco—where the statues he made are everywhere, from the Mechanics' and Volunteers' monuments on Market Street to Father Serra and the Baseball Player in Golden Gate Park—knows much of Douglas Tilden, the deaf-mute sculptor, who died only in 1935? Who knows anything but snatches of biography about William Alexander Leidesdorff, after whom narrow Leidesdorff Street in the financial district is named—one of the most interesting of all the San Francisco pioneers?

Leidesdorff came to San Francisco first in 1841 as captain of the schooner *Julia Ann*. He was a mulatto, from St. Thomas in the Danish West Indies (now the United States-governed Virgin Islands). He was in the Bear Flag revolt, and during the Mexican regime was appointed by Consul Thomas O. Larkin United States vice-consul in Yerba Buena. When Yerba Buena became San Francisco, he was the first American *alcalde* to be regularly elected in the new City Hall; he was also city treasurer. He organized the first American public school in the city; built the first wharf, at the foot of Pine Street; and erected the adobe Congress House, which later became the City Hotel. Besides being a shipowner and lumber agent, and a large investor in real estate, he ran a ship's chandlery and a general store. It was Leidesdorff who gave the great ball to Commodore Stockton at which nearly all the guests were Mormons; and it was he who, on the historic Fourth of July in 1846, read the Declaration of Independence from a stand in Portsmouth Plaza. He died suddenly in 1848, at thirty-eight, and is buried beneath the church floor at Mission Dolores, though he was never known to be a Roman Catholic. (Neither, though he held Federal office, did he ever become a United States citizen!)

Leidesdorff is described as being "liberal, hospitable, cordial, and confiding even to a fault," though he was also reticent and secretive. He never married, and always lived alone. The honor in which he was held is a living monument to the lack of race or color prejudice in early San Francisco.

Perhaps the most amusing of Leidesdorff's exploits was his pioneer steamship service between San Francisco and Sacramento. In 1847 he bought the *Nasledrich,* a thirty-seven-foot sidewheeler, from the Russians in Sitka. On November 28 the *Nasledrich* started on her first voyage. Just what delayed her is not known, but most of the impatient passengers jumped off at likely stops and flagged a stagecoach. Even those who walked got there first. The *Nasledrich* arrived in Sacramento (a distance of about eighty miles) after a voyage of six days and seven hours!

Leidesdorff had a strange posthumous career. As told by Rabbi Jacob Voorsanger, late professor of Semitic Languages and Literature at the University of California, in the *Jewish Encyclopedia,* about 1817 a Jewish youth of fifteen named Wolf Leidesdorfer left his home in Szathmar, Hungary, and never returned. Later his relatives heard that he had gone to America and had become rich and prominent.

In 1854 some surviving cousins of Wolf Leidesdorfer brought suit in San Francisco for the million and a half dollar estate of William Alexander Leidesdorff, claiming that they were one and the same person. The litigation continued, without success, until expiration of the statute of limitations.

Leidesdorff had died intestate. Captain John L. Folsom, a well-known pioneer after whom Folsom Street was named, was appointed temporary administrator. He visited Jamaica (not St. Thomas) and bought the claims of various persons, including that of a Negro woman who said she was Leidesdorff's mother and that his father was a Dane. In 1854 Governor John Bigler recommended escheat of the estate and proceedings for its recovery from Folsom, but this was never carried through.

The claim from Hungary seems to rest on very improbable foundations. All Leidesdorff's acquaintances took it for granted that he was a mulatto; he was described as far more "swarthy" than any Jew could ever be. Leidesdorff never talked about his ancestry or his early days, but the reason for that is obvious; he was probably the only Negro in San Francisco in his time. The relatives' suit said Wolf Leidesdorfer went from Hungary to Jamaica and thence to New Orleans, where he became captain of the port. From then on the careers of the two men were said to be identical. It seems most unlikely that any man would claim to be a Negro when he was not; Jews have always been an integral part of San Francisco's life and there was absolutely no prejudice against them in the early years. The ages of the two men were discrepant also. But if by some queer chance Leidesdorff actually was Leidesdorfer, it seems sufficiently obvious that he desired to have no relations with his family, and would have been most unwilling for them to become his heirs.

There was another early pioneer whom everybody knew but who was in reality a stranger to everybody.

In his native Wales his name had been Thomas Williams; before he came to San Francisco during the gold rush he had changed it to Thomas Blythe. He had been a draper's clerk and then a contractor in England; in San Francisco, like so many others, he became a multi-millionaire through the purchase of real estate. At one time he owned a tract which is now the heart of the Grant Avenue shopping district. He also bought 40,000 acres of swamp land in Riverside County, site now of the town of Blythe, and intended to turn it into rich farming country by diverting the Colorado River, but he died suddenly of a paralytic stroke before the work was fairly begun.

Blythe was a familiar San Francisco figure, dressed always in black, accompanied always by four huge dogs. In 1873 he revisited England, and had an affair with a girl there who bore him a daughter. Blythe never saw his daughter, but he became passionately devoted to her. He planned to have her come to him when she was grown, and he built a house for her on Russian Hill which still stands. Litigation for his big estate began immediately upon his death, and continued for years. For a year, Blythe was not even buried; his body lay in a coffin in a downtown mortuary, next door to a firehouse whose staff used to look in every morning before they went on duty and "wish Tom good morning." Eventually the greater part of the $4,000,000 estate was awarded to the daughter, who became a noted member of society not only in San Francisco, but in the East and in Europe as well. She died in Oakland in 1941, having survived three husbands, the last of whom was a nationally famous San Francisco physician.

Another interesting old-timer, with a less honorable career, was Henry Meiggs, builder of Meiggs Wharf. Meiggs came to San Francisco in 1850 with a shipload of lumber, which he sold immediately at twenty times what it cost him. He was one of the first of innumerable "boosters." His special field was the North Beach, now the Italian section, which he claimed was much nearer the Golden Gate than was the district around Portsmouth Square, then the city's center. (It is.) He built his two-thousand-foot wharf from the north end of Powell Street, graded the streets around, and fathered a boom. But it wasn't quick enough, and soon he was heavily in debt. He got hold of a book of city warrants for street work, already signed by the mayor and comptroller—a slack custom of these easygoing days—and hypothecated $800,000 worth of them to moneylenders, with no funds to back them. It was a long time before he was discovered, for he was a councilman and a great deal of a public bene-factor, with a good reputation. A music lover, he had built Music Hall and given an organ to Trinity Church. Nobody thought of suspecting him of forgery and theft.

But of course the discovery did come eventually, and Meiggs lit out just ahead of arrest. He went to Peru, where he became famous as a railroad builder. He built the Oroya Railroad between Lima and Cerro de Pasco, 14,000 feet up in the Andes, which had been given up as impossible by British, French, and Belgian engineers. He became one of the wealthiest men in South America. He paid back every cent he had stolen, and began to besiege the authorities for permission to come home. On one occasion the Legislature passed an amnesty act allowing his return, but the governor vetoed it. Meiggs died in Peru, still pleading for permission to become again a San Franciscan.

Another enigmatic figure of a slightly later period was Rufus A. Lockwood. Lockwood came into port as a sailor before the mast. He hunted up a prominent law firm and asked to be taken on as janitor. He was a good janitor who kept things clean and himself out of the way. One morning one of the partners found on his desk a beautifully full and accurate brief dealing with a case, the transcript of which he had left on the desk the night before. He called Lockwood and asked where that had come from. "I wrote it," said the janitor. "I am an attorney." A week later Rufus Lockwood was a member of the firm. He became one of the best-known criminal trial lawyers in the city, famous for his caustic wit. Once he had a witness who was notorious for his perjury. "I want to ask you just one question," purred Lockwood suavely. "Would you believe yourself under oath?"

Amelia Ransome Neville tells a story of a time when a friend noticed that Lockwood looked depressed. Thinking he was in money difficulties, the friend followed him on the street and offered to lend him any money he needed. By this time they were on Meiggs Wharf. Lockwood pulled from his pocket a handful of double eagles and skidded the gold pieces one by one over the bay. "I can keep that up as long as you can," he said. Whatever his mysterious trouble was, it was not financial. Samuel D. Woods, in *Lights and Shadows of Life on the Pacific Coast*, relates that as suddenly as

Lockwood appeared in San Francisco he disappeared, and was never heard of again. But Mrs. Neville, in *The Fantastic City*, has another version of his end. She says she made a voyage from New York on the same ship with Lockwood when both were returning from a visit to New York. He grew very tired of the monotonous voyage and remarked that if he were ever foolish enough to set foot on a ship again he hoped he would drown. A few years later he was on the *Central America* when it foundered off Cape Hatteras. Lockwood locked himself into his cabin, and went down with the ship.

One San Franciscan who had ample reason for his shyness of identification was a mild, gentlemanly man who called himself Charles Bolton (or sometimes Bowles), and who lived in a boardinghouse, where he said he was a mining man. Mr. Bolton didn't smoke or drink or swear; he was a primordial Casper Milquetoast in a derby hat. Periodically he disappeared for a while, presumably to visit his mining interests. As one of those dependent on the Wells-Fargo Express for safe shipment of his ore, he was particularly bitter about the elusive highwayman, "Black Bart," who held up only Wells-Fargo coaches, never molested the passengers, but simply ordered the driver to throw down the treasure box. After the man in the flour-sack mask had vanished, searchers would sometimes find pinned to a tree some badly written verses (signed "Po8") in which Black Bart had wooed the Muse and dared the law to find him. At last Black Bart made his first mistake; he dropped a handkerchief bearing a laundry mark.

Yes, they arrested quiet Mr. Bolton. He went very

meekly. The only thing he didn't like was their making fun of his verses.

But probably the most thoroughly mysterious people who ever lived in San Francisco were the Bell family and their remarkable Negro "housekeeper," Mammy Pleasant. Thomas Bell, a pioneer banker, lived in a big house on Octavia Street which was long known as "the house of mystery." With the Bells lived Mammy Pleasant, born Mary Williams in Philadelphia. Her father was either a Cherokee Indian or a South Sea Islander, her mother a Negro woman from Louisiana. She was married first to a Cuban planter, then to his overseer, John Pleasant. She was reputed to have been a friend of John Brown's, and to have contributed $30,000 to the Harper's Ferry raid. She came to San Francisco in 1849, and ran the leading boardinghouse in the city. About 1875, she had the Bell house built and registered in her name, and moved in as manager. Officially she was a servant, but actually she ruled the household. There was no more familiar figure in the city. She was seen on the streets daily, in the Bell carriage, tall, slender, ebon, with a white kerchief tied around her neck, a long black shapeless dress falling to her feet, a red blanket about her shoulders, and a broad hat tied under her chin.

Under her wool-covered skull was one of the wiliest brains that ever lived. She had a genius for finance, and is said to have become rich through shrewd investment in mining stocks, though no one knows what she did with her money. She certainly advised Judge Bell and many other distinguished San Franciscans on investments. What is more, she was credited with knowing damaging secrets about half the prominent men and women in town. The strange relationship between the judge and his servant was almost that of a voodoo priestess and her disciple. He asked her advice on every matter and always obeyed it. It is said that it was by her suggestion that he actually paid for his children—giving several thousand dollars to his young wife for every child she bore him. He was finally found dead, in 1892, at the foot of a staircase—with Mammy Pleasant's red blanket enigmatically caught in the ledge. Seven years later Mrs. Bell ordered Mammy Pleasant out of her own house. She died in 1904, at eighty-nine. Until the house was torn down, it was reputed to be haunted by her ghost.

When Sarah Althea Hill sued Senator William Sharon on an alleged marriage contract, it was brought out in court that Mammy Pleasants was tied up in that notorious and unsavory case too. She had given the flamboyant Althea a love charm which was sure to win the elderly senator's heart—and apparently did. After she lost the suit, Althea married her lawyer, Judge David S. Terry. Terry was a formidable man. While a state supreme court justice he had stabbed an officer who was arresting one of his political supporters; the Vigilantes took him in custody and thought of hanging him, but eventually let him go. In 1859 he killed Judge David C. Broderick in a duel on the shore of Lake Merced. He was tried for murder and acquitted, and when the Civil War broke out he joined the Confederate Army. After the war he returned to San Francisco. He had announced openly after losing the Sharon-Hill suit that he would avenge himself and his new wife on the judge, Stephen

J. Field, who on appeal had decided the case against him. (Terry had been on the state supreme court when Field was its chief justice.)

Field was the brother of Cyrus W. Field, inventor of the trans-Atlantic cable, and of David Dudley Field, the famous lawyer. He was a scholarly New Englander, who, when he first came to California, kept a diary in Greek. He became a justice of the United States Supreme Court, but still spent most of his time in California. After he had been warned that Terry was out to get him, he never traveled without a bodyguard. In 1889 he was on his way from Los Angeles to San Francisco. At Lathrop the passengers all got out to eat in the station restaurant. Terry, who with his wife was on the same train, saw Judge Field in the restaurant, walked up to him, and struck him in the face. The bodyguard instantly shot Terry dead.

In 1892 Sarah Althea Terry was found wandering the streets in San Francisco, hopelessly insane. She was taken to the State Hospital for the Insane in Stockton, Mammy Pleasants signing the commitment papers, and there everybody supposed she had died, until in 1936 a newspaper reporter discovered her, quite mindless but still alive. She died the next year at eighty-seven, never having recovered her reason.

Figures less remarkable than Mammy Pleasants, and less violent than Judge Terry, but still sufficiently off the beaten track, have always abounded in San Francisco. One was a man named Fletcher who founded the first Japanese importing business in the city, known as the Ichi Ban. The business failed, and he disappeared, but he returned later, to enjoy a brief nation-wide fame as Dr. Horace Fletcher, inventor of the "Fletcher System" for avoidance of bodily ills, which consisted in chewing one's food some unbelievable number of times before swallowing it.

Another odd character was Dr. Henry Daniel Cogswell, a pioneer dentist. Dr. Cogswell wrote his own biographical sketch for the *National Encyclopedia of American Biography*, in which he told how he was born in 1819 in Connecticut, deserted by his father at nine, and after a miserable boyhood which included slavery in a cotton mill at fifty cents a week and a period in the county poorhouse, taught himself dentistry and practised in Pawtucket, Rhode Island. Always more of a Yankee mechanic than a scientist, he invented a vacuum chamber to replace the springs then used to keep false teeth in position, and on the profits moved to California in 1849. He ran a general store in Stockton, then went to San Francisco and until 1855 practised dentistry there and also dealt in dental supplies. As soon as he became sufficiently prosperous, with an income of $54,000 a year (more from real-estate operations than from fillings and extractions), he retired from his profession and spent the rest of his life in travel, the conservation of his fortune, and the exercise of philanthropy. As he was an arbitrary man, who thought very highly of himself, his benefactions were not always received with unmixed gratitude. He gave the regents of the new University of California a lot and building he owned for the establishment of a dental college, but when after nine years the college had not been founded he took his gift back. He also offered to endow a chair of Moral and Intellectual Philosophy, and to donate a fund for the use of indigent students, but the conditions were so onerous that neither of these came to anything. The same fate befell a projected home for "fallen women." He did, however, establish the Cogswell Polytechnic College (the oldest technical school west of St. Louis), still in existence as a manual-training high school for boys, and he built a statue, in what was then a cemetery, to Mrs. Rebecca Lambert, founder of the Sailors' Home Society. The statue still stands in what is now the Lincoln Park Golf Course.

But Cogswell's great interest was in teetotalism, and his pet philanthropy was the erection of drinking fountains, each equipped with a patent cooling apparatus for the improvement of what he called "Nature's own beverage." His ambition was to provide one public fountain for every hundred saloons, but he never achieved that. He gave away twenty fountains and statues in all, about half of them in San Francisco. One once adorned Boston's Public Gardens, and others, much the worse for wear, in San Jose, Washington, D.C., Pawtucket, Rhode Island, and Fall River, Massachusetts. In 1945 Senator Sheridan Downey introduced a resolution to tear down the Washington fountain, as an eyesore and an offense to San Francisco, whose name is on it. Each fountain was topped by a life-size figure, sometimes of some celebrated and temperate man like Benjamin Franklin, but usually of Dr. Henry D. Cogswell. He was very bitter about the reception accorded these fountains. Most of them were never set up, and of those

that were, all were mutilated very quickly by people
who preferred Nature's own beverage to be alcoholically
improved before drinking. One fountain still stands in
Washington Square, San Francisco, in rather poor condition, but the rest have vanished. A diver once reported
"a stone man" lying at the bottom of the bay near the
Marina, and that may be one of Dr. Cogswell's well-
meaning gifts—perhaps the one a committee of artists
tore down one dark night; but as the good dentist has
been dead since 1900, no one is interested enough to dive
again and find out.

Perhaps the strangest of all San Francisco stories
concerns a little old man named Jack Bee Garland, who
for forty years was a familiar figure on the streets and
in the parks. Garland had been a newspaper correspondent, and occasionally he worked as an advertising solici-
tor for one of the newspapers. But what he lived for
was to do good.

He was poor, with a small inherited income, from
which he took barely enough for food and lodging. The
rest went to people in trouble. Dressed always in a
shabby blue suit, with big clumsy shoes and a hat pulled
low over his eyes, the little old man haunted lonely
places after dark. Perhaps there was a girl crying on a
park bench, or a frightened boy wondering if his first
holdup must supply his next meal. Perhaps it was a
thin-faced mother with a scrawny baby, or a jobless
man who dared not go home and face his hungry family. Somehow Garland got it all out of them; and into
their hands was pressed the money that often meant the

difference between despair and hope. Forty years before, he had happened to see a callous instance of

> "Organized charity, scrimped and iced,
>   In the name of a cautious, statistical Christ"

and his heart had revolted. The rest of his life was given
to those who did not fit into the pattern, those too bewildered or too insecure to be cases for the "proper
authorities," but to whom this obscure, frail, simple
man came as a rescuing angel who would not even listen
to thanks.

Often he himself went hungry. One night in 1936
he came to the home of one of his few close friends and
asked for carfare to the room in which he lived. He
had just given his last dollar to a boy who had run away
from home and was ragged and hungry. He was ill,
dying on his feet. His friends begged him to rest, but
he shook his head. "Hunger is a hard taskmaster and
must be served," he said. A few nights later he collapsed
on the street and was dead of peritonitis before he
reached the hospital.

And then it was discovered that Jack Bee Garland
was a woman. Her name was Elvira Mugarietta, and
she was the daughter of the first Mexican Consul in San
Francisco. During the Spanish-American War she had
been a Red Cross nurse in the Philippines. It was soon
after her return to California that she began her anonymous dedication to charity. Finding that the beggars
and waifs resented help and advice from a woman, and
that her selfless "journeys to the end of the night" involved her in unpleasant misunderstandings, she adopted

men's clothing and took a masculine name. Only her few friends and her sister knew the truth, while for nearly half a century this merciful masquerader trudged the city looking for people who needed the pittance of her money and the largesse of her compassionate heart.

San Francisco from its beginning has been a strongly pro-labor town, as the chapter on Kearney and Haskell will show. A few other interesting figures in the labor movement deserve some mention. General A. M. Winn was probably the most picturesque. His title was honorary, but doubly so: he had been a brigadier general in the Mississippi state militia, and in 1850 he achieved the same rank in the militia of California. Although a Virginian by birth, he moved to Vicksburg in early youth and learned carpentry there. There also he joined the Master Carpenters' and Joiners' Society, one of the earliest trade unions; and though he never worked at his trade after coming to California in 1849, he retained his interest in labor. With so many others of the pioneers, he made his money in real estate in Sacramento and San Francisco. He was a great "joiner," and what he could not join he organized. Like Cogswell, he was a strong supporter of the temperance movement and belonged to various societies and groups of an arid nature. He was active during his San Francisco years—remembering his trade union past—in organizing branches of a secret order of union men known as the Ecumenic Order of United Mechanics, which lasted only a few months. In California, General Winn is known (if at all) as the founder of the Native Sons of the Golden West (though he himself was not eligible for membership) ; and that honor is inscribed on his tombstone in the old City Cemetery in Sacramento. (He founded it in 1875, following an abortive attempt in 1869—when all the Native Sons he could discover turned out to be turbulent 'teen-agers.) Winn also belongs to state history in that he married the widow of James King of William, the fearless editor of the San Francisco *Evening Bulletin,* whose murder led to the formation of the first Vigilance Committee.

But actually the General should be remembered as the father of the agitation for the eight-hour day in the state. He organized the first local group dedicated to this end, the House Carpenters' Eight-Hour League. It was followed by numerous other craft leagues, and soon was uniting with similar movements in the East. In 1869 Winn went to New York in the interests of the movement, and was elected chairman of the first National Eight-Hour League's executive committee. It was not until after the Haymarket tragedy in Chicago in 1886 that the eight-hour-day fight was finally won. By that time General Winn was dead; but long before his death in 1883 he had withdrawn from the labor movement and devoted himself entirely to the organization of the Native Sons.

Frequently associated with Winn in the agitation for the eight-hour day was Alexander M. Kenaday, another Southerner who had had a stirring career before coming to California in 1849. He was born of Irish parents in Wheeling, but grew up in St. Louis, where he attended a Jesuit college and then became a printer. He had

been a Mississippi steamboat captain and had served
through the Mexican War, being promoted to sergeant
for bravery under fire. The Mother Lode in 1849 was full
of Mexican War veterans at loose ends, mostly Southerners, hoping to find wealth in the mines. Kenaday
was not the only one who failed to strike it rich and so
went to San Francisco to earn a living. He was more
fortunate than most in that he had a trade, and he soon
found a job as a printer. He organized the Typographical Union and became its president; he was secretary
and then president of the San Francisco Trades' Union,
a very early central labor council; and he founded the
first labor paper to be published on the Pacific Coast,
the *Journal of Trades and Workingmen.* His attempt
to establish a San Francisco branch of the National Labor Union was not so successful; the early California
unions were highly independent and suspicious of national affiliations. He, too, in his later years branched
out into organization of groups outside the labor movement. He was founder and secretary of a local society
of Veterans of the Mexican War, and in 1874 organized
a National Association of Mexican War Veterans and
became its secretary as well. In 1868 he made a vain
trip to Washington to lobby for an Old Soldiers' Home
on the Pacific Coast. It seems strange, in view of the
number of Mexican War Veterans in California—the
Civil War veterans were of course at this time still all
young men—that it was not until much later that such
a home was established.

No one in San Francisco will for a long time forget
old Andrew Furuseth. San Francisco is a seaport, and

it is sea-conscious to an extent unknown to most cities.
For many, many years, Furuseth, that hard-bitten old
Norseman, practically *was* the sailor's union, first when
it was the Coast Seamen's Union, of which he was secretary from 1887, then when it became the Sailors' Union
of the Pacific. Conservative, almost reactionary in his
political and economic views, Furuseth no longer felt at
home in the complex labor situation of the post-War
and especially the depression years. He had many enemies, even when he had withdrawn from active life into
a bitter sort of retirement in Washington. He died
there in 1938, at almost eighty-four. But his worst
enemy could never say that the old man had not lived
selflessly, fanatically, for the welfare of his fellow sailors
as he saw it. He had been at sea from the time he was
seventeen, and five years after he came to California he
joined the first organization of coastwise sailors to have
more than the most temporary existence. He was a hard
fighter, with a lashing tongue and a bulldog stubbornness; he fought factions within his own group just as
he fought the employers. But even those who hated
him respected him. "Andy" Furuseth was no velvet-
padded "duke of labor," letting his hands grow soft in
a mahogany office while he forgot the days of hard
manual toil. All his life he lived poorly, on a sailor's
wage, just as sailors had lived and eaten and dressed in
his youth. He was a lonely man, who detested women
and had no time for "social nonsense." He could never
see beyond the needs or aspirations of his own limited
group, and he set his granite face obstinately against
change even when change meant progress. But he was

in his way a saint of labor, vowed to an austere devotion. "You men see life from a parlor, I see it from the hold of a vessel," he wrote to the Ruskin Club of Oakland. And he had the immense patience of his native snow fields. "Tomorrow is also a day," Andrew Furuseth would say to those cast down by lost battles.

"Tomorrow is also a day" might have been the motto as well of a very different sort of man, E. J. Baldwin, who was known always as "Lucky" Baldwin. Tomorrow usually brought him trouble, but it brought wealth too. Whether it ever brought him happiness is another question; probably to him the real happiness of life was in acquisition and power. He was one of the chief beneficiaries of the fabulously rich Comstock Lode; his racing stable is still famous; he built and owned the Baldwin Hotel and Theater. He was worth twenty million, but was always being sued for debts which he would not pay without a court judgment. In later life he went broke, then founded a new fortune. He had come to San Francisco in 1853, after a career as farm hand, horse trader, and saloonkeeper in the East and Middle West. Almost his first act was a sort of advance display of the Yankee shrewdness which was afterwards to make his name synonymous with luck. He decided to buy the hotel in which he had been staying for three months, and dated the lease three months back so that his former landlord owed him board and lodging for that period!

His private life was equally complicated. He had four, or perhaps five, wives—"I was so mixed up on Baldwin's ladies," said a court witness, "that I could not swear to any of them. He had a manner of introducing them that way, as his wife." He was shot more than once by irate ladies or their relatives, and many times sued for breach of promise. The woman he loved was his third wife, a beautiful young girl who died in 1881. To the end of his life this hard, shifty man kept carefully in a cabinet a pair each of her dainty little shoes and her tiny gloves. Yet he had no scruples against pleading as his defense in one breach of promise suit that his public reputation was "such that every woman who came near him must have been warned against him in advance."

Compared with this sensational career, the lives of other financial tycoons of San Francisco seem a trifle flat. But there is some color in the histories of nearly all of them, as if even a life of money-making must take on vividness when projected across the screen of "the amazing city." Adolph Sutro, for instance, in San Francisco itself was known only as its honored mayor and benefactor, but he had gained his fortune in the first place by an almost unequaled feat—the building of the tunnel which drained the lower levels of the Comstock mines in Nevada and made its resources available. Sutro was derided when he proposed the tunnel, and every obstacle was put in his way, even by such usually far-seeing men as William C. Ralston, but he persevered and lived to enjoy the embarrassment of those who had flatly called him a fool with a monomania. It was he who planted the half-wild Sutro Forest on what had been bare hills, and gave it to the city. At the edge of the ocean he bought a cliff he called Sutro Heights, built his house on it, and dotted the formal garden with quaint statuary in the German style. When he died, his daughter, Dr. Emma Sutro Merritt, deeded Sutro Heights to the city, though she continued to live in the house until she died, at eighty-two, in 1938.

Dr. Merritt herself was an interesting figure, one of the pioneer women physicians of the Pacific Coast. Her father was horrified when, instead of contenting herself with social gayety and a husband hunt, she insisted on going to Vassar. There she discovered that the college physician was a woman — the first time she had ever heard that women could practice medicine. There was another tough tussle with her father when, after graduation, she announced she was going to enter the Medical School of the University of California, but she won that fight, too. She and another medical student, George Merritt, fell in love, and in 1883 they were married by the American consul general in London, while both were doing postgraduate work in Paris. They came back to San Francisco together, and were near their golden wedding when Dr. George Merritt died. Dr. Emma Sutro Merritt, after her father's death, gave up her practice and devoted herself to handling his estate, including the famous Sutro Baths. She adopted a nephew, and lived with him in the old house, now torn down. Golden Gate Park gardeners now care for the huge garden. In Adolph Sutro's day it had taken thirteen full-time workers to keep it in condition.

As an ironic aftermath to the story, after Dr. Emma Sutro Merritt died, the mayor of San Francisco received a letter from a cousin of the Sutros in Germany, asking if it would be possible to let him live in the old house on Sutro Heights. (Adolph Sutro was of German-Jewish descent.) Unfortunately there was no legal way to provide for this refugee cousin in what was now city property.

A story typical of early San Francisco was that of the pioneer hotel man, John Henry Brown. Brown was an Englishman, born in Devonshire in 1810. According to his own naive book, he shipped as an apprentice on a packet, deserted after his third voyage, and for years led a roving life, which took him to Havana, New York, Philadelphia, Cincinnati, and the "Cherokee Nation." Somewhere along the route he had become skilled as a carpenter and a painter. He first reached San Francisco (then Yerba Buena) in 1844, then went to Sacramento, where he was Sutter's overseer in the kitchen and butcher shop. He returned to Yerba Buena in 1846 as a sailmaker and carpenter on the *Portsmouth*, Lieutenant Montgomery's ship. It was then that he started the town's first hotel, painting the *Portsmouth* free of charge in return for the right to give its name to his inn, the Portsmouth House. The sign over the hotel, incidentally, was the first painted sign to be displayed in the infant city. At the time he opened the hotel, he remarks, there were just two "white ladies" in Yerba Buena. In 1849 he gave the precipitating push to one of California's severest early problems when for three months he employed Chinese in the City Hotel, which he had taken over after selling the Portsmouth House. Brown led a rather varied career thereafter, never content very long in one place or one occupation, living in several places between San Francisco and Santa Cruz, and functioning sometimes as hotelkeeper, sometimes as grocer, and sometimes as farmer. He died in Santa Cruz in 1905, at the age of ninety-four.

The stories of San Francisco's colorful nabobs (whose mansions gave its nickname to Nob Hill) go as far back as the fifties and sixties, or even the forties. It was a decade or two later, in the late sixties and seventies, that blossom time arrived for the budding *literati* of the young West Coast metropolis. It was then that Mark Twain lingered briefly on the threshhold of fame; that Robert Louis Stevenson, trudging to Rincon Hill to call on Charles Warren Stoddard, first heard of the beauties of Samoa, where he was to die; that Bret Harte, very much henpecked by his singer-wife, worked in the mint and at the same time edited the *Overland Monthly*, with its symbolic emblem of a locomotive and a grizzly bear. Harte was in San Francisco for nearly two decades, from 1857 to 1871. There is considerable confusion as to his first California years. Just how much time he actually spent in the Mother Lode country, whether he ever was actually a stage driver for the Wells-Fargo express as he claimed, is open to much doubt. Certainly he taught school in the mining country for a few months, but it is probable that most of the material on which his stories are based came at secondhand. Several northern California towns claim, without much evidence, to have been his residence. In San Francisco he worked as a druggist's clerk, and as a typesetter on the *Golden Era,* until he secured a secretarial post in the mint.

Harte had a gift for doing a dozen things at once. He was a beau and a bit of a flirt, a skilled croquet player, a Bohemian who was always in debt; and at the same time he gave satisfactory service at the mint, edited the *Overland* in its first great days, and produced most of his writing that has any prospect of survival. Some accounts of his life say that for two years he also taught at the University of California, but such versatility was a little beyond even Bret Harte. It is true that he was offered the Chair of Recent Literature, plus the curatorship of the library and museum, at the new university, at a salary of $300 a month, but he refused the offer and went to New York instead. He never saw San Francisco again, and indeed soon after entered into his permanent exile in Europe.

The literary trinity of those fine young years consisted of Harte, Charles Warren Stoddard (more an accomplished *litterateur* than the authentic poet he thought himself to be), and Ina Donna Coolbrith—a diminutive of her name used in her first poems, and thereafter retained as her own. Ina was born Josephine, daughter of a father who died soon after her birth; her mother remarried Don Carlos Smith, brother of Joseph Smith, the founder of Mormonism. She was brought across the plains from Illinois in 1851, when she was ten years old. The Smiths settled first in Plumas County, then in Los Angeles, at that time a somnolent *pueblo*. There at a very early age the future Ina Coolbrith married one Carsley, from whom she was divorced after three years. When she was seventeen the family moved again to San Francisco, and she soon became the center and queen of the growing literary group which had arisen in Harte's early San Francisco years. He found her teaching school, and made her co-editor of the *Overland Monthly*. From teaching she turned to library work. In Oakland she directed the public library for more than twenty years, and befriended Jack London when he was a ragged, book-hungry newsboy. Then she became librarian of the Mechanics-Mercantile Library in San Francisco, and finally of the celebrated Bohemian Club. For nearly thirty years she was the only woman member the club has ever had, the only one allowed to enter its doors except on infrequent "ladies' nights."

Harte was desperately in love with her, and wanted to divorce his wife to marry her. Stoddard threatened to kill himself for her sake. She was the first to encourage Isadora Duncan; she corresponded regularly with Tennyson, Dante Gabriel Rossetti, Whittier, and other famous poets (the letters were all destroyed in the fire of 1906); through Joaquin Miller she secured the reburial of Byron in Westminster Abbey. She took into her home and educated Miller's daughter, Cali-Shasta, by a Digger Indian squaw. During the Panama-Pacific International Exposition in 1915 she was crowned by the regents of the University of California the first poet laureate of California. She had a graceful and delicate talent, but was never more, as a creative writer, than a regional versifier. As a fructifying influence, however, she did much to keep literature alive in San Francisco in the barren decades that followed the first flowering. In her later years—she did not die until 1928—she reigned as a sort of empress, the last living link with the great days of the past. She had known well every writer of importance who ever lived in the city, and her salons were crowded, if not with the younger authors, at least with the professors and historians to whom the past was of interest.

Another quasi-literary figure, a little younger than Ina Coolbrith, was Ella Sterling Mighels (pronounced "Miles"), who was born in 1853 and died in 1934. Mrs. Mighels wrote always under the pseudonym of "Aurora Esmeralda," the name of the Nevada mining town where she had spent her childhood. She was a Native Daughter, born near Folsom, and was a posthumous child—men died young in those days of adventure and hardship—both her father and her stepfather being '49ers. From 1901 she lived in San Francisco, where she wrote innumerable volumes of reminiscence and conducted a children's society, the Ark-adian Brothers and Sisters of California, "based on the kindness of the miners to the children of Aurora Esmeralda." In 1919, since California already had a laureate, the legislature made her "the first literary historian" of the state. They had either forgotten or they ignored the fact that some years previously she had staged a public bonfire of books of which she disapproved—including such classics as "Camille" and "Madame Bovary."

The seventies and eighties were the period of greatest power and influence for that strange, thwarted writer, Ambrose Bierce—the period during which he wrote his witty, venomous "Prattle" for the *Argonaut* and the *Examiner,* attacked the Southern Pacific's "Big Four" in the *News Letter,* edited the *Wasp,* and wrote most of the macabre stories on which his fame rests. His tall, slender figure, his beetling brows and curly fair hair, his beautiful hands of which he was so vain, his asthma which drove him constantly to futile searches for a climate in which he could breathe without discomfort, were all as familiar to San Franciscans of the late nineteenth century as were his daily column and his volumes of stories and essays and poems. He called himself bitterly "a mere failure, a hack," but eager young people from Seattle to San Diego bought the *Examiner* religiously, reluctant to miss a word their glittering idol wrote. But Bierce, as I have said, has been too much written about to need more than a mere mention here.

In February, 1939, a woman died in San Francisco, her birthplace, who might almost be called "the great unknown." She was Agnes Tobin, most of whose life was spent in London. George Meredith, Sir Edmund Gosse, Alice Meynell, and Arthur Symons were among her devoted friends. Yeats called her the finest American poet since Whitman. Conrad dedicated to her his "Under Western Eyes." Mrs. Patrick Campbell asked her to make the first translation into English blank verse of Racine's *Phèdre*. She was the first to translate Petrarch into English in his own Italian metres. Yet in her own city (though a perspicacious few, like George Sterling and Joaquin Miller, knew and admired her work), and indeed in the world at large, her name meant nothing. Nearly all her translations from Italian, Greek, and Latin poets, and her own exquisite poems, were privately printed and distributed only among her friends. She belonged to a wealthy and distinguished family and had no need to go out into the marketplace from which she shrank. She was a sort of nun of poetry, living as closely in her symbolic ivory tower as Robinson Jeffers lives in his actual tower of stone. Now that she is dead and need not mind, it may be hoped that all her scattered writings will be gathered into a volume where lovers of beauty may possess their treasure.

Two other writers who for a short time were identified with San Francisco may be mentioned here, not because either of them was of first or even second rank, but because of their strange and pathetic careers and personalities. One was Edward Maitland, surely the oddest of all the '49ers, for he joined the gold rush in a "leave of absence" from his conscience, to make up his mind whether in spite of religious doubts he should become an Anglican clergyman! He soon found that, clergyman or not, he should never be a miner; and he drifted from the mining country to San Francisco. After several obscure years, he went on to Australia, returned to England, and ten years later began producing a series of mystical novels. In his last years he was quite insane, but his was a great natural talent gone to waste. The only interest in his San Francisco residence is that he seems to have begun work as a journalist on one of the early newspapers of the city.

Richard Realf was in San Francisco for even a briefer time, only a few months, but they were his fatal months. He was, besides, one of Bierce's "discoveries," like George Sterling and Herman Scheffauer, and so has a legitimate tie with the city's literary history. Few men have had such complex and tragic stories. Realf (pronounced "Relf") was the son of an English market gardener who had become a country constable. He had hardly any schooling, but from earliest childhood poured out verses which made him the talk of the neighborhood. When he was ten, in 1844, he was sent to Brighton to his sister, who was personal maid to an aunt of Charles Stewart Parnell, the Irish patriot. Brighton in those days was a literary center, with Samuel Rogers, Harriet Martineau, and Lady Byron living there. They made a pet of the handsome, talented boy, and completely turned his head; in 1852 (when he was eighteen) they even paid for publication of a volume of his poems, *Guesses at the Beautiful*. Then, tiring of the youth who was growing too old to be treated longer as a sort of amusing lap dog, Lady Byron sent him to her nephew to learn to be assistant manager of his farm. There he committed the unforgivable sin—he had a love affair with a girl of his master's own family, and was caught. He was beaten horribly and cast adrift. Weeks later his frantic father found him wandering the roads, a half-crazy beggar, and as the only solution he could think of shipped the boy to another sister who was a servant in Maryland. But Realf never went to Maryland; instead, for two years, he worked as a missionary in the New York slum formerly called the Five Points. Somehow he met John Brown, the Abolitionist, became heavily involved in his plot, and was saved from execution at Harper's Ferry only because he was then in England trying to raise funds for the scheme. He served through the Civil War in the Union army, for most of the time as colonel of a Negro regiment.

Then began his tortuous matrimonial career. At the end of the war he married a Maine schoolteacher, promised to follow her north after he had been discharged from the army, and never saw her again. He claimed to have heard she was dead, but never produced any evidence of it. As a matter of fact, she long outlived him, but there was no vengeance in her heart; she never betrayed their secret while he was alive. In 1867 he met his nemesis. It is not surprising, after such a life, that Realf was an alcoholic, who alternated between drinking bouts and lectures on temperance. He was intoxicated when he married Catherine Cassidy — of course a bigamous marriage, though that is one thing about him she never knew. When he realized what he had done, he divorced her, but she had the decree annulled. Thereafter, wherever he went, whatever he did, he was followed by a woman bent on revenge. She lost him every job he got, she denounced him to every editor and lecture manager, she made his life a hell. To crown the painful tale, he had fallen deeply in love with a very different sort of woman, had married her as well, and she had borne him four children, three of them triplets. She became an invalid, he grew almost blind; in extreme poverty he struggled to support his family, followed always by the inexorable Catherine. Finally a kindhearted friend paid his way to San Francisco.

The six months or so that followed were Realf's happiest time. For a while he had to work as a laborer; then, like Harte, he found a place in the mint. He met Bierce, who became enthusiastic—a bit too enthusiastic for their merit — over the rather florid, melancholy poems Realf poured out profusely. Later Bierce was disgusted to find that some of the poems he had published and paid for had been sold before, several times over—but one cannot be too hard on a poor devil in Realf's position. In any event, he was securing recognition at last, the first he had had since the almost forgotten days in Brighton; and he was earning a steady living, saving enough to bring his family from Pittsburgh—to build up, he dared to begin to hope, a home at last, a life such as he had dreamed of before disaster first spoiled the dream.

One evening in October, 1878, Realf went from the mint to his room near by. At the door his landlady met him. "Your wife has come!" she exclaimed. "She's waiting for you now, in your room!" His wife! Was it possible? How? Had she brought the children? He dashed upstairs and flung open the door.

It was Catherine.

That night Richard Realf took a room in a hotel in Oakland. The next morning he was found dead by poison. By his side were three sonnets—by far the finest poetry he ever wrote.

The streets of San Francisco echo with the ghostly tread for so many men and women whose names evoke a story! Here little Isadora Duncan, a passionate, wilful child maturely confident of her genius, taught a dancing class of adults for which her mother pounded the piano. Here, for a moment, lingered the dizzying Lola Montez, pausing long enough to add another to her list of husbands. Here David Belasco and David Warfield, each to achieve fame on opposite sides of the footlights, were stagestruck boys glad to serve as ushers or to walk on in silent roles. In San Francisco, William Walker, the fabulous filibuster, who had already been a lawyer and a physician, turned journalist before he sailed on his expeditions into Mexico and Nicaragua. The second of these expeditions led directly to his death before a Honduran firing squad five years later, in 1860. And in San Francisco, in 1850, Heinrich Schliemann, the German businessman who excavated the sites of Troy and Mycenae, became an American citizen, thus bringing it about that some of the world's greatest archaeological discoveries are credited to the United States, though Schiliemann spent most of his remaining forty years in Greece.

A queer ghost of a man, "the last Stone Age man on the continent of North America," lived out the last five years of his pathetic life in San Francisco. His name was Ishi, and he was the very last of the Yahi Indians.

He was found cowering, cornered by dogs, in the corral of an Oroville slaughterhouse in 1911, his only clothing a rabbitskin around his shoulders. He was a man in his fifties, the only survivor of what had once been a powerful tribe in the Sierra foothills. Dr. T. T. Waterman, of the department of anthropology in the University of California, was perhaps the only man in the state able to speak to Ishi in his own tongue. He brought the Indian to San Francisco, and made him assistant janitor of the university's anthropological museum, which was then in the city near the medical school. There the professors studied him, learned from his lips the history, customs, and language of the Yahi, and introduced him to the white man's civilization. For most of his life he had lived by hunting in the mountains. He proved to be very teachable, amiable, and seemingly quite happy. To him everything he saw was magic, and the white men were great magicians. He loved to stand on Market Street watching the crowds and marveling that there should be so many people in the world. He learned a little English, and became passionately fond of ice cream sodas and the movies. He disliked both alcohol and tobacco.

Unfortunately, city life was fatal to Ishi. Arrested tuberculosis flared up again, and in 1916 he died. Five of his guardians in the university gave him a Yahi burial. With his bow, a quiver of arrows, ten pieces of Indian money, some dried venison, some corn meal, and his fire sticks, his body was cremated, and his ashes were placed in an Indian pottery jar. "Thus lived and died," says Robert O'Brien, "the last of the Yahi, and the last direct link to primeval America."

Just as Major Andrew Rowan, the man who "carried the message to Garcia," lived until 1944, a very old man, in San Francisco, so to the city have come many men at the end of eminent if sometimes incongruous careers. Everyone has heard of Captain John S. Mosby, the Confederate guerilla leader. But how many know that when the Civil War was over and he was restored to citizenship, Mosby was for a long time United States consul in Hongkong, and then settled in San Francisco, where he became a lawyer for the Southern Pacific Railroad? The choicest story told of Mosby, however, does not date from his rather dull and stodgy San Francisco days, but from the war. As Don C. Seitz tells the tale in his *Uncommon Americans,* Mosby and his men raided

Fairfax Court House, in Virginia, and found the Union officer in possession of the town, Brigadier General E. H. Stoughton, asleep in bed. Apparently the general slept "raw," for the dashing captain of Mosby's Rangers awoke him by "slapping his bare skin." Stoughton sat up, alarmed, half-asleep still, and bewildered. "Have you ever heard of Mosby?" demanded the stranger standing at his bedside. "Yes—have you got him?" asked the general excitedly. "No," retorted the stranger grimly, "but he's got you!" The man who was capable of that sort of adventure deserved a better fate than to settle down to the routine of a corporation lawyer.

Another interesting figure of Civil War memories lived in San Francisco not after, but long before, the war. This was Hinton Rowan Helper, the best-hated man in his native North Carolina and throughout the South, because of his antislavery book, *The Impending Crisis*, published in 1857. It was the first book to oppose slavery on an economic, as opposed to a humanitarian, basis; it drove Helper into permanent exile from the South, and had a definite effect on bringing the break he predicted to a head. It was eight years before this book that Helper had gone to California as a '49er. He stayed for five years, most of the time not in the mines but in San Francisco, where he wrote *The Land of Gold: Reality versus Fiction*. Helper was an early "debunker." He did not like California at all and said so; the only thing he did like was free instead of slave labor in the mines, and to his indignant disgust his Baltimore publisher removed all passages referring to this before he brought out the book. "It is my unbiased opinion,"

Helper remarked acidly, "that California can and does furnish the best bad things that are obtainable in America." This slightly cryptic dispraise seems to refer to the miners' liquor, gambling halls, and women, for Helper was considerable of a Puritan.

It would be a pity to leave to Hinton Rowan Helper the last word on a state or a city that had so many lovers. Let us give it instead to Rudyard Kipling, who ended his visit in 1889 by saying: "I find only one drawback in San Francisco. 'Tis hard to leave." And if he called it also, "a mad city, inhabited for the most part by perfectly insane people," he meant it as a compliment. He liked them that way. For those who share his taste, this book is written.

This is too informal a volume to weight it down with a bibliography. I need say only that in its preparation I have read some hundreds of books, magazine articles, and newspaper accounts. I have also written and talked to innumerable, and uniformly kind and helpful San Franciscans. Most of them I must thank in a mere blanket avowal of gratitude. A few compel special mention: the late Austin Lewis, a mine of information in half a dozen fields; William McDevitt, who was a classmate of George Sterling's in Maryland; Rudolph Blaettler, for information from his unique Sterling collection; the late Albert Bender, patron saint of San Francisco's artists and writers for a generation past; Archibald Treat, who knew Corbett before he was a champion; Ethel Turner, with her invaluable recollections of early days in Carmel; the late John D. Barry, long and closely associated with Fremont Older; Bruce Porter, who knew

Lillie Hitchcock Coit and her mother; Lawrence Esta-van, who let me take advantage of the research done by the W.P.A. Project on History of the San Francisco Theater relating to Tom Maguire; Professor Ira B. Cross, of the University of California, who read the chapter on Kearney and Haskell; Mrs. Anna George deMille, who sent me data concerning her father, Henry George; and Dr. Loren Taber, who is writing a book on Cogswell. For interpretation of the characters and careers of my subjects, no one, of course, is responsible but myself. Several of them I knew personally. I have endeavored in every case to be scrupulously fair, to say nothing that might offend a still living friend or relative, but to be as objective and candid as the nature of such a biographical study demands.

In conclusion, for remembered stories of old San Francisco "before the fire," and recollections of nearly all the persons of later date of whom I treat, I have to thank one whose counsel and help, if he were still living, would have made this a far better book—my husband, Maynard Shipley.

CHAPTER I

The Miser Who Brought the Stars to Earth:
JAMES LICK

IN THE DECADE following the Civil War, a melancholy-looking old man, with a smooth-shaven but not overly clean face bordered by a heavy muff-like beard, was a familiar sight on the streets of San Francisco. Though he was upwards of eighty, his abundant black hair and beard never showed a streak of gray. He rode around the city in a decrepit buggy mended with wire where it had sagged and broken, driving an old horse whose shabby harness was tied with string. When he was at home he lived in a single hotel room, a room furnished with cheap red plush chairs, an aged bed, a worn, faded carpet, and tattered lace curtains. The five windows were never washed, and they and the curtains were black with dust; the room was seldom swept. This was through no neglect by the hotel servants, but by his express orders.

His income at this time was about $250,000 a year. He owned the hotel, the best in the city. He owned property in Santa Clara County, innumerable lots in choice sections of San Francisco, all of Catalina Island. He hated to pay anything to anyone for personal services; when he was dead it was found that he had carried this reluctance to the point where he had made no ar-

rangements for his burial. He had few friends, though
he was president of the Society of California Pioneers
and was on amicable terms with his fellow members.
His only amusement was cabinetwork; his tool chest
stood always in his bedroom, and he enjoyed showing
he had not lost the skill which had made him an excellent
builder of organs and pianos. His general reputation was
that of an eccentric recluse, an avaricious skinflint, sel-
fish, unlovable, unwashed, and unsocial.

His name was James Lick. He was the greatest benefactor San Francisco ever knew.

Lick was born in Fredericksburg, Lebanon County,
Pennsylvania, in August, 1796. The name originally was
Lük, and the family was from the Palatinate. So are the
so-called "Pennsylvania Dutch," by whom the Licks
were surrounded; but the Licks were much later immigrants. James Lick's paternal grandfather had come
from Germany as a young man. He had served in the
Continental Army during the American Revolution, and
was one of the soldiers who survived the awful winter
in Valley Forge. He survived much more, for he did not
die until he was a hundred and four.

Lick's mother was of English descent; her maiden
name was Sarah Long. Not much is known of her except
that she died in 1812, when her son was only sixteen.
There was a daughter, too, who died young. James seems
also to have had a younger brother, but apparently they
were not on good terms in later life; he provided for
granite monuments in Fredericksburg to his grandfather,
his parents, and his sister, but not to his brother.

After very little schooling, Lick was apprenticed to a

carpenter and cabinetmaker in Hanover, the nearest large town, and showed immediately a natural bent which made him in the end a superb craftsman who could construct a bureau drawer with the joint and dovetail so exquisitely set that the drawer could hold water. A cabinetmaker of this variety was wasted on a small town, though for a time Lick settled down in Fredericksburg. At the end of 1817 he suddenly moved to Baltimore. One of the reasons became apparent when early the next year Barbara Snavely, a Fredericksburg girl, gave birth to a boy whom, with no one to dispute her, she named John Henry Lick.

James Lick, who never married, never denied this child, and toward the end of his life formally acknowledged him as his son. He was the only living relative whom his father did not disown. But the legacy, the contest, and the compromise settlement were all half a century in the future when young James Lick found a job in Baltimore as piano maker for Joseph Hiskey.

Of Barbara Snavely nothing more is known, how old she was, of what sort of family, how she lived with her illegitimate child under the scornful eyes of the village, whether her affair with Lick had been brief and casual, or whether she really had loved him. It is almost certain that he did not love her, for it was during these same years that he met the only woman he ever did love, whom he loved for fifty years after she lay in her grave, and whose name nobody knows.

It is an obscure and confused period in Lick's history. He was nobody of importance, and no one cared to keep account of his doings. He spent two or three years in

Baltimore making pianos and organs for Hiskey, and
he may or may not, in 1820 or 1821, have gone to New
York, tried to succeed at his trade there, failed, and
sailed for South America. All that is sure is that he did
go to Buenos Aires in one of those years.

He may have met in Baltimore or New York this girl
who kept him all his life a bachelor, but it is more probable that he had known her before he left Fredericksburg, and that his desertion of Barbara Snavely was
more complicated than it appeared. For the unknown
girl's father was a wealthy miller, which suggests a
country rather than a city background. The two
youngsters fell in love, and Lick, in his simplicity of
class barriers, went to her father and asked his consent
to the marriage. There is no doubt that every word of
the rich millowner's reply was branded on the young
man's mind until he died. He never repeated it, but,
helpless when he had to stand and listen to it, he made
his answer in polished wood in California thirty years
later. He, a poor young cabinetmaker, a man who
worked with his hands for a wage, to dare to ask for
the daughter of a man who could afford to employ
twenty such creatures as he! It is not unlikely that the
rather discreditable affair with Barbara Snavely was the
rebound from Lick's humiliation after this interview.

At all events, he made no further attempt to see his
beloved. Soon afterwards he went to Buenos Aires. He
remained in South America—in Argentina, Chile, and
Peru—for nearly twenty years, with only one visit back
to the United States: that was in 1832, when he visited
New York and Philadelphia. In one of those cities he

learned that his sweetheart was dead. Now that her home was the grave, he was no longer forbidden her presence. He went to her with his arms full of roses. And for the rest of his life, wherever he was, no matter how he begrudged the spending of money for other things, it is said that there were always fresh roses heaped around the tombstone of a girl who never grew old.

Lick was all his life solitary and uncommunicative. He told no stories of his exploits in South America, where ostensibly he made and sold pianos, but presumably invested his earnings and savings in far more profitable enterprises. There is an interim also after he returned to the United States permanently, probably to New York. The next time anything is definitely known of him is when he appeared in Yerba Buena, the sand-and-adobe village soon to be called San Francisco, in 1847. After that moment his inner life may have continued to be secret, but his outward career was known to everyone in the town.

The celerity with which Lick began buying up real estate suggests that it was by this means he had gained the $30,000 with which he reached California. A year after his arrival, San Francisco had gone insane over gold. Sailors deserted their ships, merchants their counters, surgeons their operating tables, in a crazy rush to the Mother Lode gold fields. Lick watched them go. He had tried his hand, briefly, at mining. Thereafter the only gold he was interested in was the gold to be secured by buying land and letting the growth of the city increase its value. A quarter of a century later, another San Franciscan wrote a book which called this

James Lick at the time he announced his legacies.

the source of all economic evils, and proposed a remedy which the author named the Single Tax.

Lick immediately invested in as many fifty-*vara* lots as he could buy in San Francisco, Santa Clara, and Los Angeles Counties, and around Lake Tahoe. Later, he bought extensively also in Napa County and in Virginia City, Nevada. (A *vara* is a Spanish yard, thirty-three and a half inches.) Most of this property he snapped up before others had sensed its future value. It is said that he bought the sand waste which was the site of the Lick House for $300. However, he had a long struggle with squatters over the titles to many of his purchases, so that they were not so cheaply obtained as might at first appear.

It was in 1854 that this hard-headed, miserly man made a fantastically romantic gesture of defiance to the wealthy miller back east who was probably long ago dead, and in any event had in all likelihood forgotten him. In San Jose, near the Lick homestead which was long in building and never was finished, he erected such a flour mill as was never seen before, and has never been seen since. He lived in a shack near by while it was in course of construction, and did most of the fine cabinetwork on it with his own hands. It was built of Cedar of Lebanon and other exotic sweet-scented woods, and of highly polished solid mahogany, finished in California laurel. The building alone cost over $200,000. Yet with magnificent carelessness he built it on ground so low that it was inundated yearly during the rainy season—and he paid a quarter of a million more for this undesirable ground! Nothing mattered except to consummate this strange revenge on perhaps the only man who had ever successfully deprived him of something he very much wanted. There is not one chance in a hundred thousand that the man who had refused to be Lick's father-in-law ever heard of the mill, or would have understood or been concerned about it if he had.

Finally, the constant floods and the emptiness of the gesture brought Lick to his senses. His grandiose and hollow vengeance embarrassed him. He decided to give the mill away. He presented it, grounds and all, to the Paine Memorial Society of Boston, which promptly sold it for $18,000. Lick was angry; he would have bought it back for $50,000. Eventually it was burned down.

But what he considered the ingratitude of the Paine Memorial Association did not impair Lick's interest in the eighteenth-century freethinker who wrote *Common Sense* and *The Crisis* and *The Age of Reason*. He had paid $18,000, in effect, to build Paine Memorial Hall, in Boston, which was destroyed by fire in 1940. In later years he wanted to erect a statue of Thomas Paine in San Francisco, but was dissuaded on the ground that it would be thought an "outrage," and would be torn down. Only a few months before he died, when he was confined to his bedroom, his old acquaintance Mrs. Addie Ballou called on him. Mrs. Ballou was a disciple of Edward Bellamy and his semisocialistic utopia; she was also a spiritualist, and like a great many spiritualists of that day, she was, like Lick himself, a freethinker. The year was 1876, and San Francisco was going to commemorate the country's centennial by a parade which would pass the Lick House. Mrs. Ballou was an amateur painter, and from portraits and descriptions she had constructed a pretty fair picture of Paine which she had offered to the organizers of the parade to carry as a banner, together with other representations of the Founding Fathers. Although without Paine there might never have been a United States of America, the parade organizers indignantly refused.

Mrs. Ballou took her story to Lick. "All right," said the old man, "if they won't march with Paine, they shall march under him." He had a line run from his bedroom window to the window opposite, and had Mrs. Ballou's painting strung on it. The entire procession marched that day under the portrait of Thomas Paine.

Up to 1874, when Lick made the first announcement of his startling benefactions, to most of San Francisco his name suggested just one thing—the Lick House. The Lick House, on the west side of Montgomery Street between Post and Sutter, was San Francisco's first palatial hotel. From the day of its great opening banquet, in 1862, until the opening of Ralston's Palace Hotel thirteen years later, its dining room was the focus of fashionable life. People who "mattered" in Society felt it necessary to be seen dining there on Sunday evenings— though it never attained that apotheosis of glory achieved by the Palace, when social aspirants not solvent enough to live or eat there could at least hire a hack on Montgomery Street, drive into the Palace's famous Palm Court, alight at the desk, look around nonchalantly— and quietly walk out again!

Nevertheless, the Lick House had its own day in the sun. Its owner might allocate to his own use only a small room on the third and top floor of the red-brick building; he might feel that he could not afford to have his meals in its remarkable dining room; but it was his accomplishment—in part literally his own handiwork. The lobby had flagged marble for its floor, but the dining room, eighty-seven by sixty-four feet and thirty-two feet high, was made entirely of rare woods imported from South America and the Orient. Its floor was a mosaic of oak, walnut, ebony, mahogany, and limewood, in 87,772 intricate pieces. Its roof was arched, the ribs covered with ornamental plaster, with ground-glass skylights and three crystal gaslight chandeliers which cost a thousand dollars each. The plaster walls were divided by ornate Corinthian pillars and pilasters. Around the walls large French plate-glass mirrors with carved rosewood frames alternated with paintings of California scenery by William Keith and Thomas Hill, the two most celebrated Western painters of the day. The elaborately carved and gilded redwood frames for these paintings were made by James Lick himself, sitting with his toolbox beside him in the shabby room where he lived while the hotel was being built. The cabinet workbench he used is now the property of Lick Observatory, his toolbox of the Society of California Pioneers.

All this acme of Victorian grandeur was gutted by fire in 1877, a year after Lick's death, but was restored in exact imitation of the original by his trustees. The Lick House itself was eventually sold by the trustees to the estate of James G. Fair, one of the "bonanza kings" of the Comstock Lode, for $1,250,000, and its site is now covered by office buildings and stores. Across the street, on Post Street, is the Mechanics' Institute, of whose pioneer library Lick was an early supporter, though it was not one of the beneficiaries of his deed of trust.

On July 16, 1874, this eccentric, repellent Scrooge suddenly became the outstanding philanthropist of his time. On that date James Lick announced that, being in poor health and not expecting to live many years longer, he was signing a trust deed, to be executed by a board of seven trustees, who would be charged with distribution of his wealth—estimated at between three and four million dollars—to a list of beneficiaries drawn up by himself.

This list is an interesting revelation of Lick's character and interests. The residuary beneficiaries were the Society of California Pioneers and the California Academy of Sciences. There were to be free public baths in San Francisco, a home for destitute old ladies, and a school of mechanical arts. Granite statues were to be erected in his native town to his soldier-grandfather and his undistinguished parents and sister. Sacramento was to have some statues which—probably without much regret by the capital city—were taken away again in the second deed of trust. San Francisco was to have a statue of Francis Scott Key, author of the words of "The Star Spangled Banner," and a huge monument representing various periods of California history. San Jose, where the marvelous flour mill had been built, was to establish an orphan asylum. Relatively small sums were to go to the Society for the Prevention of Cruelty to

Animals and the San Francisco Protestant Orphan Asylum. One hundred and fifty thousand dollars was given to the donor's acknowledged son, John Henry Lick, of Lebanon, Pennsylvania. Most important of all, California was to have the world's largest telescope; incidentally and casually, the instrument was to be housed in an observatory.

That Lick did not look upon this division of his property as a legacy, but expected to live to see some at least of the money distributed, is evidenced by the fact that when he revoked his deed of trust, on March 27, 1875, he gave as one of his reasons the fact that his health was better and he hoped to be able to attend personally to the liquidation and distribution of his property. He now had five hundred thousand dollars reserved for his own use. This was in the second deed of trust, which also provided that the proposed telescope and observatory should be given to the regents of the University of California.

Lick's main reason for the revocation of his first deed, and the drawing up of a new one, was the refusal of the board to discharge its chairman, Thomas H. Selby, to whom Lick had taken a dislike. The second board had as its chairman Captain Richard S. Floyd, a graduate of Annapolis and a commander of a Pacific Mail liner. It was a completely new board, and it contained one strange name—that of John Henry Lick.

It has been said that Lick acknowledged his son because he considered it "expedient" to do so. But is there not a touch of pathos, of the longing of the lonely man for something near to him when life is almost over, in the naming of John Lick on that second board? If this really was an appeal from the father to the son he never saw, it was wasted; the younger Lick never served on the board, never appeared in San Francisco until his father was dead and he arrived to try to break his trust deed. The next September, James Lick once more revoked the deed of trust and appointed still a third board, with only the chairman remaining unchanged. Since he died ten days later, this was his last opportunity to keep under his own control the body which was charged with giving away his fortune.

The second revocation came on September 4, while Floyd was in Europe on Lick's business. He came home after Lick's death, to find an entirely new set of trustees. Fortunately for the continuity of the trust, the changing boards had had since 1875 an unchanging and very efficient secretary, H. E. Mathews, who served, sometimes under great difficulties, until the trust was finally discharged in 1895. A generation later, in a diary for 1918, Mathews, then an old man, wrote in longhand his memories of the James Lick Trust, and gave this invaluable document to the San Francisco Public Library. It is the only account in existence by anyone personally concerned in the distribution of Lick's millions.

Appointment to the board could hardly have been called an empty honor. The trustees set about turning Lick's property, mainly in real estate, into money. Times were bad in those years immediately following the Jay Cooke panic, and if the property had been sold for what the trustees could get—as the two residuary legatees kept urging—not enough would have been raised to carry out all the provisions of the deed. As soon as Lick was dead, his son arrived to contest the deed, and though a compromise settlement was reached with him, other litigation continued for nearly twenty years. Even before Lick died, a crisis arose when the Independent Order of Odd Fellows tried to buy the lot at Fourth and Market Streets, could not get it for the price they wanted to pay, and had their attorney claim that the trustees' title was not safe and that Lick was insane. No one had thought him crazy when he was making and saving his money, but now that he was giving it away it took an examination by eight physicians to declare him legally competent. He had taken to his bed at the beginning of 1876, and never left his room again, but his mind was clear and capable up to his very last hours.

The curious thing is not that Lick gave so much for some of his benefactions, but that for others he set aside so little that his wishes could not be carried out. For example, he left $100,000 for the Lick Old Ladies' Home. It was enough to build and equip the home but not to run it. Finally his name was eliminated from the title, others were appealed to for donations, and the institution got under way as the University Mound Old Ladies' Home, under which name it still exists. In the same way, the $25,000 he left to establish an orphan asylum in San Jose was ridiculously inadequate. No attempt was ever made to build an asylum, but the money was used for the general benefit of San Jose orphans until it was exhausted. Lick left $150,000 for a free public bathhouse in San Francisco. Erection of the brick building at Tenth and Howard Streets—in a neighborhood where it must certainly have been needed —used up all the money except $25,000. When this was gone, in the five years from 1890 to 1895, the trustees made a charge of five cents a bath. Soon it was apparent that the bathhouse was still running at a loss, so the charge was raised to a dime. The consequence was a boycott, which reduced attendance from ten thousand to five thousand a year. Still the Lick Baths struggled along until April, 1906, when they went down with everything else in San Francisco. They were rebuilt in May, 1907, and now charged fifteen cents, in spite of which the boycott was withdrawn. But to rebuild, the trustees had had to mortgage the new building, and in a few years the mortgage holder, the Hibernia Bank, foreclosed. There are now no free public baths in the city.

Others of Lick's benefactions fared better. The California School of Mechanical Arts, for which he left $540,000, was not opened, thanks to the long-drawn-out litigation, until 1895, but it still functions in the original brick building. It is now one unit of a group of three; the Lick School, training boys in the machinery trades; the Wilmerding School, training boys in the building trades; and the Lux School, training girls in various occupations from photography to chemistry, and from domestic economy to nursing. The three together, all of them free to students of high-school age, are commonly known as the School of Mechanical Arts, though properly this name belongs only to the original school founded by Lick.

The $60,000 statue of Francis Scott Key stands in Golden Gate Park; and at Hyde and Market Streets, near the Civic Center, is the massive group of five separate figures, by Charles Happersberger, which is known as the Pioneer Monument. Lick had ordered it placed before the City Hall, and it was; but the catastrophe of 1906 destroyed the City Hall, and when the new one was built in another location, the Pioneer Monument was left in its former site. When everything else had been done, the two residuary legatees, the Society of California Pioneers and the California Academy of Sciences, each received about $600,000. The Academy of Sciences Building in Golden Gate Park was put up with this money. Another reminder of Lick in Golden Gate Park was none of his doing. He had imported from England the materials to build a conservatory at his "homestead" in San Jose which should be a duplicate of the one in Kew Gardens, in London. After his death San Francisco citizens subscribed $2,600 to buy the materials and erect the conservatory in the park which was just beginning to be transformed from the sand dunes by that inspired old Scot, John McLaren.

But of all the Lick benefactions, the greatest and most important was the observatory.

Nobody knows who first suggested to Lick the idea of building as a memorial an astronomical observatory containing the largest and most powerful telescope then on earth. His original idea — since he firmly believed that this was the only life he would know, and that immortality consists only in what a man leaves behind him—was to construct a giant pyramid, a megalomaniac monument in imitation of the ancient kings of Egypt. The $20,000 he reserved for the monuments of his relatives in Pennsylvania would have been multiplied ten times over for this. Fortunately, someone diverted his mind from this bombastic plan. It may have been W. C. Ralston, as Julian Dana thinks; it may have been a business associate named D. J. Staples; it may have been some member of the Society of California Pioneers; or he may simply have evolved the idea himself.

Perhaps it was George Davidson, himself a remarkable man. Davidson was for fifteen years president of the California Academy of Sciences; Mount Davidson was named for him. He was a scientist whose field ranged from the stars to the microscope, from ethnology to geography. His published works ran into the hundreds, his awards and honorary degrees came from all over the world. Yet his formal education ended with high school. He was brought from England to Philadelphia at seven, in 1832, and by the time he was seventeen his knowledge of astronomy had given him a position as night observer and computer in the observatory at Girard College (a school and home for orphan boys, founded by Stephen Girard) in that city. In 1850 he came to San Francisco as head of an astronomical and geographical expedition of the United States Coast Survey. Soon he set up a telescope in Lafayette Square, which constituted California's first observatory. It was through Davidson's telescope that Lick first viewed the wonders of the sky. Quite possibly it gave him his first impulse to build a far greater telescope—and may have contributed also to some of his naive misconceptions about telescopes and observatories.

Be that as it may, once he had settled on the project, Lick began at once to get the thing done on a large scale. To Lick, making a telescope was merely like erecting a building—you simply ordered the size you wanted, furnished the money, and there it was. He ordered a refracting (equatorial) instrument of forty inches diameter. At that time the most powerful telescope in existence was at the observatory in Pulkowa, Russia: its aperture was thirty inches. The great astronomer, Simon Newcomb, was sent to Europe to interview the leading telescope lens-makers; they all agreed that to construct a forty-inch lens would be impossible. (The present largest telescope, now in course of construction and to be set up at Palomar, California, will have a lens of two hundred inches.) Finally, after eighteen failures, a thirty-six-inch lens was made by Feil and Mantois, of Paris, and it was ground and polished by Alvan Clark and Sons, of Cambridge, Massachusetts.

Before there could be any thought of a telescope, however, Lick discovered, rather to his surprise, that the location of the observatory to house it was of primary importance. His first idea had been to build the observatory on his lot at Fourth and Market Streets, in downtown San Francisco! Such a location might have refuted the people who think it is always foggy in San Francsico, but it would otherwise have been quite unsuitable. At this time he intended to set aside $1,200,000 for the enterprise; eventually the sum given was $700,000.

Next, a site was considered on the shores of Lake Tahoe—meteorologically just as bad a situation. That was abandoned. Then George Schonewald, who kept a hotel at Calistoga, suggested the slopes of Mount St. Helena, an extinct volcano, one of whose prehistoric eruptions left in its wake the celebrated Petrified Forest. Lick went to visit Schonewald and inspect the proposed site. He was far past the age when he could climb mountains, but the hotelkeeper rigged up a wagon with a mattress laid in it, and Lick started to the summit. Part way up, the wagon's tailboard slipped, the mattress slid out, and Lick landed heavily on the rough road. That killed any thought of putting the Lick Observatory on Mount St. Helena! He held no grudge against Schonewald, though, and named him as one of the final Board of Trustees.

The first suggestion of Mount Hamilton, in Santa Clara County, was made by Captain Thomas E. Fraser, who was Lick's foreman at his "homestead" in San Jose. The site was then given scientific investigation by Professor S. W. Burnham. This mountain of the Coast Range (named for the Reverend Laurentine Hamilton of Oakland) has an altitude of nearly 4,500 feet. Fortunately the land belonged to the United States Government, which was willing to sell 3,130 acres at an elevation of 4,256 feet (4,209 after leveling). Building of the observatory was begun in 1879. The two residuary legatees, the Society of Pioneers and the Academy of Sciences, chafed particularly at the delay in concluding the largest of Lick's bequests. But aside from all other considerations, it was impossible to construct the dome of the observatory until the focal length of the telescope became known, and until the dome was measured the diameter of the foundation for the walls could not be estimated. The mounting for the telescope was being built by Warner and Swasey, of Cleveland, the greatest telescope makers of their time in America. In H. E. Mathews' manuscript record of the Lick Trust there is a photograph he had made, showing the telescope, without distortion due to perspective, and giving the entire height of the pier when the floor is lowered to the fullest extent. The original of this photograph was destroyed in the fire of 1906, and so this copy in the San Francisco Public Library is the only one in existence. The observatory and telescope were not handed over finally to the regents of the University of California until June 27, 1888. In June, 1938, Lick Observatory celebrated its fiftieth anniversary by an "open house" and a display of its instruments and work. By a distressing coincidence, the celebration was almost contemporaneous with the tragic death of its great ex-director, Dr. William Wallace Campbell.

Much of this highly important work done by Lick Observatory during its half century of life is too technical to be appreciated properly by the layman. It was here that the first successful photographs of the Milky Way and of comets were made. Valuable studies have been made of the moon, Mars, and Jupiter, and it was here that the fifth, sixth, seventh, and ninth moons of Jupiter were discovered. The observatory has discovered also 4,700 double stars, and found the companion of the double star Procyon. It has been a pioneer in spectroscopy, the analysis and study of the wave lengths of light.

On January 9, 1887, a year and a half before the observatory was turned over to the university, it became the burial place of its founder. Though he had made no arrangements before his death for the disposal of his remains, he had said more than once that he would like to lie on Mount Hamilton, near the observatory. Ten years and three months after his first burial in the Masonic Cemetery in San Francisco, Lick's body, sealed in a lead casket, was removed to San Jose and placed under the supporting pier of the great thirty-six-inch telescope, where it will remain as long as the observatory lasts. A bronze tablet marks the spot.

Although Lick had been bedridden for so long, his death was unexpected. On Saturday, September 30, 1876, he suddenly became very ill. The cause, says a contemporary account, was "general decay of all his physical faculties, with no disease." The actual reason for his end was probably some form of cardiac disorder.

As soon as rumors of his approaching death ran around the city, his dirty, shabby bedroom became crowded with members of the Society of Pioneers, newspapermen, and a miscellany described as "personal friends." Two reporters were actually allowed to remain in the room while he died; and nothing can emphasize more the intolerable loneliness of this old man than the callous manner in which these two hard-boiled pressmen noted his ashy skin, his hard breathing, his fallen jaw—and even the faded carpet and the frayed, dusty lace curtains. The doctor complacently said it was the most painless death he had ever witnessed, and chatted to the reporters about Lick's "cheerful con-

versation" earlier in the day and his last regret that he
would not live to see all his bequests carried out. But
the look of gloom—which the newspapers called "a
heavy scowl"—overspreading the dying man's face be-
lied the doctor's optimism.

In all that curious crowd there seems to have been
only one person who had a throb of human feeling for
old James Lick. That was a young German druggist
("for whom he had formed a strong attachment"—another evidence of his pathetic isolation) who, late in the
afternoon, asked him in German (the druggist could
speak no English) if he would not take some medicine.
Lick nodded in answer to his friendly words. It was
his last sign of consciousness, and the last speech he ever
heard was in the language which must have been familiar to him in his childhood home.

As soon as Lick was declared dead, Pietro Mezzara
took a death mask which was afterwards cast in bronze.
The body was then dressed in a decent old black suit
found hanging in his closet, and in a shirt and collar "of
a style many years past." Doubtless they were the only
kind he had. It was taken to Pioneers' Hall, where it
lay in state until October 4, in an iron coffin mounted
with silver.

Lick had practically built and subsidized Pioneers'
Hall, and he left the society which conducted it $600,-
000. Nevertheless, in 1889, when the San Francisco
Free Thought Society asked permission to hold its meetings there, Lick's fellow freethinkers were denied their
request. Moreover, it could not have been by Lick's
request that he was given a religious funeral; there is

no record of his ever having entered a church of any denomination. Since he was a lifelong Mason (on the basis of several reports, though the California Grand Lodge has no record of him in its files), it might have been expected that he would have been buried by Masonic ritual, but he was not. The services consisted of several hymns and prayers, and an address by the Reverend Dr. Horatio Stebbins.

Dr. Stebbins, faced with the necessity of eulogizing the subject of his speech, was hard put to it. It would scarcely be tactful to refer to Lick's lavish bequests, but what else was there to say except that he was a cranky, eccentric old skinflint? He was obliged to fall back on Lick's mechanical ability, to describe his watertight bureau drawers. At that, he hit Lick off very aptly:

"He was a believer in reality.... The boundaries of his nature were expressed in mechanics; the affinities of his character were expressed in real estate. In thought he did not transcend the fact; in action he never stood upon the verge of enterprise. He lingered on the barren shore till the tide came in. He waited in simplicity of manners and frugality of living until society made him rich."

Having summed up Lick's essential nature so well, Stebbins then spoiled it by adding that his life had been "without romantic incident or exploit." Had he forgotten the fabulous flour mill in San Jose?

Hardly was James Lick settled in the Masonic Cemetery, waiting for the building of his final resting place, before the son he had never seen arrived to contest his deed of trust. John Henry Lick was, by this time, himself nearly sixty years old. He was a prosperous small-town businessman, with no particular ability or distinction. He did not succeed in breaking the deed of trust; eventually he compromised with the trustees for a settlement of $533,000, out of which he agreed to compensate all collateral relatives who might be considered as heirs. The $150,000 left him by his father was also included in this settlement. He went back to Pennsylvania, invested his new fortune, and lost it all. A few years later he died a poor man.

As soon as John Henry Lick had been satisfied, the third Board of Trustees, without allowing themselves to be hampered by minor litigation, set about liquidating the real estate which had constituted James Lick's fortune. The monuments were ordered, the School of Mechanical Arts, the Old Ladies' Home, and the Free Public Baths were started, the Mount Hamilton property was acquired. Santa Clara County borrowed from the trustees $78,000 with which it built a road to the summit, the loan later being repaid by county warrants. The thirty-six-inch telescope, the largest in the world, which when finished would bring the moon to the equivalent of a distance of sixty miles, was already in preparation. Lick had wished that the telescope, like the bathhouse, should be free and open to the public; he had no conception whatever of the demands or difficulties of astronomical observation. However, the trustees and the director of the observatory, when it was completed, found a way out: to this day Lick Observatory is open every Saturday evening to anyone who wishes to visit it, and tens of thousands of persons go every year to have the great equatorial telescope and the other later instruments explained to them by the staff, and to gaze for themselves at "the wonders of the heavens." The most popular view is that of the vast, far-off star-clusters, especially of the Great Cluster in Hercules, of which the astronomer Harlan True Stetson tells the story of a tourist who, after gazing in awe at this group of a hundred thousand suns each mightier than our own, gasped: "Well, I guess it doesn't matter much, after all, who is nominated for president!"

So, gradually, all James Lick's legacies were carried out, until in 1895 the money had all been spent and the trustees were discharged. Lick's body had then been eight years sealed under the great telescope. The observatory, far more than any grotesque pyramid would have been, is his memorial and his monument. Once one might have said it will remain forever to remind the world of the strange man who deprived himself of every comfort, and gave away his millions; now one can say at least that only an aerial bomb could cause its destruction. Curiously, a few years ago an airplane crashed on it and damaged one building.

In the city where Lick spent the last thirty years of his life, and where once he was a familiar sight to every resident, all that officially commemorates his name is a junior high school and a narrow alley midway in the block where once stood his ornate hotel.

CHAPTER II

The Spirit of '49:
SAM BRANNAN

"THERE'S THAT damned flag again!" cried the Mormon elder, flinging his hat on the deck. Some report he said "rag."

He could hardly be blamed. He had come all the way from New York, around Cape Horn, a journey of five and a half months, to settle his two hundred-odd Latter Day Saints under the protecting aegis of Mexico. And there, as the *Brooklyn* sailed through the Golden Gate, he saw fluttering over the village of Yerba Buena the very same Stars and Stripes that had exiled his people from Nauvoo and sent them on their wanderings. Captain John B. Montgomery, of the United States Army, had preceded him by three weeks; California belonged to the United States.

But it took more than a mere change of government to daunt Sam Brannan. On board ship he had already excommunicated four of his followers for "wicked and licentious conduct"—an action which was to bounce back on him later and explode. He had been supreme dictator and he intended to remain so. When two children were born during the voyage he ordered the boy named Atlantic and the girl named Pacific, after the oceans which had heard their first squalls. He found only sixty non-Spaniards in Yerba Buena, and his Mormons formed an easy majority. He meant to keep them in control. His mind was thoroughly made up: as soon as he had his people settled, to find Brigham Young and his overland party and persuade them to join him in California. He did not realize that Brigham Young matched him in stubbornness and will power; that he was equally big and broad-shouldered and deep-chested, equally loud voiced, and equally bent on having his own way.

Meanwhile, there was immediate work for Brannan to do. He arrived on July 31, 1846. (Two weeks later he preached a sermon—the first non-Roman Catholic sermon ever preached in California.) Soon after, he performed the first non-Catholic wedding, when he married Lizzie Winner to Basil Hall, the scene of the festivities being the only public hall in town—the calaboose. This pioneer couple met with melodramatic tragedy: four years later, in Washington, D.C., the bride was burnt to death by a woman slave she had mistreated.

Brannan, who attracted "firsts" to himself, also figured in the first trial under American occupancy—as the defendant! The excommunications he had handed out so freely had rankled; some of the Saints brought charges against him of improper administration of their funds. The jury was hung, and the case was dismissed. It is quite likely that Brannan had handled the company's money in a free and easy fashion; he was always a plunger, a spender, and a speculator, but he was as openhanded as he was acquisitive, and doubtless thought of the general fund as given to him to dispose of as he saw fit. This trial had historical significance far beyond its practical importance; it was the result of grafting the Anglo-Saxon jury system on the Spanish form of government by *alcalde*, or mayor. It also created the first schism among the Mormons, between Brannan's friends and his foes, and thus kept them, in spite of their great preponderance in numbers, from dominating the town.

As soon as Brannan had his flock settled in adobe shacks and tents, a matter of some ten months, he hurried back by land across the mountains to find Young and persuade him to bring his party to California and join in establishing a strong Mormon state. He found Young in the Green River country in eastern Utah. He used all his oratory in vain; Young remained adamant, unwilling to bring the Mormons into contact with people as competitive as were their fellow Americans, and knowing the hopelessness of trying to colonize a seaport. "Let us go to California," he said, "and we cannot stay there for over five years; but let us stay in the mountains, and we can raise our own potatoes, and eat them; and I calculate to stay here." Brannan had to go back empty-handed, but in revenge he told his followers that the Utah land was poor and that they would be fools to move there.

This very peculiar young Mormon elder, with his shaggy hair, his sideburns and imperial, his flashing black eyes and resonant voice, his dandified dress and coarse, aggressive manner, was "a State of Maine man." He had been born in Saco, York County, Maine, in

March, 1819, the son of Thomas Brannan, a farmer. He was christened Samuel, but was never called anything but Sam. He had very little schooling, and that of the most primitive variety. When he was fourteen, his older sister Mary Ann married a man named Badlam, and Sam's mother sent him with the newly married couple to Lake County, Ohio, where he was apprenticed to a printer. Three years later he "bought his time," and started out as an itinerant journeyman. By 1842 he had traveled in every state then in the Union, making his way as a printer but also speculating in land, without success. He had also failed as the editor of literary weeklies in Indiana and in New Orleans.

The year 1842 found him in New York, and, rather surprisingly, a Mormon missionary. He had been converted to the faith in Ohio, and given his commission by Joseph Smith himself. There has been much speculation as to how much of Brannan's Mormonism was an honest religious conviction, and how much of it was a shrewd intuition that the Mormons were economically on the upgrade, and that tying up with them was a short cut to prosperity. But in those earliest years he seems to have been sincere enough, though he profited immediately by his connection, being made publisher of the denomination's organ, the *Messenger* (later the *Prophet*). In November, 1845 the persecuted Church of Jesus Christ of the Latter Day Saints held a convention in New York (at which Brannan was present), and decided to strike west from Nauvoo, Illinois, and seek a more peaceful home somewhere in the wilderness. Brannan, a full-fledged elder, was selected to charter the 372-ton *Brook-*

lyn and lead the contingent which preferred to go by water. He started the same day that Brigham Young and his party left overland from Nauvoo.

On his way back to California after his rebuff by Young, Brannan went via Sutter's Fort, where Captain John Sutter had established the domain which he called New Helvetia. The grand scale on which Sutter operated and the vast potentialities of the region at the delta of the American River fascinated Brannan. Real estate always produced in him a sort of intoxication. Sutter was building a mill, and Brannan seized the opportunity to start a store to furnish supplies for it. He called the place where the mill was being put up, Coloma, and another spot where he established a second store and a mill of his own, Natoma—both after Indian tribes of the neighborhood.

Mills, indeed, were one of Brannan's passions. Before he left Yerba Buena for Utah, he had already started the first two flour mills in California, about where lower Clay Street now runs in San Francisco, near the water front. The equipment had been brought in the *Brooklyn*. The ship had also carried a complete printing press, for Brannan after all was a printer and had been a publisher. One of his first enterprises, while he was settling his colonists, was to start Yerba Buena's first paper, the *Yerba Buena California Star*, with "Dr." Elbert P. Jones set up as editor. The *Star* made its first appearance on January 9, 1847. The site of its publishing plant is now that of the only all-Chinese telephone exchange outside of China.

Brannan's enterprises in the district around Sutter's

Fort did not prevent frequent visits to San Francisco—as the village of Yerba Buena was now called—to attend to his affairs there. In the attitude of the *Star* toward the proclamation changing the town's name, lay a story of newspaper rivalry. For the *Star* by now had a rival, a paper called the *Californian*, published by Dr. Robert Semple (a dentist by profession, and six feet eight inches tall), first in Monterey, then in a little town on the north side of the bay. Dr. Semple advocated calling his town Santa Francisca, after General Mariano Vallejo's lady—and also because the first place which adopted the name of the bay would attract the immigrants and insure its rapid growth. But Yerba Buena got there first, and became San Francisco, so Semple had to content himself with Señora Vallejo's middle name, Benicia. One might have expected the *Star*, which was already indulging in very nasty personalities between Dr. Jones and Dr. Semple, to have welcomed this black eye to the *Californian*. But Brannan sulked because the name had been changed without consulting him, and the *Star* still listed Yerba Buena as its place of publication. The indignant citizens gathered, placed little Dr. Jones neatly in a hogshead, and rolled him around the Plaza (soon to be Portsmouth Square). Next day the *Star* came out with a San Francisco date line, and Brannan capitulated completely by hailing the newly baptized city as "the Liverpool or New York of the Pacific Ocean."

Soon after, Semple moved the *Californian* to San Francisco, and the two papers became more deadly enemies than ever. But the climax of their rivalry did not come until January, 1848, when James Marshal, who was building the mill at Coloma for Captain Sutter, discovered gold.

The *Californian* (though not very excitedly) acclaimed the find in March. Therefore, the *Star* was in honor bound to deride it as a hoax. Unfortunately, while this ridicule was appearing, the *Star's* owner, Sam Brannan, was up to his ears in the gold discovery. Major Stephen Cooper, one of the early pioneers, included this entry in his privately printed memoirs, in 1888:

"On the 4th of May, 1848, Sam Brannan, a Mormon, came to Benicia in a little sail vessel. He came to my house, with his saddle on his back, and dunned [asked] me for a horse, saying that he had some horses at Sutter's Fort and wanted to collect them. I furnished him a good horse. When he was about to mount the horse, he told me he was not going after horses. He remarked, I know the biggest speculation in the world, and if there is anything in it, on my return I will lead you into the secret; he was gone some four or five days. On his return my horse brought him to Knight's Landing, on the Sacramento River. He had him [the horse] run down; procured a fresh horse, which brought him to Vacaville, having also run that one down; another fresh one brought him on to Benicia. He told me he had stood over a man five minutes, and in that time had seen him wash out eight dollars, and remarked that there was more gold than all the people in California could take out in fifty years. That was the first gold excitement that ever amounted to anything."

The worthy Major Cooper decided that gold would become a drug on the market, and that he would be better advised to stay in Benicia and mind his own business—a resolution which his contemporary descendants have reason to regret. As for Brannan, he was more than satisfied. He dashed into San Francisco, rushed to Portsmouth Square, and waving a bottle (some say a sack) of gold dust, shouted in his taurine bellow: "*Gold! Gold! Gold from the American River!*"

A few weeks later the *Star* had to suspend publication. But so did the *Californian*. There were only seven men left in San Francisco. In spite of the exodus, Brannan had meanwhile got out a special edition, written by Dr. Victor Fourgeaud, a medical man from South Carolina, extolling the attractions of the state, and distributed throughout the Mississippi Valley in the emigrant supply towns.

Brannan, of course, intended to profit by the gold rush he had inaugurated. His stores did $150,000 business a month, and when the new city of Sacramento was laid out, Brannan owned a quarter of it. The day he opened the City Hotel there, he entertained the entire population for a day and a night. Naturally he was invited to name the new town's streets, but he did not show much imagination, for he gave numbers to the north and south streets and letters to the east and west. He also took time out to help found Yuba City.

In the American River, about two miles from Folsom, Brannan staked a claim on an island which he called Mormon Island. It was worked by members of the "Mormon Battalion," originally formed by Brigham Young; and as an elder of the church Brannan collected tithes of their takings. When they asked the government authorities if their "high priest" had a right to take away 30 per cent of their earnings, they were informed that he had a right to do so if they were fools enough to let him. Discipline and piety were still strong enough to keep the money flowing into Brannan's pocket, but then Brigham Young, back in Utah, heard about this unauthorized tithe taking, and sent an apostle to demand the money for the church. It was the Lord's money, said the apostle, and must be given to Him.

"You go back and tell Brigham," retorted Brannan, "that I'll give up the Lord's money when he sends me a receipt signed by the Lord."

When Brigham Young got this message back, he excommunicated Brannan forthwith, on the grounds that "his course and habits were not consistent with the life of a Latter Day Saint." Over and over again, for several years, Young sent his "Destroying Angels," or "Danites," who might be described today as gunmen, to get the tithe money from Brannan, but Brannan always had the "Angels" met in the desert by his own bodyguard, whom he called "Exterminators"; and after five years of seeing his "Angels" regularly "exterminated," Young let the matter drop. But, as someone has remarked, Brannan's life wouldn't have been worth ten cents in Utah after that.

By the late fifties, there was not much to collect; in 1851 the Mormon colonists at New Hope, on Mormon Island, quarreled among themselves and with Brannan and went in a body to Salt Lake City; and in 1858 Young called all the faithful "home to Zion," and few Mormons were left in California. They had never been the majority in San Francisco after the first year, though in 1847. when William A. Leidesdorff gave a ball in honor of Commodore Stockton, nearly every one of the invited guests was a Latter Day Saint. Since dancing and the theater were the only recreations permitted to Mormons, they were prominent in the theaters and at balls, but never seen in saloons or gambling houses.

The "Mormon Battalion" had also been dissolved by this time; it had been made up in the first place of honest farmers, carpenters, and blacksmiths, most of whom preferred to go north to work in the mines. During its time in San Francisco it had been called to arms just twice. The first time was when John Brown, of the Portsmouth House, had an arrangement with an army officer to supply him nightly with a flask of whiskey after the bar was closed, on the signal called through the window: "The Spaniards are in the brush." One night Brown was sound asleep. The officer yelled the magic words so loudly that the doughty battalion sprang to duty and fired hotly at the surrounding scenery. The second time was when a coffeepot exploded in Brown's kitchen and the noise was mistaken for the first shot of an invasion. But ludicrous as these incidents were, the Mormon Battalion was made up of brave men ready to defend themselves, and many of them did good service later in the days of the Vigilantes.

Brannan had started his first store at Sutter's Fort in 1847 with C. C. Smith as partner; in 1848 he bought Smith out. He still kept his first San Francisco holdings and interests, though the *Star* had been sold, with its printing plant which had once been the equipment of

the *Prophet,* to E. C. Kemble. This was no triumph for
the *Californian,* which also gave up the ghost at the
same time. Kemble combined the two papers as the *Alta
Californian,* which in its long lifetime was the ladder to
fame of nearly every San Francisco writer.

One amusing story comes out of the two years which
Brannan spent in and around Sacramento. It concerned
a character almost as unusual as Brannan himself—
Charles Edward Pickett, known as "Philosopher"
Pickett.

Pickett, a Virginian, had founded the Coast's first
newspaper, in Oregon, in 1845—a sheet entitled the
Flumgudgeon Gazette and Bumble Bee Budget. Coming
to California, he brought from Hawaii five Merino sheep,
the first wool-bearing sheep imported to the then terri-
tory, and settled in Sonoma as a landowner. The gold
rush ended this, and Pickett became a merchant at Sutter's Fort, where he tangled with Brannan. In subsequent years he became the political gadfly of California,
ending with an uproarious scene in which he usurped
the seat of State Supreme Court Justice J. B. Crockett,
spent eight months in the San Francisco county jail for
contempt of court, and unsuccessfully sued the Supreme
Court for $100,000 for false imprisonment.

The Brannan affair arose from a little shooting match
at Sutter's Fort. Pickett didn't care to be arrested for
murder, and the recently elected *alcalde* didn't relish the
idea of apprehending him. So he resigned in favor of
Sam Brannan. Brannan invited "Philosopher" to bring
himself in. Pickett's arsenal was laid on the table, together with whiskey and glasses. The matter was then

talked over amicably, except at one point when Brannan stepped down from the judge's bench and, doubling as prosecuting attorney, began an eloquent plea against the defendant. When the trial was not finished at the end of the day, Pickett was allowed to carry his guns home and bring them back the next morning. The jury disagreed. Pickett was tried again, not before Brannan, and acquitted.

In 1849 Brannan returned to San Francisco to live. He formed a partnership in the China trade with a man named Osborn, but his chief source of income was from real estate, his earliest passion. Only one legend remains of Brannan the China trader. The bulk of his imports consisted of tea, which was auctioned off in public. One day a group of merchants began bidding at ridiculously low prices in the hope of getting a bargain; the tea was worth from $1.50 to $4 a pound, and sixty cents was the highest bid. Brannan then appeared and made a bid of sixty-one cents. The other bidders let the tea be knocked down to him at this price, expecting that they could get the rest of it for no more. "How many pounds do you want?" asked the auctioneer. "All of it," answered Brannan, and with a smile at the crestfallen faces took his goods back to hold till he could get a better price for them.

The time soon came when Sam Brannan owned a fifth of San Francisco, including nearly all the property abutting on Market Street. Rents, like prices, were incredibly high, and his returns from rented property alone would have made him the first California millionaire. The tea caddy which Sherman and Mason had sent to Washington as a demonstration, packed with 230 ounces and more of gold dust, had done its work well. A man who had got there first, like Brannan, could no more help coining money than he could help breathing.

The days of his extensive investments, spread out all over California—and finally spread out too far for his own good—were yet to come, but he was already a man of substance, and respected by those whom his brash manner and aggressive personality repelled, but who felt instinctively that gold and brains must inevitably go together. In this particular instance they were not mistaken. Brannan was made a member of the first city council, in August 1849. He was foremost in organizing the volunteer fire companies, and paid $18,000 to give the best engine yet made to the Brannan Fire Company. He helped to organize the Society of California Pioneers in 1850; three years later he reorganized it and became its president. He was the chief patron of the Music Fund.

When San Francisco's decent citizens, in 1851, found themselves faced for the second time by a state of chaos and terrorism, it was natural that they should turn for leadership to the richest man in San Francisco, who had already proved his mettle against the "Hounds."

This earlier struggle between the forces of evil and those of good citizenship in San Francisco had taken place in July, 1849. Many of the first United States soldiers sent to California and mustered out there were roughs from the slums of New York. Calling themselves at first the "Bowery Boys," and associating them-

Sam Brannan at the height of his power and wealth.

selves with rowdies drawn by the gold rush, they quickly degenerated into a gang variously known as "Regulators" or "Hounds." Several of San Francisco's devastating fires were attributed to them and their allies, the "Sydney Ducks," escaped or time-served convicts from Australia. No man's life was safe on the streets at night, but their chief animus was against the foreigners in the town, and especially against the tent colony of Chileans. So far as the "Hounds" had a political theory, they were adherents of the "Know Nothing" Party, a semisecret organization much like the later Ku Klux Klan, and with the same xenophobia.

The climax came in the summer of 1849, when the "Hounds" raided the Chilean colony, raped a mother and daughter, and murdered the mother. Brannan was the leader in the spontaneous uprising of good citizens which demanded their long overdue punishment. In return they threatened to burn his home, and indeed later it was burned by deliberate intent. This home of Brannan's was near Portsmouth Square, hard by the little redwood schoolhouse which also served as town hall, courthouse, church, and jail. As evidence of San Francisco's laxity with criminals, one of the few men ever locked up there appeared next morning at the jailer's office with the door of the jail chained to his back, loudly demanding his breakfast!

The grand jury finally indicted an assortment of the "Hounds," but the *alcalde*, Dr. T. M. Leavenworth, was afraid to order their arrest. Two hundred and thirty deputies, led by Brannan, accomplished that for him. Nine of the criminals were convicted and ordered banished from the town, but they never even left; nor did those sentenced to up to ten years each remain long on the ships in the harbor on which they were placed in lieu of a proper prison. The gangsters merely went underground and kept on operating. In spite of the night patrol organized by Brannan, there were six or more great fires in the next year, one of which consumed Brannan's house.

But even San Francisco patience had its limits. A man named John Jenkins, a "Sydney Duck" familiarly known by the simple title of "The Miscreant," actually stole a safe in broad daylight from the Long Wharf and walked off with it on his shoulders. That seemed to touch off a spark. In Sam Brannan's office, on June 9, 1851, the first San Francisco Committee of Vigilance was formed. Brannan was its second member and its first president; before long he was replaced as president by William T. Coleman, because his rashness and pugnacity interfered with the calm discharge of civilian functions which was the keynote of the righteous Vigilantes. But before he was deposed, Brannan had the pleasure of holding on to the rope by which Jenkins was hanged on the same wharf where he had stolen the safe.

The Vigilantes had made no attempt to conceal their identity. The inquest on Jenkins named Brannan and eight others as his killers. Immediately the entire committee of nearly two hundred prominent citizens published their names. The committee continued to mop up. In the midst of their housecleaning, they almost caused a serious miscarriage of justice. They were not to blame, however; it depended on one of the most unusual coincidences in history. A gambler named Thomas Berdue was arrested after being identified by numerous persons as one "English Jim" Stuart, a badly wanted "Hound." He was Stuart's exact double, even to scars and an amputated finger. Brannan was all for hanging him at once: "These men are murderers, I say, as well as thieves. I know it, and will die or see them hung by the neck." But Coleman's warning against precipitate action prevailed, and fortunately so; the next month Stuart himself was captured (and later hanged), and the mistake was apparent to everyone. Berdue, who had been held in jail in Marysville, was released immediately and given several thousand dollars in compensation. Within an hour he had started to lose the sum at the gambling table, and he soon disappeared forever.

The path of the Vigilantes was not cleared for them by the constituted officials. Corruption and cowardice were in evidence in both the city and state government. In August, Governor John McDougal attacked the committee and "the despotic control of a self-constituted association, unknown and acting in defiance of the law." The Vigilantes then published an affidavit showing that McDougal had previously met with their executive committee and had told them "in case any judge was guilty of maladministration to hang him, and he would appoint others." In spite of this showing up, the governor ordered two of the "Sydney Ducks" who had been seized to be taken away by force from the Vigilance Committee. Before long the committee got them again, and hanged them, marking the end, for all practical purposes, of the "Ducks" and their friends the "Hounds." The kindest thing to say about McDougal is that later he became hopelessly insane.

For several years San Francisco was more or less peaceful, and then came, in 1855, the depredations of Casey and Cora and the assassination of the fearless editor, James King of William. Once more Sam Brannan's brassy voice was heard, "louder than the bell at the Oriental Hotel," demanding the lynching of Cora for his murder of United States Marshal Richardson. In the hope of avoiding trouble, Brannan was ordered arrested, then released on his own recognizance. With the formation of the Second Vigilance Committee, cooler heads were in control, and Brannan played little part in the trials and executions at "Fort Gunnybags."

By 1855 Brannan was one of the principal figures in California, and one of the richest men in America. His investments were multifarious. In 1851 had occurred the grotesque episode when he headed a filibustering expedition to take over the kingdom of the Sandwich Islands, as Hawaii was then called. In the course of this rash enterprise he had bought much property and put up many buildings in Honolulu, but he was deported by King Kamahameha III, and the United States government forced him to sell all his Hawaiian holdings.

In California he had no such difficulties. He bought 160,000 acres of what then seemed desert land in Los Angeles County. He traveled to Europe and came back with blooded horses and sheep and choice wine-grape roots. He reclaimed the tule lands in the valley. He invested in the railroad, the telegraph company, the express companies, the banks.

In 1853 he was elected state senator, but resigned at once, because of "important business in New York." (What that business was will soon be seen.) The honor, however, he treasured, though he never seems to have used the title. It was the time of his greatest affluence and his greatest power; the time when the way to advertise a product in California was to announce on huge signs: "Sam Brannan Buys It!" When the exotic Lola Montez appeared at the American Theater in May, 1853, Sam Brannan, who had met her on the ship coming back from one of his New York trips, and had been added to her many conquests, paid five hundred dollars for a box at her opening night.

Brannan's rise had been sensational, and his fall abrupt.

In 1859 he became enthusiastic about the possibilities of the Napa Valley and its medicinal springs. At a place which he called Calistoga (California plus Saratoga) he built a spa which he hoped would become the Western rival of the fashionable Saratoga in the East. He backed a boom in Napa Valley lands, which, like most booms, collapsed with a bang. Brannan, the invincible, was licked. Stubborn as ever, he poured most of his fortune into the failing project. He lost everything. The Calistoga estate was bought later by Leland Stanford, one of the railroad "Big Four." The town still exists, and the resort, but it has never been particularly fashionable or prosperous.

In his disappointment, Brannan, who had always been a hearty drinker, able to carry his liquor with the best of them, lost his grip. His business acumen and his civic pride were drowned together in alcohol. As if prophetically, his last desperate attempt to make Calistoga pay was the building of a distillery. Pretty soon it was common talk in San Francisco that Sam Brannan was drunk every afternoon—drunk and noisy and reeling. He had accumulated much wealth, however; it did not all go at once. When the Civil War was imminent, he was one of the strongest of Union supporters. He gave more, during the war, to the Sanitary Commission, from his sinking fortune, than anyone else in California. Unfortunately, he had not stopped at donations. In a New York hotel, in 1860, he picked a fight with a man who had been captain of a slaver, and was arrested. Later he staged a huge alcoholic celebration of the fall of Charleston before it fell. He floated a Mexican bond issue in the fight against the Austrian emperor, Maximilian, and he paid for an American legion, known as Brannan's Contingent, which went to fight on the republican side. (In the end, this was the only one of his investments which paid him dividends at the close of his life.)

The man whom everyone in San Francisco had looked up to had become San Francisco's butt, the subject of a hundred jeering stories. In 1866 he reached the nadir.

To recount the story of Brannan's painful last years it is necessary first to unsnarl his tangled matrimonial history. Very little was known of its details before Reva Scott, a descendant of Mormon pioneers, in 1944 published "Samuel Brannan and the Golden Fleece," based on hitherto unavailable Mormon records. From this it appears that Brannan was one of the many who took advantage of the "dispensation" sanctioning plural marriage—but without the knowledge of his second wife. His first was Harriet Hatch, whom he deserted when their daughter Almira was a baby. The "important business" which kept him out of the state senate in 1853 was a trip East to see at last how they were getting on. He brought them, with Harriet's mother, to San Francisco, and established them in his own former home, where they posed as vaguely distant "relatives." Brannan supported them in return for their promise never to reveal their real status. For in 1844 he had married Anna Eliza Corwin. Eventually Harriet divorced him privately in Los Angeles and remarried; Almira took her stepfather's name.

But by then Brannan and "Lizzie" were permanently estranged. His affair with Lola Montez caused the first break. After their younger son died, Mrs. Brannan returned home, but never lived with him again as his wife. She persuaded him to take the family to Europe, then sent him back alone and stayed in France eight years with the children. The final collapse of their marriage came when she discovered he had had an affair with his own niece. She divorced him in 1870. Only Fanny Kemble, his favorite daughter, ever saw him again. Little Don Francisco had died at two. Samuel, Jr., Adelaide, and Lisa were on their mother's side. On his family Brannan settled the very last of his fortune.

Stanford had not yet bought his Calistoga estate, and the next heard of Sam was when, staying at that resort, he was shot eight times by a man who disputed ownership of a mill with him. In spite of his degeneration, he was still tough, and he recovered.

In 1880 the Mexican government, in gratitude for his help against Maximilian, gave Brannan two million acres of land in Sonora. Brannan's old grandiose ambitions revived; he planned an American colony in Mexico. It cost $100,000 to survey the land, and the surveying company took most of the property as its fee, since Brannan no longer had $100,000 in cash. Then he discovered that the Yaquis, who considered this land their home, had not been consulted about having it given away over their heads, and that it would be exceedingly uncomfortable, to say the least, for any outsider to settle there.

As if in token of his Mexican sympathies, in 1881 Brannan had married for the third time, in Tucson. His new wife was a widow whose maiden name had been Carmen deLlaguno. The marriage lasted only two years.

By 1888 he was settled on a little ranch at Escondido, in San Diego County, near the Mexican border. There he tried to raise Smyrna figs, which had become adapted to California since the Roedings, of Fresno, had imported from Syria the fig wasp, necessary for their fertilization.

Brannan was a prematurely old man by now. The gunshot wounds had caused paralysis of his right side. But there was life in him yet; he fought his way out of paralysis too. In 1887 he had come to San Francisco for the last time. He stayed at a twenty-five-cent flophouse, he who had once owned a quarter of Sacramento and a fifth of San Francisco. A curious reporter interviewed him. "Do you see those two men?" said Sam Brannan, pointing through the dusty window. "I met them yesterday, and they crossed the street to avoid me. When they had no money, I staked them; I made them the rich men they are today." That same year he had sold pencils from door to door in Nogales, Arizona.

All at once Mexico decided to make good again on its debt to Brannan, since the Sonora gift had been a fiasco. Its government settled $49,000 on him. According to some accounts (which Mrs. Scott denies) a strange transformation took place—Brannan used the money in partial payment of his debts, impoverishing himself once more; and he stopped drinking. Certainly the money went somewhere; in his last years he lived mostly on a pension from the Odd Fellows. It is pleasant to think that at the end of his life, with a last spurt of his old stubborn energy, he had reformed.

He was just past his seventieth birthday when he died, at the little Escondido ranch, of what was then called "inflamation of the bowels" (perhaps appendicitis). For more than a year his body lay in the receiving vault of Mount Hope Cemetery, in San Diego, because there was no money with which to bury him. In 1890 Alexander Badlam, son of the sister who had taken Sam with her to Ohio when he was fourteen, bought a lot in the cemetery for him. A two-inch wooden stake marks his grave.

"Graceless," "rough," "violent," "coarse-fibered," "forbidding," "saturnine," "bombastic"—these were some of the words flung at Brannan after his downfall. Charles Henry Webb called him "that thing of booty and a bore forever." But Asbury Harpending, who had often been in partnership with him, tempered some of this invective by adding that Brannan in his good days was keen-witted, resolute, and fearless. And everyone who knew him, friends and enemies alike, acknowledged his prodigal generosity. No more openhanded man ever lived: his philanthropy was often extravagant but was never grudging; he was an easy mark for every cadger.

In the city where he lived so long and played so great a part, few marks of him remain except the name of a dingy street "South of the slot." A plaque on the Chinese telephone exchange shows the site of his newspaper office; and in July, 1940, a bronze plaque was set in the sidewalk at Broadway and Battery Street, where the *Brooklyn* docked in 1846. This is all by which San Francisco remembers Sam Brannan. But H. H. Bancroft, who knew and disliked him, was fair enough to write: "He probably did more for San Francisco . . . than was affected by the combined efforts of scores of others."

CHAPTER III

Cabby to Impressario:
TOM MAGUIRE

THE HISTORY of Thomas Maguire, who was always called Tom, is an Alger story—with a slip at the end. Many old-time San Franciscans rose to eminence from very humble beginnings. Senator David C. Broderick, Maguire's close friend, was once a saloonkeeper in Brooklyn. Maguire started lower than that. The first glimpse of him is as a hackman in New York about 1845, with a stand in Park Row.

Exactly when he was born is not known; birth records were not kept in those days by poor and illiterate families; and besides, Maguire was as sensitive about his age as a prima donna. The probability is that he was a native New Yorker, that he arrived on earth somewhere around 1820, and that he was seventy-five or seventy-six when he died. All that was ever seen of his family in San Francisco was an old father, Irish by birth, who died in 1850 and was buried from St. Francis Roman Catholic Church in North Beach (now the Italian district).

Tom Maguire was wholly illiterate; he could not even sign his name. His numerous pronouncements to the press in later years were all dictated. When he died, in 1896, George E. Barnes, in the San Francisco *Bulletin*, remarked smugly: "Had Maguire been an educated man, he would have been a better one." The slur, if directed at his mentality, was unmerited. Without any education whatever, he was as shrewd and far-seeing as he was, occasionally, unscrupulous.

He was married twice. His second wife was a beauty, who carried her clothes well — she was called "the only woman in San Francisco who could wear a shawl properly"—and she was noted for her graceful figure and her lovely shoulders. But his first wife, who died midway in his career, who was his business associate and adviser, whose shrewdness and daring equaled his own, he brought with him from New York when he arrived in San Francisco in September, 1849. To the habitués of flashy barrooms of the period she had been known only as "little Em." Tom won her in fair fight with a rowdy named Dick Donnell, who had been her protector before him; and later on, before they came West, he married her. She was not pretty, but she had brains. No man could have had a better wife.

Maguire's New York cabstand was near the old Park Theater. By 1846 he and another man had progressed to running the bars of the theater's second and third tiers—for in those days the alcoholic rush between acts was such that every tier of a theater had to have its separate bar. This was Tom's first "theatrical" experience, but he was stage-struck for life. Later on, when he built his theaters in San Francisco, the first consideration always was the proximity of a good bar, and of accessible gambling rooms, from each of which he took due share of the profits.

In 1847 Maguire went still farther up the ladder; with Captain Isaiah Rynders, a noted Tammany chieftain of the period, he became owner of a famous and prosperous saloon in City Hall Place. Just why Maguire and Rynders parted—certainly not for political reasons, for he was an ardent Tammanyite—and why he should have abandoned this sure steppingstone to wealth and taken the long, hard journey to San Francisco, are questions that will never be answered now. The probability is that, having acquired savings enough to enable him to strike out for himself, he was fired, like thousands of others, by the unlimited prospects open to ambitious young Americans in California in those exciting "days of '49."

His first venture in San Francisco was a saloon again, housed in a large frame building on Kearny Street near Washington, opposite Portsmouth Square, which till recently had been the Plaza of Yerba Buena. The building had a vacant second story, whose barnlike interior called aloud for some public use. It became the first of the three Jenny Lind Theaters built by Maguire on the site between 1850 and 1852.

Jenny Lind, "the Swedish nightingale," never, in spite of assertion and tradition, sang in California. Barnum would not risk the expense of taking her to the Far West. Yet all over the state theaters could be found named for her, and to this day you will hear that she sang in the so-called first theater in California, in Monterey, though she never set foot in the town. Maguire's Jenny Lind Theater was not the first theater even in San Francisco, being preceded by two others.

All, however, were built within a few months of one another. Tom had struck a gold mine; he had found a city where people were stage-mad, and he exploited the passion—which indeed he shared—for all that it was worth.

The only rival he had was "Yankee" Robinson, who was called "Doctor" because he had once kept a drugstore. But in a few years Robinson went back East on a visit and died, and Maguire was left in sole possession of the field. He liked to think of his career as that of a great general, and loved to call himself "the Napoleon of Impresarios." He forgot (or rather never knew) that Napoleon had not only his Austerlitz and his Wagram, but also his Elba, his Waterloo, and his Saint Helena.

But the consideration, if presented to him, would not have dashed Tom Maguire. He always stood off bad luck intrepidly—just as once, in his San Francisco saloon, he stood off a young desperado who had killed four men and had a six-shooter pointed at Tom's ample middle. Maguire stood there without a sign of fear until the police arrived and arrested the young man. In the same way, when three times fire razed his Jenny Lind Theater—fire which each time, by some unlucky mischance, spared all the rest of the block—he merely built a new and better theater on the site. The second fire was only nine days after the theater had reopened, but Tom was undaunted. His third theater was built of stone—yellow sandstone from Australia. To offset this sunny exterior, the entire interior was painted pink, with touches of gilt on the carved proscenium boxes and backdrop which represented (a little forebodingly) "a romantic ruin."

The jinx pursued him. The third Jenny Lind had cost too much and he could not make it pay. A truly Napoleonic scheme enabled him to recoup his loss. He merely sold the theater to the city for $200,000, for use as a City Hall!

His credit re-established, he built a new theater, temporarily known as San Francisco Hall, later as Maguire's Opera House, and installed Junius Brutus Booth, Jr., as manager. The entire Booth family, with the exception of the ill-starred John Wilkes Booth, appeared at one time or another under Maguire's aegis; Edwin Booth had his first triumphs in San Francisco, first played *Hamlet* in a Maguire theater, and for a long time was one of the little theatrical colony clustered around Maguire's home on Telegraph Hill.

By 1858, Tom Maguire was the undisputed czar of the theater in California north of Monterey. He owned all the theaters of consequence in San Francisco, all in Sacramento, Stockton, Sonora, Marysville, and in a dozen towns then thriving mining centers but now mere names. He even penetrated later to Virginia City, Nevada, metropolis of the Comstock Lode. The system was for each theater to have its own stock company, which supported visiting stars. These came around the Horn or through Panama, and after their California tour frequently went on to Australia. The list of famous actors and actresses whom Tom Maguire brought to his theaters is a roster of all the most distinguished English-speaking thespians of the era. They included

Edwin Forrest; John McCullough; Charles Kean; Dion Boucicault (who appeared not in one of his own dramas but in *Hamlet*); Junius Brutus (Sr.) and Edwin Booth; Lawrence Barrett, who became Booth's long-time partner, and who while living in California built the first business block in Modesto; Joseph Jefferson, in his early performances of *Rip Van Winkle;* and three great foreign stars—Madames Ristori, Januschek, and Modjeska. It was for Maguire also that the exotic Adah Isaacs Menken, who later was Swinburne's mistress and the last passion of the aging Alexandre Dumas, *père,* appeared in the sensational *Mazeppa,* in the flimsiest of garments, strapped to a plunging horse—with Junius Brutus Booth, Jr., as leading man.

Everything was grist that came to Tom Maguire's theatrical mill—minstrels, Japanese jugglers, the earliest of burlesque shows, and finally grand opera, which became his mania. He actually introduced Italian grand opera in San Francisco, and he persisted in producing it, in spite of losses running up to twenty thousand dollars a season. In 1863, in the midst of the Civil War, he built the Academy of Music, at Montgomery and Pine Streets, as "a temple of opera." It was the beginning of his financial downfall. But the end was not yet.

San Francisco's dramatic taste matured slowly. Nobody wanted grand opera except "society," which came the first night to show off its clothes and jewels and did not appear again, and the Italian fishermen, who mobbed the Academy to sing in the chorus, but had no money even for gallery seats. As for the drama, it had not been so many years since, when the signal of an approaching steamer was heard from Telegraph Hill during the fifth act of a play, the audience arose *en masse* and deserted the theater, leaving the chagrined actors standing alone on the stage. Both the Eureka Minstrel Hall and the Opera House (not the Academy of Music) drew their largest crowds, not for serious dramatic performances, but for acrobats, black-face singers, and "the great Professor Belew, tamer of wild horses."

Nevertheless, Maguire did make San Francisco the training ground for many actors who later achieved world renown, and he did present innumerable already established celebrities in the great classics. Nearly every play of Shakespeare's was given at one time or another at the Opera House, and at least twenty interpreters of *Hamlet* appeared there. Moreover, the permanent stock companies were made up of trained, intelligent professionals; they were the real dramatic schools of the great days of the theater in America. Maguire was willing to pay whatever was necessary, not only for the visiting stars but also for distinguished members of his supporting companies. When McCullough came to San Francisco as Forrest's leading man, Maguire wanted him to stay on after Forrest left. "You can't pay me what I can get in New York," sneered McCullough. "How much do you want?" was Tom's only reply. McCullough wanted $150 a week—a prohibitive sum in those days. Maguire paid it without a murmur. Later on McCullough became manager of the California Theater, and took most of Maguire's stock company away from him.

For stars of sufficient magnitude, he often paid a hundred dollars a night. On one occasion the contract stipulated that he must furnish the costumes. That was difficult in San Francisco, so Maguire paid the man $250 a week more to provide his own costumes.

It was not only money that Tom never let stand between him and an actor or actress he wanted. In his early days in the city he had been shot at in Portsmouth Square by Lotta Crabtree's father because of a disparaging remark that he had made about the dramatic ability of California's adored Lotta. But when he wanted Lotta for his theater, he let no past quarrels stand in the way. He engaged her on her own terms and never mentioned their previous encounter.

He was a daring impresario in every way. Not only was he the first to import Italian grand opera with a full orchestra into the city, but he also defied the Victorian squeamishness of which even San Francisco had its share, and brought in such plays as *East Lynne* and *Camille*, both of which were considered rather more than risqué. Of *East Lynne*, the *Bulletin* said, in 1863: "The novel is a very painful one, but in the drama it [*sic*] is even more so. The morality and taste of such pieces is doubtful, yet people will see them and sit them out." If the sentimental melodrama of *East Lynne* attracted such notices, one may imagine the response to Matilda Heron in *Camille!*

But the great sensation of Tom Maguire's career as an impresario was his production of the pioneer burlesque, *The Black Crook*. It was said that he had to go to the Barbary Coast to secure the "Amazons" for the

Tom Maguire, the Napoleon of impresarios.

grand march; few decent women, even actresses, would appear on the stage in tights. Immediately two other versions of the show were rushed to rival theaters (for Maguire's monopoly by this time no longer existed in the city itself). One was a parody, the other a plain steal under the name of *The Black Rook*. Maguire sued for an injunction, but all he got was a lecture on censorship from the judge, who fancied himself as a dramatic critic. "It is the duty of all courts," said His Honor, "to uphold public virtue and discourage everything that tends to impair it. It cannot be denied that this spectacle of *The Black Crook* merely panders to the pernicious curiosity of very questionable exhibitions of the female person. The spectacle is not suited for public presentation." The injunction was denied.

These were Maguire's great days, when every morning at eleven he held court on the sidewalk in front of his Opera House, and transacted all his business there. He was a handsome enough figure in his years of prosperity, burly but erect, with deep-set eyes of an indeterminate color, and with prematurely white hair, "like spun glass," but his saddlebar mustache still dark. And he dressed like the gamblers he so admired—up to the minute in cut and style, polished, curled, and bejeweled, huge solitaires on finger and in necktie—a Western version of Diamond Jim Brady.

In 1869 he went East scouting for plays and actors in New York, and in 1878 he got as far as Europe. In spite of his losses in grand opera, he did have a flair for opera as well as for the drama; he knew good singing and good music when he heard them. He had imported the famous Madame Parepa-Rosa, though this great soprano was a figure of fun on the stage—so fat that she looked like a sack loosely tied in the middle. Once the shapeless object opened her mouth, however, and her glorious voice filled and shook the house, the audience forgot to look at her, lost in hearing her.

Maguire in France and Italy ("in company with Signor Verdi," the *Morning Call* noted boastfully) was looking for a successor to Parepa-Rosa. He heard Patti, then at the height of her fame, but "discounted her somewhat in a vocal sense," though he thought her "a pleasing actress." He was thrilled by *Carmen,* and above all by *Faust,* sung as they should be sung. "He was open-mouthed with astonishment, and dumb with sheer delight. . . . He irks that he cannot gratify his ambition to show his stay-at-home fellow-citizens what Gounod's work is really like. The desire was dwelling within him when, with his hat off, he stood on top of the Arc de Triomphe, one night, and saw Paris spread out before him, a star-lighted panorama of beauty." The account sounds as if it had been dictated by Mr. Thomas Maguire himself.

Tom as a dramatic critic is embalmed forever in a priceless story which comes from the *Alta California.* It is worth giving almost in full. It seems that one of the paper's reporters called on Maguire and said he had written a play which he wanted to tell about. Reluctantly Maguire told him he might outline the plot.

"Well, in the first act there is a man who goes crazy."

"Ah," said Maguire, "a daft man is a dead weight to a play. . . . How did he get cranky?"

"He thought someone had killed his father, and accused his uncle of it."

"Oh, I see. Then the detective gets to work on the clue. Of course you have a detective?"

"Oh, he does the detective business himself."

"That's bad. How in blazes could a crazy man work up a clue? You must change that. What next?"

"Well, his uncle marries his mother."

"Now, here, Cap, we can't stand that business. . . . Every time we try an immoral snap, we catch it from all sides. You must cut out the part of the uncle. It's good, sensational, but it won't do."

"Then the crazy man takes the family to a theater, and gets the actors to ring in a scene that will remind the uncle of the murder."

"All bosh, my boy. If a man should come to the theater and ask such an absurd favor, he would be kicked out of the side door by the scene shifter. There's nothing in it. Besides, how did he know his dad was salted if he didn't see it?"

"Oh, I fix that, his father's ghost tells him."

"That's dead rot, these blasted ghosts are too old-fashioned for the stage. That won't work. Cut the ghost, my boy, cut the ghost."

"Then he falls in love with a young girl who goes and drowns herself, being crazy too."

"Two cranky people in one piece won't work. You must shelve the girl."

"Then they bury the girl and at the funeral the crazy man has a row with the girl's brother and licks the officiating clergyman."

"Hold on, don't put such rot as this in. It will be hissed off the stage."

"Then the brother and the crazy fellow have a duel; he kills his man; the old lady takes poison, then he kills his uncle, and—"

"Say, young man, I've heard quite enough. This is the most infernal confounded rot I ever heard of. They wouldn't play it in a melodeon. What the devil do you call all this blasted trash?"

"*Hamlet*," the young man murmured as he escaped. *Hamlet* had been played more than twenty times in Maguire's own theaters.

After this, it is not surprising to hear that he thought Forrest was the author, as well as the star, of *Coriolanus*, and when doubted, said belligerently: "Of course he wrote it. He can do anything, that man can."

In and out of the courts; constantly being sued by disgruntled players (one of whom deposed that he called her "a fiend in human form"), or himself suing—unsuccessfully—for libel; actually arrested in New York for pirating plays, Maguire's life was one long excitement, much of it unpleasant. There is no doubt of his ruthlessness; he did steal plays and neglect to pay royalties; he had no qualms in any of his business ventures. An actor who could demand his salary or refuse to appear was a very different thing from a helpless author three thousand miles away.

He had his generosities and his kindnesses, of course—a chance given to an unknown actor, or the free use of his theater on Sundays (before the days of Sunday theatrical performances in San Francisco) to a poor woman who wished to give spiritualist lectures. He had staunch friends who stood by him in bad times and gave benefit after benefit for him. But he also had plenty of enemies, just as staunch, and frequently just as much deserved. In the end the ill will he had built up, added to his reckless extravagance as a producer, brought his empire to ruin.

He was very near financial disaster when, in 1876, he persuaded E. J. ("Lucky") Baldwin to go into partnership with him. Together they built the Baldwin Hotel, at Powell and Market Streets, and in the same building Baldwin's Academy of Music, later the Baldwin Theater. From the very beginning there was trouble between the partners. They did not like each other, and would hardly speak; their intermediary and interpreter was Maguire's secretary, a tactful young man named David Belasco. Maguire owned the land on which the hotel and theater stood, and produced the plays in the theater; therefore he thought of it as his property. Baldwin owned the two buildings, and thought of them as his. They were born antagonists, and would have been so had they met when Tom Maguire was a cabby and "Lucky" Baldwin was a horse trader.

The theater itself was in the ornate style which Tom Maguire loved. It was a "marvel of elegant filigree and red plush," with gilt scrollwork, elaborate frescoes on the walls, a satin drop curtain costing six thousand dollars, velvet draperies, and crystal chandeliers valued at sixteen hundred dollars each.

A few months after it opened with Barry Sullivan in *Richard III,* the house was "dark." Times were hard, and it was no moment to splurge in new theaters charging high admission. Indeed, Maguire was obliged to lease all his other theaters, one by one. His decline had begun. He continued, however, to produce plays from time to time in the Baldwin Theater until 1882, when Baldwin, disgusted by his extravagance, withdrew his financial support. After Maguire left, the theater continued to operate under other management until it was burnt down with the hotel in 1898.

Maguire's last important attempt to recoup his losses, in 1879, proved to be his final disaster. It was the production of a Passion Play.

No more superstitious man that Tom Maguire ever lived. It is surprising that he ever dared to produce this play, which called forth so much clerical indignation in spite of its being handled in the most reverent manner possible. But the author, a man named Salmi Morse, had secured the backing of "Lucky" Baldwin, who was still Maguire's partner, and between them they persuaded him. The play opened at the Grand Opera House on March 3, 1879.

So fervently and reverently was the performance given, that many of the audience dropped to their knees and joined in prayer throughout entire scenes. Gradually people who had been shocked were won over, and the audiences grew. But a committee called on Maguire and told him he was "marked by the devil for sacrifice" for having committed so blasphemous a deed. Maguire had a terror of death and never allowed it to be mentioned to him. Sure that he was doomed, he closed the theater in a panic.

Meanwhile the Board of Supervisors had been approached by a similar committee, made up mainly of clergymen—Catholics who were appalled by the appearance of Christ and the Virgin on the stage, Protestants who thought the Passion Play to be Catholic propaganda, Jews who were afraid it was an attempt at proselytizing them (though Morse himself was a Jew). The board obediently passed a municipal ordinance forbidding "the personation of any scriptural character upon the stage of any theater."

And then Tom Maguire, finding that the devil had not yet struck him dead, and tempted by the still persisting demand for the play and the imperative need for some profitable enterprise, reopened the Passion Play at the beginning of Easter Week, on April 15.

At the close of the performance the Christus was arrested and freed on one-hundred-dollars bail, on charge of violating the new ordinance. He was James O'Neill, a celebrated actor and father of the still more famous Eugene O'Neill. He and the other members of the cast were later found guilty and fined, and the play was withdrawn for good. Morse, the unhappy author, went to New York, where he tried in vain to secure another performance,and finally killed himself in despair. The Passion Play had indeed claimed a victim, but it was not Tom Maguire.

Nevertheless, though for two or three years he struggled to hold on and keep his head above very troubled waters, Maguire's prosperous days were over. Public sentiment veered against the Passion Play, and against him for producing it. Baldwin broke the partnership.

His other theaters had their leases broken, and he brought out no new successes. His gambler's luck had turned.

In the early eighties, realizing that he was through in San Francisco, he went back permanently to New York. For a while he kept up a pathetic front. Stories were sent to San Francisco papers of his plans to build a new theater, with his nephew and namesake as manager. Had the theater really been built, it would have been his twelfth. But it was only a wish-fulfilment dream; nobody was going to back him any more, and his own fortune, once nearly a million, had long ago vanished. As late as 1886 he inspired a touching paragraph in the *Morning Call*: "Mr. Tom Maguire has just moved into a magnificently furnished house on Thirty-third Street, New York. The California ex-manager is said to be the best dressed man in that city."

It was his last bluff. Undoubtedly the "magnificently furnished house" and the fashionable clothes, if they ever existed, were never paid for. Maguire was down and out. What became of his nephew is unknown; but the old man drifted from one cheap theatrical boarding-house to another, always downward, haunting theatrical agencies, boring actors who could not escape from his garrulous reminiscences, still dreaming of a comeback which everyone knew would never arrive. In his last years, utterly destitute, he was supported by the Actors' Fund. He died in New York in January, 1896, without ever seeing San Francisco again.

Even so, his life cannot be thought of as a failure, any more than Napoleon's was a failure because it ended on Saint Helena. He had a better end than would have been his had he remained a hackman or a bartender in New York. And in the course of building up his fortune he had brought to San Francisco the greatest actors of their time, had introduced it to grand opera when few cities outside of New York had ever heard an opera sung, and had contributed to making the history of the San Francisco theater one of the greatest in the stage annals of America.

CHAPTER IV

America's Marx and His Bebel:
HENRY GEORGE and KATE KENNEDY

NLY ONE American has been the father of an economic theory which has commanded and continues to command world-wide adherence, which possesses devoted disciples whose efforts to introduce their system into cities, states, and even nations are unabating. At every election, for instance, in California (where the theory was born) there is an open or disguised single-tax measure to be voted on. And the father of the single tax was an American, born in Philadelphia, but resident for the best years of his life in San Francisco. His name was Henry George. He is the only American analogy of that other great system maker, Karl Marx.

George's system was not revolutionary, as Marx's was and is. Dorothy Thompson, the current high priestess of economic orthodoxy, remarks shrewdly that "had the capitalists paid any attention to George's writings, they would not be in the mess they are in today." Among those who have "paid attention" to them are Tolstoy, Einstein, Brandeis, and Helen Keller. Essentially the single tax is a middle-class philosophy, the economic solution of a liberal, not a radical. But it has attracted some of the best minds of the middle class ever since its first exposition. Henry George, though he was a workingman, was not a proletarian; it may well be the absence of the class concept in his theory which keeps it from being the panacea for poverty which he and his followers thought it. Its central thesis, however—that poverty increases with the progress of civilization, that the central cause of this is the burden put by taxation on the use and improvement of land, and that the only taxation should be on land itself, so that it would no longer be possible to hold property idle for speculation —has a simplicity and hence an attractiveness (only slightly specious) that appeals to many who would become bogged down in the complications of "value, price, and profit" or lost in the mazes of "dialectical materialism."

Marx had his Friedrich Engels, his co-worker and partner from the beginning. George had no one so close to him. Several persons might compete for the title: Mayor Tom Johnson, of Cleveland; Louis F. Post, who was in Wilson's war cabinet; Horace Traubel, the friend and biographer of Whitman; Joseph Fels, the millionaire soap manufacturer. But Marx also had his August Bebel, propagandist and disseminator of the doctrine. For this position in relation to Henry George, I nominate a woman who was once well known but is now almost forgotten — an Irish schoolteacher named Kate Kennedy.

It was the Duke of Argyll who derisively called Henry George "the Prophet of San Francisco." As in many other cases, his disciples took up the jeer and wore it proudly as a decoration. George lived in San Francisco, with brief excursions to other parts of central and northern California, from 1858, when he was not yet nineteen, to 1880, when he was over forty; *Progress and Poverty,* his greatest book, was written and first privately printed in San Francisco. And, in the Old Testament sense at least, he *was* more or less of a prophet. The Duke of Argyll spoke better than he knew or intended.

One day in January, 1865, a citizen walking on a San Francisco street was stopped by a short, stocky young man with reddish hair. The young man's face was white and his eyes were wild. "Listen," he said to the stranger. "You have to believe me. I am a printer out of work. My wife is at home with a new baby—our second son. The doctor says that she and the baby are both starving —that if they don't have food they will die. I must have five dollars for them."

Something in the tone, the appearance, told the stranger that this was no ordinary panhandling story. Something made him, without a word, put his hand in his pocket and give a five-dollar gold piece to the speaker, who with a look of gratitude hurried away to buy food for his hungry family.

That was the turning point in Henry George's life. Years afterward he said: "If he had not given it to me, I think I was desperate enough to have killed him."

The young man who had come to such a pass had been born, in September, 1839, as the second child and eldest son of a family of eight, children of a customhouse clerk in Philadelphia who before that had been a dry-goodsman in New Orleans and a publisher of religious books, whose business had failed. The parents were both devout (and in the case of the mother, fanatically devout) Episcopalians; the father was a vestryman at St. Paul's Church. The boy's closest friend was the rector's son, R. Heber Newton, who became widely known in later years as a liberal clergyman and ended up as chaplain of Stanford University five years after Henry George was dead.

But George's maternal grandfather had been a sea captain. The church and the sea contended in his blood. From the former he got his sonorous style and what Broadus Mitchell calls his "doctrinaire quality of mind"; from the latter he got his start in life and his passage to San Francisco.

The boy's education was desultory. He read much, but he was an idle pupil. He was shunted from private school to public, and back to private again, as the family's fortunes fluctuated. In the fashionable Episcopal Academy he spent an unhappy year, oppressed by the snobbishness of his fellow students, and then secured permission from his father to be tutored privately for high school. The months during which he was under the tutelage of Henry Y. Lauderbach he considered the most truly educational of his life. But he stayed in high school—the old Central High School, the first in Philadelphia — only five months. Lauderbach had tutored him too well; he was too young to be there. His time there was thoroughly wasted; he was fretting to be up and about early in the world of men. Finally he was allowed to leave, at only twelve. He became a two-dollar-a-week errand boy, then a clerk in a marine adjustment office. His reading was almost exclusively of verse; poetry, not too good, was his lifelong passion. He courted his wife, later, with verse; he read it aloud to his children; his prose falls naturally into the cadences of blank verse. For the rest, he attended the lectures at Franklin Institute at night, and picked up a smattering of physical science. He was still haunting the docks in his spare hours, longing to go to sea.

At last his father gave permission, as an alternative to seeing his eldest son a runaway from home. George shipped as foremast boy, at less than fourteen, on the *Hindoo,* an old East Indiaman bound for Melbourne and Calcutta.

He was away for more than a year. He saw the world, he kept a diary, and he experienced a gold rush. In Australia the crew mutinied to go to the gold fields; they were arrested, released, and finally deported. Young Henry George didn't count as one of the crew, but years later in California he was better able to understand what happens to a country economically when gold is suddenly discovered in it. He brought back to Philadelphia the Bible and the volume of James's *Anxious* (Religious) *Inquirer* he had taken with him, and almost all of the six dollars a month he had received. His father's salary from the customhouse was eight hundred dollars a year, and he had a wife and ten children. Henry had to find work at once. But he did not find work; for six months he was unemployed. Then he was apprenticed to a printing firm to learn typesetting.

Becoming a journeyman printer was in those days of hand presses a standard American way of laying the foundation for a career. Sam Brannan had done it twenty years before George; Fremont Older was to do it fifteen years after. Benjamin Franklin had been the great pioneer in this as in so much else.

But a mettlesome lad who had been to sea did not fit quietly into a composing room. George, who always resented domination, quarreled with his foreman (he was not a paying apprentice in the technical meaning of the word) and was fired.

It is something that single taxers do not like to remember, and that their prophet in his mature years tried to forget, that Henry George, in 1857 in Philadelphia, was a strikebreaker. He worked on the *Daily Evening Argus* during a printers' strike, and earned just $9.50 by his scabbing. He was only seventeen, with no education in the ethics of labor. In California he joined the printers' union as soon as his age made him eligible, and the brief experience in the East was not held against him.

However, some ethical stirrings must have made him abandon his new trade now and ship as an able seaman to Boston and back on a topsail coal schooner. Soon after his return he heard of an opening to go as steward to California on a lighthouse steamer, the *Shubrick,* Commander John deCamp. He had a cousin in San Francisco, and he promised his mother that he would stay under the wing of this older cousin and his wife all the time he was on shore. In December, 1857, he left Philadelphia, not knowing it was forever.

Just before George left on the *Shubrick,* he had a phrenological analysis—a more respectable procedure then than it would be now. The report was, in the jargon of the pseudo-science, that his assertiveness, adhesiveness, combativeness, destructiveness, self-esteem, conscientiousness, and individuality were large; his acquisitiveness and mirthfulness small. However obtained, the analysis hit him off very well. His chief defects were irascibility and a total lack of humor; chief of his virtues were his loyalty and perseverance.

When Henry George landed in San Francisco, early in 1858, he resolved at once that he wanted to stay. Here was a city where laborers were being paid twenty dollars a day and cooks five hundred dollars a month, where there was all the rush and excitement of the Australian gold fields, but in his own, not a foreign country. He still had six months to serve as steward, but Commander deCamp had been young once too. He did not formally release Henry George, but when the boy disappeared he made no search, and he did not mark him down as a deserter. George had forfeited his wages for the trip, but he was free.

Very soon he found that the real excitement in 1858 was in British Columbia, where a new and rich gold find had been made on the Frazer River. His cousin was establishing a store for the miners in Victoria, and he hired George to work for him there.

But a lad who quarreled with an ordinary foreman was certainly not going to take much dictation from a relative. In a few months the two were at outs, and George had thrown up the job. He was penniless; he had to borrow his fare to San Francisco, and a coat to wear on the train.

Henry George at the time he left San Francisco.

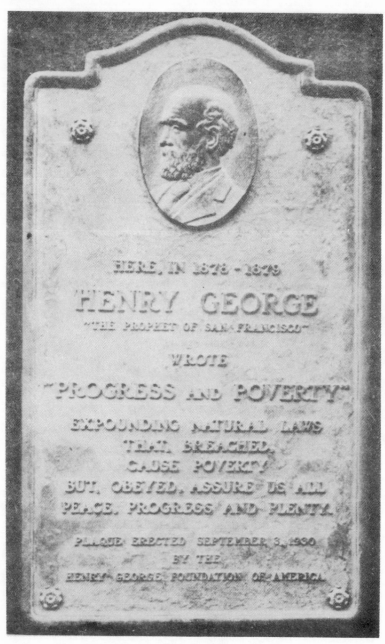

HERE, IN 1878 - 1879

HENRY GEORGE

"THE PROPHET OF SAN FRANCISCO"

WROTE

"PROGRESS AND POVERTY"

EXPOUNDING NATURAL LAWS
THAT BREACHED,
CAUSE POVERTY
BUT, OBEYED, ASSURE US ALL
PEACE, PROGRESS AND PLENTY.

PLAQUE ERECTED SEPTEMBER 3, 1930
BY THE
HENRY GEORGE FOUNDATION OF AMERICA

Henry George memorial in San Francisco.

By November he was back in San Francisco, half-resolved to find a ship and go to sea for the rest of his life. Before he could make up his mind, he was given a position at typesetting in Frank Eastman's job-printing office. Eastman was a freethinker, and under his influence George shed his early piety and became something of a rationalist, though more through emotion than through reason. He lived at the What Cheer House, a famous bachelor hotel of the day, in which no woman was ever allowed to set foot. It was a temperance hotel, whose proprietor felt a personal interest in his guests and their welfare and was very patient about the rent with aspiring and sober young men. One feature of the What Cheer House was a well-stocked library for the use of guests. Henry George read straight through it, in an orgy of study after three hard-working years.

But the printing job, which had paid him sixteen dollars a week, soon went the way of all the others, up in the smoke of a quarrel, and he was unemployed again. For a short time he worked as weigher in a rice mill. Then, with some vague hope of prospecting, he went to Hangtown (now Placerville), but all the good claims were long ago staked out, and he saw not even a glint of gold. He tramped his way back again, working on farms as he went—a hard experience for a boy who had known only cities and the sea. Luck was with him on his return; he was taken on as compositor by the *Home Journal*, though at only twelve dollars a week.

In 1860 Henry George became twenty-one. It was a momentous year for him. He shed his rather feeble rationalism and joined the Methodist Church. He became a member of the Eureka Typographical Society, the printers' union. He was promoted to foreman of the *Home Journal*, at two and a half times his salary as compositor. And he met Annie Corsina Fox.

She was an Australian girl, just seventeen, the orphaned daughter of a British Army officer; she had recently been graduated from a convent school in Los Angeles, and was living in San Francisco with a choleric uncle. She was a devout Roman Catholic, and she was already engaged to another man. She was accustomed to comfort, even to luxury, and had had no experience of poverty. This sum of obstacles made up a challenge. Henry George fell in love with her at first meeting, and loved her devotedly until he died.

But his first hopes of an immediate marriage were dashed by the sale of the *Home Journal* to new owners who promptly discharged the young foreman. For a while he "subbed" as compositor on various papers; then, with five other printers, joined in establishing a new paper with a confusing name, the *Evening Journal*. It failed in a few months because news was now brought by telegraph instead of by Pony Express, and the paper could not get along without the Associated Press service, which they could not acquire. George went back to "subbing."

It was hardly the moment for a wedding. But on December 3, 1861, Annie Fox, now eighteen, stole out of her uncle's house and eloped with a penniless bridegroom who had to borrow a decent suit in which to face the preacher. They were married by a Methodist minister, since it was a runaway match and also since it was

Advent, when Roman Catholics do not celebrate marriages; but later, in Sacramento, they were married again by a priest. Though George remained a fairly orthodox Methodist, he was always very friendly to the Catholic Church, and in later years was particularly close to Father McGlynn, the first martyr of the single tax.

The newly married couple went to Sacramento, not because he had work there, but because there was obviously none for him in San Francisco, and also to give the new Mrs. George's angry uncle a bit of time in which to cool down. George worked, as substitute typesetter, on the Sacramento *Union;* he took any work he could get, night or day, and on one occasion sold tickets at the door for a lecture by Mark Twain. Unfortunately, he still had faith in getting rich from gold, and every cent he got ahead went into mining stocks, mostly worthless. In this atmosphere, eleven months after his marriage, his first child was born.

The Georges came back to San Francisco. George went to work for the *Home Journal,* of which he had once been foreman. He did job printing for Isaac Trump, a Jack-of-all-trades who managed to fail in every scheme he promoted. He printed cards and labels in exchange for food and fuel, on a barter basis. He tried to solicit subscriptions for the *Journal;* he even tried to sell clothes wringers and carriage brakes. His wife pawned all the jewelry she had owned as a girl; she did sewing for the landlady in part payment of their rent. Then she had to stop sewing; their second son was born. There was no food for the mother, no milk for the child. The doctor said they would die.

It is probably quite true that murder and suicide were in Henry George's heart that January day when he stopped a stranger in the street and asked for five dollars.

The tide was beginning to turn, but very slowly. Twice more he was fired from San Francisco papers for quarreling with the foreman. But on a third paper, the famous *Alta Californian,* he made his first appearance in print. Into the editor's box the unregarded young printer dropped an anonymous article on the assassination of Lincoln. Next morning it was published. He was discovered, and was taken from the composing room to the editorial department, as a reporter.

Richard S. H. George, Henry George's father, had been a Democrat and a proslavery man. The son, an abolitionist in his sympathies, had joined the new Republican Party. His article on Lincoln was an elegy and a eulogy. It was written in the clear, simple style that was natural to him from the beginning. His wide reading had made up for any deficiencies in his formal schooling; though he always deprecated himself as a writer, he was a born stylist. And in the midst of the harassments and sufferings of this year, he was doggedly practising the turning out of articles as a means to "self-improvement by writing."

As a reporter for the *Alta,* George was very nearly involved in a filibustering expedition to Mexico, to help Juarez defeat the French-dictated Austrian-born emperor, Maximilian. Sam Brannan's money was in a similar expedition. But the United States Government stopped this one at the dock, and George (probably much to his relief) did not go to Mexico.

Where he did go was to Sacramento again, to work in the State Printing Office. The year he spent there this time was a more comfortable one than his first residence. He was beginning to write regularly and to place what he wrote; he had a steady job at a fair salary; and he had leisure to widen his mental horizon. At a debate in Sacramento, he was converted from protectionism to free trade, though he remained a Republican until the corruption of Grant's administration turned him into a Democrat again.

Once more in San Francisco, in November, 1868, he became first a printer, then a reporter on the *Times,* edited by James McClatchy, of a famous California newspaper family. In the two years George spent on this paper, he rose to be managing editor, at fifty dollars a week, with an extra income from correspondence for out-of-town papers. He was prospering in the world of journalism, but more and more of his time and thought were being given to the economic problem which obsessed him: why is there so much poverty in the midst of plenty? In October, 1868, the *Overland Monthly* published his first article bearing on this question. It was called, "What the Railroad Will Bring Us." The Central Pacific Railroad was about to be completed—as one local periodical put it, the United States was about to be annexed to California. Henry George praised the enterprise behind the spanning of a continent: "It will be the means of converting a wilderness into a populous empire in less time than many of the cathedrals of Europe were building." But he added that the population and the business brought to the West by the railroad would mean great wealth for a few, stark destitution for the many. His prediction was fulfilled to the letter, though he himself could not decide the reason why, until, a year later, a teamster in the hills back of Oakland gave him a clue.

When this teamster, met during a walk in the hills, told him of the enormous increases in artificial value of agricultural land because of the coming of the railroad, a light broke on Henry George's mind. "With the growth in population," he said to himself, "the land grows in value, and the men who work it must pay more for the privilege." All the remainder of his life was spent in amplifying that statement.

Meanwhile, he had left the *Times,* and after a brief experience on the *Chronicle,* as managing editor for Charles De Young (and with a printing foreman who had once fired him in Sacramento, but whom he recommended now for the position), he was sent to New York as agent for the *Herald,* to try to secure an Associated Press franchise. It was George's first visit East since he had left nearly eleven years before. In New York, with a newly sharpened gaze, he saw the end of what was beginning in California—tremendous contrasts of luxury and need which shocked him even while they confirmed his theory.

The *Herald* was refused the franchise, and an attempt by George to set up an independent wire service was crushed by the established competitor. He returned to California, and after a short time as editor of the Oakland *Transcript,* went to Sacramento for the third time. He was to edit the *Reporter,* in which he was given a quarter interest; the paper was the organ of Governor H. H. Haight, and was used by him to fight the growing strangulation of the state by that giant Octopus, the Central Pacific Railroad. George fought valiantly against the railroad's subsidies and bribery. But it was too much for him and for Haight; the railroad bought out the three quarters of the paper which the editor did not own, and he resigned. Almost forty years later, the fight was won with the help of another newspaperman named Fremont Older.

George returned to San Francisco. In 1870 he was a candidate to the state assembly, but the railroad saw to it that he was defeated. Every such experience deepened his conviction that he had the key to the economic maze. In the summer of 1871 he published a forty-eight-page pamphlet, "Our Land and Land Policy," which contains the germ of the matured single-tax theory. Every man, said George, has the natural right to apply his labor to the land; when the land is privately owned and he must pay rent for its use, he is robbed of some of his labor; taxes should be on land values only, taking for the community what the community has produced, and relieving industry of the incubus of all other taxes. The little book did not have a very large circulation, but it set a few people to thinking, and clarified George's own position to himself.

At the end of 1871, with an eccentric printer named W. M. Hinton, later a San Francisco Supervisor, George founded his last paper, the *Daily Evening Post*, the first one-cent paper on the Pacific Coast. All of the many papers with which Henry George was connected in California are dead now except the Sacramento *Union,* the San Francisco *Chronicle,* and the *Post,* which is merged with the *Call-Bulletin.* George was half owner and editor-in-chief of the new paper, which was dedicated to a reform policy and to fighting the railroad and its "Big Four." One of its first crusades was against a "hell ship," whose brutal officers it saw punished. After a year the price was raised from a cent to the customary five cents; one reason was that pennies were so scarce in San Francisco that it was difficult for the newsboys to make change. In 1875 the *Post* overreached itself; it started a morning edition called the *Ledger,* with an illustrated Sunday supplement. The money for the perfection press had been borrowed from Senator John P. Jones of Nevada, and when it became apparent that the *Ledger* was going to eat up the *Post's* profits, he called in the loan, and both papers failed. By this time there were four children in the George family, two boys and two girls, and once more their father was jobless.

But by now he had a standing in the community. He had helped found the Bohemian Club, over the California Market. He was the first secretary of the Board of Trustees of the San Francisco Public Library. He had influential friends. One of them was Governor William S. Irwin, who appointed him to the sinecure position of state inspector of gas meters, a post with few duties and a steady income. He set seriously to work on his writing, and began to build a reputation as an orator as well. In the summer of 1876 he stumped the state for Tilden, the Democratic candidate for president. (He had been a Democrat for some time now, and had been a delegate to the 1872 convention, which nominated his fellow editor, Horace Greeley.) Across the bay, in Berkeley, the new state university was being formed. Someone suggested Henry George, whose original work was beginning to command national attention, for the chair of political economy. He was invited to speak to the students on "The Study of Political Economy." After the speech he was thanked politely, but he never heard any more about the appointment. Reading the talk as it was published in 1880 in the *Popular Science Monthly* makes it quite plain why—it is an exposition in embryo of the single tax. The University of California missed the chance to have what would have been its most famous professor—even though he had spent only five months in high school and had never entered the gates of a college before.

In the summer of 1877, in a Fourth of July speech in San Francisco, George broadened his theory to include all humanity, made it a universal rather than a local question. He had formulated his ideas, and now he was ready to correlate them. He resolved to devote all his leisure time to a detailed analysis of the problem and a full explanation of his solution. On September 18, 1877, in the midst of the depression which followed the Jay Cooke panic, he started to work on *Progress and Poverty; an Inquiry into the Cause of Industrial Depressions, and of Increase of Want with Increase of Wealth.* All around him were strikes and unemployment—ready object lessons. At first he thought merely of a definitive magazine article, but soon he found that he must write a book. It took him a year and a half. In between he

ran as a delegate to the convention being held to draft a
new state constitution, led the Democratic ticket, but
was defeated. He performed the perfunctory duties of
his office as meter inspector, and he lectured frequently,
his most popular subject being Moses in his aspect as
leader of and provider for his people. The rest of the
time he worked on the book. Like Lincoln, he did his
reading lying down, flat on his back with his book held
above him. Every morning before starting the day's
research or writing, he read poetry aloud to his children.
The oldest was a grown boy now, getting ready to become his father's secretary, assistant, and finally his political successor.

Progress and Poverty was finished in March, 1879.
George took the manuscript to his friend John Swett,
the great California educator. "All I know about
English grammar," he said, "I learned in a printing office. I may have made mistakes." But Swett could find
no fault with either the grammar or the rhetoric; he
greatly admired George's natural, easy style.

The next thing was to submit the volume to the New
York publishers. Appleton's, the first to which it was
sent, said it was "very aggressive, and not likely to sell."
Harper's called it "revolutionary," in no complimentary
sense. Scribner's rejected it flatly. George resolved to
publish the book himself. He set up the first two stick-
fuls of type on Hinton's old press—perhaps the last job
he ever did as a printer. Hinton set up the rest, and
made plates for an author's edition of five hundred.
John Swett gave George twenty-five dollars for ten
copies. "Swett," said the author, "this is the first money

I have ever received for my book." Although it had little sale, when the book was sent again to Appleton's in printed form, they liked it better, and a few months later, early in 1880, they published a regular edition from Hinton's plates.

Progress and Poverty is the single taxer's Bible, and the definitive exposition of Henry George's theory, since all his later books were merely amplifications or excursions into ramifications of the main thesis. Proudhon, the French anarchist, said: "Property is theft." Henry George, forty years later, made the milder assertion that "economic rent is robbery." "Take the economic rent in taxation, and abolish all other contributions to government"—this is the heart of the Georgian theory. When he started his economic writings, he knew nothing of the classic economists, though later he was influenced by Ricardo; he was truly original. He never was thoroughly familiar with either Spencer, the great individualist, or Marx, the great collectivist. Instinctively, however, he leaned toward the individualist school of economic thought. "Adam Smith and John Stuart Mill," remarks Don Seitz, "were master logicians; George was an expounder and inventor."

It should be added that the book makes interesting and even exciting reading—a rare phenomenon for a theoretical work on political economy. The late Harry Weinberger remarked of one chapter, "The Central Truth," that it "is the most beautiful piece of writing in the English language, and stirs the blood like a clarion call."

At the beginning of 1880, George's principal book

had at last achieved regular publication. By January, 1881, he was able to write to Dr. Edward Robeson Taylor (lawyer, physician, and poet, later mayor of San Francisco): "The book *is* a success. The sale seems now to have commenced in good earnest, and orders are coming in from all parts of the country. . . . It has at last got a show in Europe. . . . In one way or another, I am getting pretty well advertised."

He had established the Land Reform League of California (mother of all single-tax societies) to carry on propaganda for his theory, and a four-page weekly paper, *The State,* for the same purpose. There seemed to be no reason why he should not continue publicizing his theory for the rest of his life in San Francisco. But the state administration changed; Governor Irwin was out and a Republican in; the position as gas-meter inspector which provided the means for Henry George to do his more important work was taken away from him and given to a good Republican. Once more he was faced with the necessity of supporting himself and his family by his wits— and impractical as George often was, he knew he could not do that by writing and speaking on economics in far-off California. John Swett was urging him to seek a wider field; flattering invitations were coming to him from the East. As with thousands of San Franciscans before and after him, the path to success and fame led through New York.

In August, 1880, Henry George left San Francisco. Ten years later, while on his way to Australia, he visited for the last time, briefly, the city which had seen all his youth and early middle age, and in which his

world-famous theory had been born. It was a triumph,
with dinners and official greetings and admiring resolu-
tions.

The rest of his story belongs to New York, and may
be summed up in a few paragraphs. In 1881 he published *The Irish Land Question,* and spent the next year
in Ireland. *Social Problems* came in 1883. He spent
1884 in England, organizing and building up the English
Land Reform Union. *Protection or Free Trade* was
published in 1886. The same year George ran for mayor
of New York on an independent ticket, against Abram
S. Hewitt and a young man named Theodore Roosevelt.
Hewitt, the reform Tammany candidate, won, but
George snowed young Roosevelt under. He felt with
some justification that he had been counted out by
fraud, and became an active advocate of the Australian
secret ballot, now in use throughout the United States.
He established *The Weekly Standard* and spent much
energy on organization of Land and Labor Clubs. When
one of his earliest New York disciples, Father Edward
McGlynn of St. Stephen's Church, was excommunicated
for his adherence to the single tax, George led the fight
which led to rescinding of the excommunication by the
pope. (The essentially non-revolutionary nature of the
single tax is evidenced by the fact that many Roman
Catholics have been prominent adherents of the theory
and that since the McGlynn case no objection has been
made by the church; whereas conversion to socialism
is a stated cause for excommunication.)

In 1887 George was candidate of the United Labor
Party for secretary of state, and was defeated. The next

two years were spent again in the British Isles, and in 1890 he visited Australia, for the first time since the voyage on the *Hindoo* in 1855, stopping at San Francisco on the way. The first national single-tax conference was held in New York later in the same year.

Soon afterwards, George suffered a cerebral hemorrhage resulting in aphasia, and went to Bermuda to recuperate. Though he returned ready to work, he was never really well again. Two more books came out in the next two years, *An Open Letter to the Pope,* bearing on the McGlynn case, and *A Perplexed Philosopher,* an indictment of Herbert Spencer for changing his mind on the land question. This was Henry George's last book except the posthumously published *Science of Political Economy.* He campaigned for Bryan and the silver standard in 1896.

In 1897, against the advice of his physician and the pleading of his family and friends, George allowed himself to be nominated again for mayor of New York, and again in a three-cornered fight against a Tammany Democrat and a Republican. He had promised solemnly to make very little of a campaign, but once he felt the harness and heard the firebells he could not be held in. He spoke four or five times a night, though often so ill that he could hardly climb on to the platform. Late on the night of October 28, George arrived at his home in Fort Hamilton, exhausted.

Shortly before midnight he suffered a second stroke of apoplexy, and in a few hours he was dead, at fifty-eight.

He was buried in Greenwood Cemetery, Brooklyn, where later a bust sculptured by his second son, Richard, was placed over his grave. The older son, Henry, not yet twenty-five, was hastily drafted to take his father's place as candidate. It was no surprise when Tammany again elected its mayor.

This bald little man with the bright blue eyes, the full reddish beard, and the unexplained "English accent," who somebody said "looked like Socrates," was one of the very few world influences whom America has so far produced. There is no part of the civilized world where *Progress and Poverty* has not penetrated, where there is not some semblance at least of a single-tax movement. Millions of people have read the book and adopted the theory. Henry F. Pringle has pointed out the double effect of single-tax propaganda on United States history—its part in "shattering the confidence of the Republican Party and its series of presidents . . . who had won fame in the Civil War," and its impress on the Populist and Greenback movements at the end of the nineteenth century. In 1889, William F. Herndon, Lincoln's law partner and biographer, exclaimed with pious Republican horror: "I see that the idea of Single Tax is growing and so is Communism; Anarchism and all wild *isms* are struggling for life. The devil seems to be in hand all around everywhere." Half a century later, the yoking of the single tax with communism seems quaint; but it is evidence of the importance which Henry George's theory thus early assumed.

Henry George achieved the acme of American provincial glory; a cigar has been named in his honor! In 1946 the Y.M.C.A. held a national exhibition of objects made in prison camps by American army prisoners of war. One is a scratch-pad contrived of the reverse side of cigarette packages. On the top leaf is a list of books this unknown officer wanted to read when he was free. The very first of them is the notation of an English edition of *Progress and Poverty*. In San Francisco, there remains to commemorate George only a plaque placed by loyal single taxers on the site of his early struggles as a printer and editor. But when he left San Francisco for New York, there remained behind one of his most interesting disciples. Kate Kennedy, in 1880, had still ten useful years to live, and her most important work was still before her.

Kate Kennedy was born in Gaskinstown, County Meath, Ireland, in May, 1827. She had one brother, older than herself, and five younger sisters. Her family were not peasants, but gentleman farmers fallen on evil days; they had their coat of arms, a hand and dagger— a not inappropriate symbol for their eldest daughter, whose life was one long battle. The laws which forbade higher education to Roman Catholics in Ireland had only recently been repealed; when Kate Kennedy was a child she spent long hours reading aloud to illiterate older people. It was good training; together with her Celtic aptitude, it made an orator out of her.

Her first school was two miles away over rough roads; it was a one-room cottage with baked mud walls, a trodden earth floor, and a thatched roof. From there she was sent, in a temporary upward surge of the family fortunes, to the convent school at Navan, from which she was graduated at the head of her class. But any

Courtesy of Charles S. Cushing.
Kate Kennedy in her years of greatest activity.

hopes of going farther—difficult for the most ambitious girl in the 1830's, and almost impossible in Ireland— were dashed when her father, Thomas Kennedy, died in 1840. There was to be no convent school for her little sisters, but Kate, at thirteen, was set to be their teacher. She made a good job of it; four of the five grew up to have strong intellectual interests, and one of her sisters in later years was a public-school teacher for forty-six years, though she was married and had four children. The older girls all spoke French fluently; Kate spoke German, Italian, and Spanish as well.

But the famine of 1846-47 struck people like the Kennedys as hard as it struck the poorest and most ig- norant peasant. People were dying all about them, with the failure of the potato crop which had become desti- tute Ireland's only standby; the roads were full of sick and starving men, women, and children, going from nowhere to nowhere. The scene must have been very like the tragic happenings in the Dust Bowl of America in recent years. The Kennedys were caught with the rest—still with a little money, a roof over their heads, a bit of food, but with everything going fast and no way of getting more.

The only solution for those of the Irish who could raise a few dollars for steerage fare was emigration to America. In 1849, Kate Kennedy, with her brother and one sister, made the voyage to New York as part of the great Irish influx. The two girls worked at embroidering cloaks and vests, and since most of this work was done by Frenchwomen, they frequently acted as interpreters —for at that time there were few English-speaking women in New York who were familiar with the French tongue, and almost none among the workingwomen. Meanwhile Kate studied diligently, with the hope of becoming a teacher in a public school. Already her chief interest, outside her technical studies, was in political economy, and her sympathies, in spite of her middle-class origin, were with the unskilled workers.

In 1851 their mother and the four other sisters joined them, and in 1853 two of the girls made the long trip to California. Eventually the whole family was reunited there. Kate arrived in San Francisco in January, 1856; as the *Examiner* said after her death, she was "virtually a California pioneer."

For a year, gathering experience for a city school, she taught in a little town of Suisun, between Oakland and Sacramento. In 1857 she was given her first San Francisco appointment—in a frame building on the present site of the Palace Hotel. In front of the school was a huge sand dune, over or around which the pupils climbed on their way to their classes. It was the same sand dune on which little Lillie Hitchcock used to play, long years before she was the dashing Mrs. Howard Coit.

From here Kate Kennedy was transferred to the Greenwich School, and then she became principal of the North Cosmopolitan Grammar School. Her next pay check was for the salary paid the principal of a primary school; she was only a woman, and could not expect to receive a man's wage.

Perhaps she should not have expected it, but Kate Kennedy was Irish and stubborn. She was a pioneer woman suffragist, and she was probably the only teacher of her period who was a member of a labor union—the Knights of Labor, which antedated the American Federation of Labor. The organized schoolteachers of today ought to remember this woman, who fought their battles eighty years ago. She was to do much for them. Now she threw herself wholeheartedly into a struggle for equal pay for equal work, regardless of sex. Eventually she was also to secure teachers' tenure of office.

By 1873 the state legislature had authorized women to hold school offices, such as supervisorships. The next year the hard fight for equal pay was won; according to state law, "females employed as teachers in the public schools of this State shall in all cases receive the same compensation as allowed male teachers for like services, when holding the same grade of certificate." In 1875 an attempt was made to repeal both these ordinances; Kate Kennedy, now principal of North Cosmopolitan at the regular grammar-school principal's salary, rushed to the fore again and helped to hold the gains the women had made. She was the first woman, anywhere in the world, to receive, as a salaried employee, equal pay with men for equal work. It is no wonder that Susan B. Anthony and Elizabeth Cady Stanton, the grand matriarchs of the woman suffrage movement, when they came to San Francisco, called formally on Miss Kennedy at her school, to congratulate her on her achievement.

Indomitable and fearless, Kate Kennedy grew into leadership in a dozen different fields. She was a fine public speaker, and, careless of her position, she spoke constantly, from all sorts of platforms, on woman suffrage, proportional representation, the organization of labor, opposition to the railroad's control of the state, political corruption, and, finally, on land reform, which in time became her chief topic. She was one of the earliest readers and followers of Henry George, one of the first members of the Land Reform League, one of the primordial single taxers.

She had her lighter and softer side, of course. She was an attractive and vivacious young woman, with plenty of admirers. She was the only one of the six sisters to remain unmarried, and if she ever had a love affair which touched her to the heart she kept it well hidden; but that she had plenty of opportunities to marry, her whole family knew. The Kennedy house on Clay Street, near Powell, was always full of laughter and bustle and hospitality; they were a fun-loving, witty, openhanded clan, devoted to one another beyond the average. Her family meant much to Kate Kennedy; all her life, except for a few weeks between her mother's death and her own, she lived with one or another of them.

In her public life she was utterly without precaution or discreet self-preservation; what she felt to be her duty she did, whatever the danger. Naturally, the school department liked then no better than it would like now a teacher who spoke from soapboxes and openly helped striking unions. Unfortunately for her critics, she was also one of the most efficient and best-liked teachers in the city, a strict disciplinarian but with a generous sympathy which made her popular with pupils and teachers alike. She violated no laws, and for a while there was nothing the authorities could do except fume and bide their time.

In 1878 she took a year's leave of absence and traveled all over the British Isles and the Continent, investigating educational and economic conditions, and particularly the higher education of women. It was her first visit to Ireland since she had sailed from it more than thirty years before. From Europe she sent home a series of brilliant letters—really travel articles, but more concerned with people and their welfare than with scenery or historic remains—which were published in the San Francisco *Bulletin.* During the year she visited nearly every university in Europe. Her linguistic ability enabled her to enter circles closed to the ordinary tourist. Her articles, though never collected in book form, are still worth reading for the picture they give of Europe at the beginning of the political grouping which ended with the World War.

In 1882 Miss Kennedy moved across the bay, to Oakland, where she bought a house on 13th Street, opposite that of one of her married sisters, and installed her mother as mistress of it. She still kept her principalship in San Francisco, no. rule then demanding that teachers must live within the city limits. In 1886 she announced her candidacy for state superintendent of public instruction, in accordance with the law of 1873 which made women eligible for school offices. Neither she nor any other of the women teachers could vote, but she received enough votes from male electors to cause the defeat of the regular Democratic candidate, who was added to the list of her enemies.

Kate Kennedy's stout heart was beginning to fail her. By 1887 she was sixty, and nearly eligible to retire on pension—not to rust away into old age, however, but with the intention of devoting all her time and energy to what was now her chief interest, the single tax. In February her health had become so bad that she applied for two months' leave of absence, expecting to return to her school on May 1 and retire at the end of the term. The leave was granted. As soon as she was out of the way, all the forces against her leaped to destroy her. This assertive woman, who pushed herself into privileges that should be reserved for men, must be shown her place. On March 16, 1887, the board of education transferred her from the North Cosmopolitan School, whose principal she had been for nearly twenty years, and made her principal of the little Ocean View School, at the same time reducing her salary from $175 to $100 a month. On May 18 she was dismissed from the school service altogether, avowedly "for political reasons."

Sick or well, Kate Kennedy accepted the double challenge. Her brown hair was gray now, but she could still set her chin and start fighting. On May 31 she sued the city for reinstatement in her old school, with back pay from the time of her transfer. The test case lasted for nearly three years—three hard years during which her beloved mother died and she was left alone in the little house in Oakland. The lower court finally declared for her, and the board appealed. Early in 1890 the state supreme court rendered its decision, the foundation of teachers' tenure in California ever since that date: "A teacher of any particular grade and with a proper certificate cannot be placed in a lower grade or dismissed except for misconduct or incompetency." Political activity, even in unpopular causes, was not to be construed as "misconduct or incompetency."

The board was obliged to reinstate her, and she then sent in her resignation, to take effect immediately, and sued for thirty-three months' back salary. She received a check from the city for $5,700.75, the largest salary warrant ever issued to a teacher in San Francisco.

Teachers' tenure was safe in California. But the winning of it killed Kate Kennedy. The strain had been too much. Too ill to care for herself alone, she moved to her sister's house across the street, and there she died, on March 18, 1890. It was just before Henry George made his last visit to San Francisco; one wonders if he knew.

Kate Kennedy had long ago left the church in which she had been born. It is a touching evidence of the devotion of the Kennedy family to one another, that, though most of them remained devout Catholics, Kate and another sister who desired it were buried as they requested, without ritual. She had said that she wanted to die "as she had lived, outside of church or creed"; she had her wish. Her funeral was held two days later, and she was buried at Laurel Hill Cemetery, where so many San Francisco pioneers then lay. (When the cemetery was abandoned in 1940, her remains were removed to Cypress Lawn, in Colma.) The ceremony was non-religious, the only speaker being Judge Maguire, her old friend, attorney, and ally, and her fellow member in the Land League Reform. "Regardless of the distinctions and classifications prevailing in human society," he said at her grave, "regardless of the division of races, parties and creeds, she loved her fellow-creatures one and all; she sympathized with the poor and hoped for the restoration to them of their natural heritage."

When her will was opened, it was found that in spite of her wide generosity — she had forgiven $10,000 in debts—Miss Kennedy's simple living and wise investment of her money had left her, for a teacher, very wealthy. Her estate amounted to nearly $50,000, much of it in real estate. Judge Maguire had been left $10,000 "to promote the Single Tax." She had also wanted her *Short Sermons to Workingmen,* seven simple articles on the single tax which had been published in the San Francisco *Star* in 1887, under the pseudonym of "Cato the Censor," to be printed as a book and sold for the benefit of the single tax. But in spite of the bequest to Judge Maguire, this was not done until 1906, and then it was her uncle who paid for it.

What is left of Kate Kennedy in San Francisco, to which she gave thirty-three of her sixty-three years? In the Noe Valley district there is a Kate Kennedy School, which has her teacher's certificate on the wall (though it does not possess a portrait of her), and there is a Kate Kennedy Parent-Teachers' Association. The North Cosmopolitan School, whose pupils staged a riot when she was removed from it in March, 1887—the school which meant so much to her that it was mentioned in her funeral notices—was destroyed in the disaster of 1906. When it was rebuilt, a copy of *Short Sermons to Workingmen* was placed in the cornerstone of the new building.

There is one more memorial of her. She had been a member of the first California Educational Society, a sort of honor society open only to holders of life teaching certificates or state diplomas; she joined it when it was founded, in the early 1860's. That society no longer exists, but the teachers of San Francisco have not forgotten the woman who gave them their tenure of office. In 1911, San Francisco teachers founded the Kate Kennedy School-Women's Club, "to further teachers' rights professionally, to secure equal salary for equal work, to gain recognition for positional promotion for like achievement and like credentials, regardless of sex."

Kate Kennedy would have liked that; she would have been proud to think of her name at such an association's masthead. There is only one thing she would have liked better. That would be to be remembered as a pioneer in spreading the gospel of Henry George and his single tax.

CHAPTER V

Reconstructed Rebel:
ASBURY HARPENDING

HE OLD Dutch Reformed Church in New York bears a coat of arms, with the motto: *Dando Conservat*—"He saves by giving." It is the coat of arms of Baron Harpending, who came from Amsterdam to New Amsterdam and built the church. Early in the nineteenth century one of the baron's descendants brought suit for recovery of the property, with Henry Clay and Daniel Webster as his counsel, but after appeal lost his case in the New York supreme court. The disappointed Harpending moved to Kentucky, where he married a Miss Clark, a Virginian. Though thus allied with the South, Harpending was and remained an antislavery man. But his son Asbury, who was born in Hopkinsville, Kentucky, at the end of 1839, was a fiery rebel from the very first stirrings of secession.

Asbury Harpending was large for his age, and precocious; at fifteen he was already in some unnamed college, probably not one with very strict scholastic requirements. But study was the last thing in the world to hold him, and he ran away to join William Walker, the filibuster, in his unlucky expedition to Nicaragua. There he was promptly arrested, but he escaped and somehow made his way home again. A boy of this tem-

per was not easy to hold, and his wise father made the
best of things by giving permission for Asbury to sail at
sixteen for California.

Combined with Asbury Harpending's mettlesome nature was a genius for money-making. He set sail for
San Francisco via New Orleans with five dollars in gold
over his fare, and a revolver. He spent most of the five
dollars in New Orleans for bananas and oranges, which
he sold on board, and he reached California with four
hundred dollars in his pocket.

Adventure and a chance to make a huge sudden fortune were both much less likely in California in 1856
than they had been in 1849. Harpending was restless,
and he had his revolver and his four hundred dollars.
He soon found his way to Mexico. There he located a
rich gold claim. In 1860 the "tall, slender, dark-haired"
lad, not yet twenty-one, returned to San Francisco—
for a brief visit, he thought then. He owned at this
time a quarter of a million dollars in the bank, and a
gold mine in Mexico worth a million more! This would
seem incredible, except that he immediately used his
money in real-estate operations which, as Dr. George D.
Lyman says, "made San Francisco gasp." In the next
two years, he poured out money with both hands, yet
more kept coming in—"Dando Conservat." In 1938
one of his direct descendants was a relief client in San
Francisco!

This downfall of the Harpending wealth was not,
however, due to any prodigality on the part of Asbury
Harpending, who had made and lost several fortunes
during his lifetime, but had never lived with unusual

extravagance. This first fortune was his largest by far, and it was all confiscated by the United States Government in 1863.

When Harpending returned from Mexico, relations between the Northern and Southern states were very near the breaking point, which arrived the following April. California, with 30 per cent of its population from the South, and most of its many foreigners also Southern sympathizers, came close to joining the Confederacy, as the similarly acquired state of Texas actually did. Thomas Starr King, the Unitarian minister, is credited with having done much to save California for the Union; Asbury Harpending may be given what credit is due him for putting as many obstacles as possible in King's and the other Union spokesmen's way

His first move was to organize an early branch of the Knights of the Golden Circle. Each of the thirty members was to be responsible for finding and equipping one hundred fighting men. California was very poorly guarded; there were only a hundred soldiers at Fort Point, a hundred on Alcatraz, and a mere handful at Mare Island and Benicia, where there were thirty thousand stands of arms in the arsenal. If the Knights could raise the needed three thousand followers, it would not take a very large original society to have a trained force sufficient to seize the state government. The avowed object was the formation of the Republic of the Pacific, which would then ally itself with the Southern states in the war which Harpending very well foresaw.

The commander of the Army Department of the Pacific at the beginning of 1861 was Albert Sidney

Johnston, of Texas. When Texas seceded, Johnston resigned and joined the Confederacy; he became one of the most noted of the Confederate generals and was killed at the Battle of Shiloh in April, 1862. But as long as he was a United States army officer, he was uncompromisingly loyal to his trust. The Knights of the Golden Circle were so secret an organization that members had sworn not to tell their plans even to their own wives. But one of the Knights was a Virginia lawyer, Edmund Randolph, an excitable, noisy man who could not keep his tongue still. He talked and hinted once too often. Johnston sent for Harpending and calmly informed him that he was privy to the entire scheme. "If the conspiracy is not dropped," he said, "I will defend the property of the United States with every resource at my command and with the last drop of my blood."

With that message to consider, a majority of the Knights in San Francisco voted to disband. It was the sensible way for Johnston to handle the situation; matters were in too ticklish a state to risk publicity. But here is a curious thing: Randolph, who undoubtedly caused discovery of the plot in the first place by his garrulity, was so incensed at its collapse that he wrote to President Lincoln, told him all about the affair, and demanded Johnston's removal! Lincoln made no reply; he wanted to keep men of Johnston's caliber as long as possible, not to lose them to the Confederacy. Then Randolph, who had practically betrayed his own comrades, turned around and became the fieriest advocate of secession in the state. Perhaps he was unbalanced mentally; he died very soon after.

In any event, so far as Harpending was concerned, the first attempt to help the Southern cause had failed; the next thing was to find another means. It came to him early in 1862. He slipped down to Mexico, and then found his way through the blockade to Richmond. He managed to see Jefferson Davis, and with the Confederate president's approval he was commissioned by Judah P. Benjamin, then Davis's secretary of war and later his secretary of state, as an officer in the Confederate navy —though he had no naval experience whatsoever. During his few months in Virginia, and before he became a naval officer, he fought for a short time as a private, and was cited for bravery at Shiloh, where Albert Sidney Johnston was killed. Harpending, however, was not enlisted under his old adversary, but was one of Beauregard's men.

The next step was to return to San Francisco, again running the blockade. This time he carried with him letters from the South to California sympathizers, discovery of which would have caused his instant arrest. On board the Pacific Mail liner from Panama, he met Lady Fairfax. The Fairfax family, who kept their title both in Virginia and in California, whose ancestor was Washington's friend and a character in Thackeray's *The Virginians*, and who owned spacious estates in Marin County which were the scene of the last duel ever fought in the state, cry aloud for an historical novel that has never been written. This Lady Fairfax, also known as Mrs. Charles Fairfax, was a niece of John C. Calhoun, and her sympathies lay exactly where Harpending's did. When the ship arrived, he was searched, but nothing contraband was found on him. The incriminating letters at that moment were sewn inside the lady's crinoline.

Harpending's scheme was so simple and so daring that it takes the breath away. It was nothing more or less than to charter a ship, sail it to Mexico, lie in wait for the next Pacific Mail steamer, seize it, and send its cargo of California gold to the Confederacy. With luck, he hoped to be able to use the first seized Pacific Mail ship as a privateer, and to capture at least two more before he was caught. The Pacific Mail was at that time the chief line operating out of California; fifteen years later, it was the Pacific Mail docks that Kearney and the sand lotters threatened to blow up, because by that time the main cargo was not gold, but Chinese laborers.

Harpending had been careful to secure his naval commission, so that in the event of arrest he would be regarded, not as a pirate, but as a Confederate officer. He proceeded in every detail with the utmost caution, remembering what had happened the year before. But when he got in touch with the former Knights of the Golden Circle, he found only one who was willing to go with him into this dangerous enterprise—Ridgely Greathouse, another Kentuckian, and a relative of the well-known Tevis family of San Francisco. There is some confusion about this Greathouse, since in the old City Cemetery in Sacramento there is buried a Dr. Ridgely Greathouse, of Kentucky, who died in 1852, the last victim of a cholera epidemic in which he had served heroically. Probably the two men were cousins, or they may even conceivably have been father and son.

Casting about for more help, Harpending found young Alfred Rubery, an Englishman. Most of the leaders of English politics at this time were strongly pro-Confederate, but Rubery's family was the one prominent exception, for he was the favorite nephew of John Bright, the celebrated economist, who was chief English advocate of the Union. But Rubery, whether through conviction or love of adventure, was heart and soul for the plan. The three young men—Harpending himself was still only twenty-three—raised among them a quarter of a million dollars, of which Harpending contributed $50,000; the thirty Knights of the Golden Circle had spent a million dollars to get nothing at all, so this was cheap. They chartered the ship *J. M. Chapman,* and loaded her with boxes labeled "machinery," which actually contained arms purchased from Mexico on the claim that Harpending needed them to protect his Mexican mining property. A few trading goods were put on board to carry out the pretense that the *J. M. Chapman* was going to Mexico on a mercantile expedition. Twenty men with experience as soldiers were hired for the voyage to Manzanillo. Besides the small arms, the ship had two twelve-pound cannon aboard.

Since neither the Confederate naval officer nor his two companions had ever had any nautical experience, it was necessary to hire a navigator and a sailing master. William Law was engaged for the first, Lorenzo Libby, a Canadian, for the second. March 15, 1863, was set as their sailing date.

On the night of the 14th, Harpending, Rubery,

Asbury Harpending. The boy prodigy as he came to San Francisco.

Greathouse, and Libby, with the twenty fighting men, went on board. Law was to join them in the morning. Everything was set, and Harpending fell asleep in his berth, his heart high with hope.

He was awakened by the approach of a United States gunboat. Law had betrayed them.

There was now no time to make more than a feeble gesture of resistance. Harpending frantically tore up and burned the papers proving his guilt. He was not quick enough; the officers collected the charred scraps and pieced them together again. The entire crew was put under arrest, but only the three conspirators and Libby were held for trial. They were taken to Alcatraz, then a United States disciplinary barracks.

There Libby, who after all was a Canadian and far from eager to die for another country, turned state's evidence and confessed the whole conspiracy. "If I had known Libby's name was Lorenzo," said Harpending sourly in later years, "I would never have engaged him. I have three times in my life been cheated by men named Lorenzo." Law, who had come highly recommended, he had distrusted from the first, not liking his face; but he was in a desperate hurry and could not immediately find another competent navigator.

At the trial Law and Libby both testified, and Harpending, Rubery, and Greathouse were convicted of high treason. The court took cognizance, however, of the fact that they had accomplished precisely nothing, and also of the actual conditions of war. They were sentenced, not to death, but to ten years and ten thousand dollars' fine. This last was a mere gesture, since all

Harpending's property was confiscated. He had power-ful friends still: Rubery and Greathouse were remanded to Alcatraz, but Harpending was sent to the San Fran-cisco County jail—probably the only person guilty of high treason ever to reside there!

With remarkable common sense, the government, having proved its case, refused to take these young hot-heads too seriously. First Law and Libby were sent safely away to China. Then Greathouse was released under the Amnesty Act. Rubery was pardoned by Lin-coln and sent home to England, where he must have had an embarrassing reunion with his Uncle John. Harpending got off almost as easily; at the end of four months he was let out, the last of the prisoners.

A short time later, while he was looking about and trying to decide what to do next, he heard that Great-house had been rearrested. As a matter of fact, Great-house was merely questioned on another matter and released, but by that time Asbury Harpending was gone. He fled to Tulare County, and hid in the mountains. There, with his accustomed Midas quality, he discov-ered the immensely rich Kernville gold field, centering in Havilah!

Local officials, thinking that Harpending was "want-ed" in San Francisco, notified the authorities of his whereabouts. They replied that he was free to return at any time; but Harpending himself did not learn that for a year or more. Meanwhile he was very busy piling up another fortune of $800,000, and helping to carve the new county of Kern out of a part of Tulare.

In the summer of 1865, when he turned up again in

San Francisco, just after the end of the Civil War, he
was once more a very rich man. He was also not quite
twenty-six.

He plunged at once into more of his dizzying real-
estate operations. It was then that he conceived the plan
of "Montgomery Street Straight South."

Montgomery Street, which is now the financial center
on San Francisco in its first blocks, and "the sea-coast
of Bohemia," mixed with a transplanted Italy, for the
remainder of its length up Telegraph Hill, was in the
city's earlier days its main business thoroughfare. It
stopped at Market Street, and opposite it, to the south,
there was at that time a huge sand dune and nothing
more. Most of the property opposite Montgomery Street
was then owned by the Roman Catholic Church.

Harpending's idea was to carry Montgomery Street
across Market, and straight through to the bay; in other
words, it would run the whole length of the city, with
the bay at either end. This meant not only buying an
immense amount of land, but also tearing down many
buildings already erected, and cutting through Rincon
Hill, then the most fashionable residence quarter. It
meant even more, for Harpending also intended to widen
Montgomery Street itself, to make a continuous broad
avenue of it and its extension. He began immediately
buying up real estate adjacent to Montgomery Street
and south to Market Street as well.

William C. Ralston, of the Bank of California, was a
maniac about San Francisco; Julian Dana called him
with justice "the man who made" the city. He was
ready at any time to plunge a fortune into any scheme

to improve the city he adored. He, with all the rest of the city, heard about Harpending's project. He sent for the young man to come to his office, questioned him about his plans.

Though Ralston was not a gambler, he had the gambler's temperament. He said once that he had picked William C. Sharon as his chief business associate because when they played poker together at the Comstock mine, source of their common wealth, Sharon always won. Now he exclaimed: "It sounds like a noble game. How would you like me for a partner?"

Ralston, the great Maecenas, was worth untold millions. He was ten years yet from his incredible collapse and enigmatic death. Nothing could have pleased Harpending more. They formed the Montgomery Street Real Estate Company, pledged unlimited support by the Bank of California, with Ralston taking a quarter interest, and Sharon buying in as well.

Finally they acquired the Catholic church property (now the site of the Palace Hotel, built by Ralston in 1875), and the property next to it, owned by Selim Woodworth, son of the author of "The Old Oaken Bucket." This last property was bought in a way that made the partners laugh. In 1868, San Francisco experienced the sharpest earthquake of its career, the worst it has ever known except 1906. Going down to survey the damage, Harpending met Woodworth. "Well," said Harpending, "looks pretty bad, doesn't it?" "Bad?" quavered Woodworth. "San Francisco is through! I'm going to Oakland." "If that's so," retorted Harpending, "I'll take that Market Street property off your hands.

I'll give you $150,000 for it." Looking at Harpending as if he thought him crazy, Woodworth clinched the bargain on the spot. Until the night before, he had obstinately set his immovable price at half a million!

On Woodworth's lot, in 1869, Harpending built the Grand Hotel, the most important in San Francisco between the opening of the Lick House and of the Palace. After the latter was built, an ornamental bridge dubbed "the bridge of sighs" connected the two hotels.

But meanwhile "Montgomery Street Straight South" had struck a snag. At Folsom Street, three blocks south of Market, M. S. Latham had his home, and he refused to sell. Harpending was desperate; he even managed to get a bill through the legislature condemning the property, but it was repealed. In the end, he had to give up. Today New Montgomery Street, as it is called, extends only from the south side of Market Street, at an angle from Montgomery Street itself, two blocks down to Howard Street.

Harpending, who was so willing to cut through Rincon Hill, was by this time living there himself. In 1866 he bought Ralston's house on Fremont Street, when the banker built his magnificent mansion at Belmont, on the San Francisco peninsula. Asbury Harpending was now a married man; by 1872 he had three daughters. That he was also still a fire-eater is evidenced by a newspaper item of 1868 which records his arrest, with that of his father-in-law, I. D. Thompson, "two well-dressed, intelligent-looking men," on a charge of fighting on Montgomery Street. Harpending was charged also with "using vulgar language." Apparently, like many others, he had "in-law" trouble and did not suffer it meekly!

"Montgomery Street Straight South" did not engage all his energies as a real-estate operator. Besides the Grand Hotel, in the same year he built the Harpending Block, a $400,000 office building on Market Street between First and Second. It burnt to the ground in 1871, a total loss. Harpending had the golden touch, but he was as fated to lose money as he was to make it. Nevertheless, he was no reckless fool, but a shrewd and fearless financier, whose judgment was respected by such men as Ralston and Sharon, and by Sam Brannan, who was his partner in several enterprises.

Ralston remained his closest business associate, except when he operated alone. His nearness to Ralston and Ralston's trust in him were evidenced by a curious episode of July, 1869.

The Comstock Lode, source of most of Ralston's wealth and the focus of investment and speculation in California, took as well as gave money. The bank it had built up was the loan center for every California enterprise; for example, the Central Pacific Railroad had drawn on the bank for three million dollars in actual cash, all of which had gone East; other enterprises for two million more. In consequence, though there were millions of dollars' worth of Comstock gold in the bank's vaults, there were often times when it could summon only $50,000 in coin—and gold bullion was not legal tender. Solvent as Ralston was at this time, there was always the terrifying possibility of being caught short, with a consequent run on the bank, refusal to accept explanations, and causeless failure.

Meanwhile, the San Francisco Mint was turning out plenty of coin to exchange for bullion—or had been; for when Grant became president he closed the mint temporarily, and arbitrarily refused to let the bankers deposit gold bars and get coins in exchange at the United States Subtreasury. Ralston kept the telegraph wires hot begging for permission, but received not even a reply. Finally he became desperate. In his extremity he chose Harpending and another man named Maurice Doré to help him, though without telling them why he wanted them to come to the bank late at night in rough clothes.

They soon found out. Nobody knows to this day how Ralston made the arrangements to have the doors of the Subtreasury open for him. Undoubtedly the police on the beat were "fixed." Legend says that throughout the events of that night a high Army officer stood by the unlocked door, a smile on his face, his arms folded. From after midnight to dawn, Ralston, Harpending, and Doré carried bags of gold coin to the Bank of California and brought back five tons of gold bullion which they deposited in the Subtreasury. Neither Sharon nor Ogden Mills, the bank's first president, ever heard the story. The very next day the threatened run began. The bewildered tellers were told to put more men to work; the gold was piled high in their cages. The run stopped as suddenly as it had started; and later in the day Ralston saved another near-by bank in the same manner, by offering to cash all its checks. Three days later Grant reversed his ruling, and California finance could function again.

Harpending would have done more than this for Ralston, and proved it. One of Harpending's enterprises was the San Francisco and Humboldt Railroad, which he had built and for which he had secured a franchise from Sausalito, north of San Francisco, to Humboldt Bay—practically the route of the present Northwestern Pacific Railroad. Leland Stanford and his associates of the Central Pacific's "Big Four" watched Harpending's venture with sour glances. They considered the new railroad a threat to their own, especially at its northern terminus, where it turned inland. Stanford knew better than to go to Harpending about it, but he also knew how to reach Harpending. He had promised Ralston that when the Central Pacific was finished, Ralston should have the concession for building the cars. Now he went to Ralston and said he would withdraw the concession unless Harpending gave up his railroad. Ralston sent for Harpending and told him the whole story. Harpending immediately sacrificed his interests, and sold his railroad to Peter Donahue, who was willing to play ball with the "Big Four." To this day the Northwestern Pacific belongs to the Southern Pacific, successor to the Central Pacific. Donahue got rich by means of the railroad Harpending sold him at a sacrifice price. And, after all, Stanford double-crossed Ralston and gave the car-building concession to someone else!

But by this time Asbury Harpending was in London. He had all along continued to engage in mining operations and mining stocks, and it was this that took him to England. His chief purpose was to expose the so-called "Emma Mine scandal," a mine utterly worthless, yet with a paper value of $16,000,000, an investment in which many English buyers had been rooked through its promoter, Baron Grant. In order to expose Grant, Harpending established the *London Stock Exchange Review*, with a man named Samson as his financial editor. Alfred Rubery, his old comrade in the Civil War episode, was also associated with him now. So far as Harpending knew, though he still retained some of his San Francisco holdings and his Kern County mining land, the rest of his life was going to be spent in London, or between London and New York.

In December, 1871, he received from Ralston a cablegram that had cost $1,100, and that convinced him Ralston must have lost his mind. Other cables followed it, each more urgent than the last. Harpending must return to San Francisco at once. Something absolutely unbelievable had happened.

What had happened was this. Two men, Philip Arnold and John Slack, had come to the Bank of California with some uncut diamonds. They claimed to have found the diamonds "somewhere in the desert" while prospecting for gold. Both men, especially Arnold, had good reputations; he was a '49er. Harpending had known him, and had used him often to investigate mines; he was a fellow Kentuckian. The diamonds were undoubtedly genuine. The men were willing to sell their claim, which they described as breath-takingly rich in diamonds, rubies, sapphires, and emeralds.

The biggest businessmen in San Francisco were involved in what became known later as the Great Diamond Hoax. The Rothschilds in London took an immediate interest; in the face of Harpending's skepticism, Baron Rothschild told him there was no reason why America should not contain diamond fields. David D. Colton, who used to be called derisively the "half" of the "Big Four-and-a-Half," resigned as an official of the Central Pacific to devote his time to exploiting the great diamond find. By this time, May, 1872, Harpending had returned to San Francisco. A few days later a wire came from Reno from Arnold and Slack, who had previously taken Henry Janin, a well-known engineer, to their claim, blindfolded, and shown him "a diamond field worth at least sixty-five million, even the ant-hills sparkling with diamond dust." Soon after, they had gone back alone to bring Ralston a real sample, a sackful of their precious find. Now, from Reno, they telegraphed that they were afraid to travel farther with such wealth, and wanted someone to accompany them the rest of the way.

Harpending went. The heavy sack was completely full of diamonds and other precious gems. Harpending kept them in his own vault, until they were taken to New York, to the famous jeweler Tiffany. He examined them in the presence of Horace Greeley, General Gorge B. McClellan, and General B. F. Butler, and pronounced them genuine, and worth $150,000. And what he saw was one tenth of the contents of one sack!

The board which finally took over Arnold's and Slack's claim and paid them $660,000 for their rights included a representative of Baron Rothschild, as well as General McClellan, Ralston, and practically every important financier in San Francisco. Main offices were in San Francisco, with a transfer office in New York. The company was capitalized at ten million dollars.

The whole world was on the verge of a speculative frenzy that would have made the Comstock Lode look like a country auction.

As for Arnold and Slack, they took their $660,000—very modest pay for a claim worth countless millions—and disappeared.

And then the United States Government sent Clarence King, one of its best-known geologists, to Wyoming to make a final definitive report on the value of the find.

The one thing Arnold and Slack had not counted on was investigation by a trained scientist—one who would know, for example, that diamonds, rubies, emeralds, and sapphires do not appear in the same beds. King found diamonds pushed into the crevices of rocks, in artificial anthills, in the forks of trees! He found not a single one in bedrock where it belonged. As a climax he found a stone showing unmistakable signs of having been cut.

That was the end, before it began. The mine had been salted. Later it was disclosed that Arnold had been in London and Amsterdam, buying low-grade stones. The diamonds were practically worthless "niggerheads" from Africa.

Since investment had scarcely started, a world panic was averted. The two million already paid into the capitalized stock Ralston repaid. Arnold was traced to his old home in Kentucky, and in exchange for having charges dropped against him, disgorged $150,000. He kept $300,000, and with charming aplomb opened a bank with it! When a few years later he was killed in a duel, he left a neat fortune to his relatives. As for Slack, a minor character altogether, he was never seen again. He may have died in the desert. He may even have been murdered by his accomplice for his share of the spoils. No one knows.

The unfairest thing of all was that Harpending immediately became the target for unlimited abuse. Ralston was beyond possibility of blame, especially in view of his quick repayment of all invested money. But Harpending, who had had to be persuaded by Ralston against his will, who had investigated the claim reluctantly, and who had been honestly taken in by it together with Ralston and all the rest, was accused of having been a party to the entire fraud and of having deceived Ralston. The London *Times* printed an article to this effect, inspired by Baron Grant, whom Harpending had been exposing for the Emma Mine swindle, and by his former editor, Samson, who had gone over to Grant. Since Harpending was not in London, and Rubery had been left as his representative there, Rubery brought suit for libel in his own name and got a judgment of ten thousand pounds, with which he left for Australia and a prosperous career there. Everything ended quite happily for Rubery, but not for Harpending. London might have been silenced, but voices in New York and San Francisco were still yapping at him.

"Crushed by suspicion," he auctioned off all his San Francisco and California property of every description. He sold Ralston and Sharon his share in the Montgomery Street Real Estate Company, and with the proceeds, estimated at a million or more, he went back to Hopkinsville, Kentucky, where Philip Arnold was establishing his virtuous bank.

But Harpending was hardly one to sit and vegetate in a country town. Before long his wounds had healed, and he was once more engaged in mining operations. He had been forsaken by his magic touch. He lost money in Wall Street; he lost more in silver mines in Colombia and gold mines in Mexico. His great days were over. He salvaged enough to retire on and care for his family, and came back to California, where people had something new to talk about, now that the Bank of California had failed and Ralston was dead.

He settled in Fruitvale, at present a part of Oakland, and lived there until 1918. The fire of the young Confederate zealot turned privateer had long ago died down. He was a worthy patriot now, and was careful to run up the flag of the Union over his little house on every appropriate occasion. His three daughters were married, one to the Greek consul, another to the editor of a Greek paper in San Francisco, the third to an Irishman. It seems probable that the last daughter moved to New York, for in 1918 Harpending went there, and she was with him when he died, in January, 1923. He had amused and consoled his last dull years in California by writing a sort of autobiography. But he passed hurriedly over the really exciting story of his young career, and his lasting hurt and resentment are shown by the title he gave his book—*The Great Diamond Hoax.* It had long ago been proved abundantly that Harpending had been a dupe, not a conspirator, but the suspicion still rankled.

Few men have filled eighty-three years with more varied and picturesque experience.

CHAPTER VI

Lady Fire Buff:
LILLIE HITCHCOCK COIT

IT WAS a night in the 1860's. Knickerbocker Volunteer Fire Company No. 5 had just received a call. As the men in their red shirts, black trousers, high boots, and black helmets pulled No. 5 engine from its housing in the station at Bush and Battery Streets, they glanced at an upper window in the fashionable Oriental Hotel across the way. A light shone there, in signal that their Honorary Member had heard the call. Hours later they returned, and again they looked for the light, which was still there. All was well, and No. 5 was rehoused. If the light had been out, their Honorary Member would have been fined. All daytime calls the Honorary Member was supposed to attend; at night it was necessary only that she show a light in her window until the engine was back.

The Honorary Member was a pretty young woman with dark hair and eyes, a firm mouth, sensitive nostrils, and an habitual expression of humor and courage. She was Lillie Hitchcock, daughter of Dr. Charles McPhail Hitchcock, an army surgeon who had formerly been stationed at West Point and among the Cherokees, and who was now Medical Director of the Pacific Coast. His daughter had been named Honorary Member of

Knickerbocker Engine Company No. 5 in October, 1863, soon after her return from Paris. She was a belle and a bit of a bluestocking, a true child of San Francisco in its most romantic days, though she was eight years old before she ever saw the city, in 1851.

She took her fire-company membership very seriously. It had started when she was a child playing with other children in the sand dunes where the Palace Hotel now stands, or fishing for rats under the board sidewalk near the present site of the Donahue Mechanics' Monument, in downtown San Francisco. There was a special kind of white rat with red eyes which was a tremendous fighter, and which the young hunters particularly prized. Lillie was good at catching them, but one of the boys had to do the killing—not that she had the slightest fear, but she could not bear to hurt them. In later years she was a famous shot, but still her courage was always softened by tenderheartedness.

In those early days, before the fire department was put on a paid basis in 1866, membership in the various companies, all keen rivals, was an honor eagerly sought after by the wealthiest and most important men in the young city. Sam Brannan, for example, was delighted to have a company named for him and to buy its engine. San Francisco had already been devastated by fire several times; just before the Hitchcocks arrived, in May, 1851, the worst of three fires to date had laid waste all the central portion of the town. Protection against fire was a major social duty of the city's leaders.

Knickerbocker No. 5, which was a near neighbor of the Oriental Hotel, where the Hitchcocks made their first home in San Francisco, had come to the city only seven months before them. October 17 was its "birthday," when every year, even after commercialization of the department and the retirement of the old engine, the volunteer company held a big dinner. The Honorary Member provided the table decorations. Late in the evening, when the toasts began, she would appear, in a black silk skirt, a red fire shirt, a black tie, and a veteran's belt, carrying her black helmet. When she was abroad, she never forgot to send a cablegram. Then the men would give their annual toast: "Our lady friends in general and our lady friend in particular— here's to our Lillie!" At the banquet in 1888 the company gave her a gold pin, a replica of their helmet, set with a diamond; and in their meeting room was a statuette of her, which was destroyed in the fire of 1906.

When they held their parades, "Our Lillie" (if she was not actually atop the flower-decked engine) was at her window, in uniform, waving a red handkerchief. The windows of her suite would be crowded, for she always invited a number of her friends and provided each of them with a red handkerchief to wave too. When the company came home tired after a hard fight, she ordered supper for them all. And, just as she never forgot to leave her light burning when the bell clanged for a night call, so she obeyed the rules and never missed a daytime fire. Once she was returning from the rehearsal of a wedding at Grace Church (now Grace Cathedral), where she was to be bridesmaid. Suddenly she heard the engines, and No. 5 turned the corner of Market Street. She had her coachman stop the carriage, and rushed to her post, bridesmaid's gown and all. The hoseman of another company sneered at No. 5, called their Honorary Member a "featherbedder." No. 5's hoseman promptly turned the stream full on to Miss Hitchcock, to prove that she could "take it"!

In the de Young Museum, in Golden Gate Park, there is a painting of Lillie Hitchcock Coit done by F. Wolf about 1877. It was painted during her blonde period, but the dark eyes and the stubborn little chin are a good likeness. She is wearing a red dress—probably the same elaborate dress of magenta and garnet taffeta and velvet, with panels and bustle and silk fringe, that stands in the glass case below; and on her curls is a black hat with a sweeping, gallant white plume. Plainly visible on the bosom of her dress is a little pin, simply the figure 5. As long as she lived, Mrs. Coit wore that pin night and day; even when she was in evening dress, it was always there. She was buried with it. She always signed her name, "Lillie Hitchcock (later Lillie Hitchcock Coit) 5"; and "Lillie Hitchcock Coit 5" was marked on all her clothing and woven into her lace fans.

All this, and more that is yet to be told of her, sounds like the description of a crackbrained eccentric. But that she never was. Unconventional, yes; daring and supremely individual; but her oddities were those of a great lady who is not afraid to be herself. She had been nurtured by her father in a military code of honor, courage, loyalty, and independence; she had been born in the United States Military Academy at West Point, and reared with soldiers for playmates in Florida, Indians in North Carolina. About the only place she and her mother had not followed the army surgeon was to the Mexican War; and even there Dr. Hitchcock's care of young Jefferson Davis following the battle of Buena Vista had repercussions years later on his daughter's life. Lillie was the only child, and was trained by her father as he would have trained a son destined for the army. Even on board the ship coming to California, she showed her mettle; a big, ill-tempered boy picked a fight with a smaller and weaker boy and had him down; little Lillie, smaller than either, pitched in and pummeled the aggressor till he yelled for mercy. Once in her childhood, walking with her parents past the sand dunes south of Market Street, a bullet whizzed by her ear; before they could move she was scrambling up the dune to see whence it had come! She was the same child who was to grow into the woman who looked out of her window one night on her Napa Valley ranch, and saw a burglar on the porch roof. She got her rifle, and climbed out after him. The burglar escaped, merely because Mrs. Coit did not want to shoot him unless she had to; but he was so paralyzed with fear that he could scarcely run.

In 1851 there were very few children in San Francisco, fewer still who were from American families. The Oriental Hotel was for a while a sort of headquarters for most of these family groups. The first Christmas the Hitchcocks lived there, nearly every man in town deluged the six or eight youngsters with gifts; the children were community pets, surrogates for young ones left behind back East. There were no toys to be had in all San Francisco, so most of the Christmas pres-

ents were gold. Amusements also were few; the children fished for rats; played in the sand dunes or in Captain Macondray's barn; dressed up and imitated the
actors and actresses they were taken to see in the first
theaters of that drama-mad city; and when the bell
sounded that meant the call to the First Vigilante Committee, they were all trained to scamper home and stay
there, for the streets were not going to be safe for children for a while. As a special favor, the children in the
Oriental Hotel were sometimes allowed by the friendly
firemen across the street to pull on the rope of No. 5's
bell; and it was little Lillie Hitchcock who most often
had that privilege and to whom it meant most. Once,
it is said, she even helped pull on the rope of the engine
so that No. 5 could get ahead of Nos. 2 and 3.

When she was thirteen or so, her mother began to
worry about her education. Mrs. Hitchcock herself
was an unusual woman. She had been Martha Taliaferro
Hunter, of Virginia (Dr. Hitchcock was a Mary-
lander), and was cousin to several distinguished Virginians who later played important parts in the Confederacy. She was a clever writer, who contributed
whimsical essays to the *Alta Californian* and the *Overland Monthly,* and was a friend and patroness of the
Overland's young editor, Bret Harte. Harte, who
had refused even to consider any of Joaquin Miller's
manuscripts, sent to him so regularly and hopefully,
paid Mrs. Hitchcock twice his usual rates for anything
she would give him. But she was a friend of Miller's
also; visiting her one day, the future "Poet of the
Sierras" read a letter written by Mrs. Hitchcock's little

daughter, and exclaimed: "Thank God, Lillie, *you* have not tried to write, or I would never have had a chance!"

Lillie had, up to this time, been educated entirely by her mother. Part of her training was to write a daily letter (though mother and daughter were hardly ever separated), as a device to develop a readable style. Lillie read omnivorously every book she could get hold of in San Francisco; she was a natural linguist, whose French in later years was so much a part of her that she hardly realized she was translating when she spoke aloud in English a book she was reading in French; and she had a native aptitude for mathematics, all her life loving to do algebra problems for her own amusement. But all this was hardly fitting her to take the place in society expected of the daughter of a high-ranking army surgeon and a Southern lady.

So, pale but tearless, she was dispatched to a convent school in San Jose. She did not rebel; she obeyed all the rules, she studied diligently, she did as she was told. But she stopped eating, and nothing could persuade her to swallow a morsel of food. At the end of four days, the sisters sent her back in despair to the home she loved enough to be willing to die away from it.

There was no more talk of exiling Lillie, but when the Girls' High School was founded she was sent to it. In the middle of her senior year a skylarking classmate accidentally stabbed her in the eye with a slate pencil—which in those days was part of a high school student's equipment. Lillie was obliged to spend months in a darkened room, blindfolded. But two or three of the young army officers who always surrounded Dr. Hitchcock as disciples and admirers undertook to coach her by word of mouth in mathematics and languages; she emerged from her bandages to pass her examinations near the head of her class.

The schoolgirl evolved into (as Amelia Ransome Neville called her in her book of reminiscences, *The Fantastic City*) "the most dashing belle San Francisco ever knew, with her gay spirits and spectacular independence." After high school had come several years in a school in Paris, the first of her recurrent journeys to "the heaven of all good Americans." Then she was ready to "come out" in a city which, however raw and crude, had always set great store by its social life and its rather heterogeneous aristocracy.

She was almost eighteen when the Civil War broke out. Not for nothing was Lillie Hitchcock a romantic daughter of the South. She threw herself heart and soul into the Southern cause. She did the most daring and indiscreet things. Several young Southerners in San Francisco who were burning to get away and join the Confederate army were helped to make their escape through the influence and ingenuity of Lillie Hitchcock. One young man she disguised and helped to a job as stoker in a steamship. Then she had the audacity to call on the captain and ask to be shown through the ship, where she had the satisfaction of seeing her friend, grimy and sweating, shoveling coal into a furnace.

Her mother, whose cousins were all active in the Southern cause, aided and abetted her; but her father, son of a border state and his sympathies with the army he had served so long, was frightened. After all, young

Asbury Harpending was soon to be sent to prison for little more than the doctor's daughter was doing. Against their will, the alarmed doctor forced his wife and daughter to go to Paris until the danger was over. Very soon Lillie found that she could serve the Confederacy in France as well as in America. The United States minister refused to receive the Hitchcocks because he well knew where their sympathies lay; but Empress Eugènie was charmed by the American girl and saw to it that she and her mother attended all the court functions. Soon Lillie Hitchcock became the official translator of all the documents transmitted to the French government by the Confederate officials. For two years the entire correspondence, much of it of the most extraordinary importance, passed through the hands of a girl not yet twenty.

In 1863 the two returned to San Francisco, very indignant because they were not given permission in Washington to pass through the lines so that Mrs. Hitchcock might visit her relatives in Virginia! But Lillie, apparently, had had her fill of political intrigue; she had missed her father and San Francisco badly, and perhaps had come to a sobering realization of the seriousness of her gay defiance of military law. She plunged into the excitements and diversions of a city in wartime when the war is at a safe distance. And once more she devoted herself wholeheartedly to Fire Company No. 5.

This time what had been an endearing whim in an amusing child became an embarrassment to the parents of a marriageable daughter. Dr. Hitchcock laid down an ultimatum: if Lillie would not stop going to fires, she would be exiled for two weeks, with a maid to watch her, to the ranch in Napa Valley, the isolated house appropriately called "Lonely," six miles from Saint Helena. Lillie agreed sweetly that this was only fair—and kept right on attending all No. 5's daytime calls. After each one she obediently packed up and went with the maid to "Lonely." As soon as she was back she would start all over again. Finally her parents gave up in humorous despair; Lillie and No. 5 were engaged in a lifelong romance, and there was no use in trying to separate them.

In November, 1868, Company No. 5 acquired a rival, when at the Church of the Advent, Lillie Hitchcock married Benjamin Howard Coit, "caller" of the old Mining Exchange on Post Street—a very important office in early San Francisco. He was a large, heavily built man, a lover of sport and thoroughly masculine, but with a high-strung nervous system as well. Often, after the strain of a day in the Mining Exchange, he would come home so utterly exhausted that he could not bear to speak or hear a word. Then Mrs. Coit would put him and their pet dog in the carriage, and drive for miles and hours without a sentence between them until her husband's nerves had quieted and he was himself again. She was a magnificent driver, and, later on, her husband hired an old-time stage driver to teach her the fancy tricks of the trade.

Lillie Hitchcock had no intention of settling down into dull domesticity just because she was now Lillie Hitchcock Coit. She was a real companion to a husband who was, above all, a man's man. They went everywhere together. She joined in his poker games with his friends —W. C. Ralston, the great financier of the Bank of California, the principal one—and she was an expert player. Ralston had an impish humor which matched hers; once she and he plotted against a game at the Cliff House in which Howard Coit and William C. Sharon, the bonanza king, were two of the participants. By a trick she called all the players away for a minute, during which Ralston quickly changed the cards. When the game was resumed, each man discovered to his amazement that he held four aces! Ralston and Mrs. Coit stood by, helpless with concealed laughter, to watch the bidding that ensued, and the disgust at the end of the hand.

A husband had to be free of prejudice and ready for anything, however unorthodox, to live comfortably with Lillie Coit. One day, with her love of experiment, she bleached her dark, curly hair to a sickening peroxide yellow. Coit was furious. Unabashed, she went to a hairdresser, had her head completely shaved, and until her hair grew in again, used three wigs—black, blonde, and red. She alternated them from day to day, choosing the one which harmonized best with her costume, utterly insouciant in the face of surprise and laughter.

It was soon after this that Coit, doubtless feeling rather overpowered, resigned his post at the Mining Exchange and took his wife for a long trip around the world. Lillie was fascinating and adorable, but what was an essentially conventional man to do with a wife who changed the color of her hair every day, or would

Lillie Hitchcock Coit wearing her fire-company pin.
From a painting by Wolf.

leave a dance in her low-necked gown and satin slippers
to answer a call from her fire company?

Dr. Hitchcock apparently agreed that his daughter
could be most herself in a less restricted environment
than any city, even San Francisco, could provide. For
when the Coits returned from their trip, he built Lillie
a house on part of his large holdings in the Napa
Valley. (It was burned to the ground in October,
1938.) She called the house "Larkmead," for the place
was thick with meadowlarks, and she saw to it, for all
her hunting, that it remained a sanctuary for them. The
place was full of pet animals, the king of them "Baby
Mule," a burro which had once saved Howard Coit's
life by its speed when, in his youthful days in Arizona,
he had been pursued by savage Apaches. Mrs. Coit sent
for the mule, aged now, but still sturdy, and till it died
it was the boss of the ranch, following its master and
mistress around like a dog.

But the childless marriage between two affectionate
and well-intentioned but utterly ill-assorted beings was
near its end. A few years later the Coits separated permanently. They were never divorced, but remained friends,
and when Howard Coit died in 1885, six weeks after
Dr. Hitchcock, he left his entire fortune to his wife.
After she and her mother became widows almost at the
same time, they moved to "Larkmead" and lived there
all the year round, with a French maid and Chinese
servants. Mrs. Coit, mounted on her fine hunter, Mace,
was a familiar figure in the countryside—and a shocking one to rural eyes, for she dared to wear short skirts
on horseback. Once when she alighted from Mace at

a country store, a loafer, gazing with wonder at the skirt under the severe coat and stock and hat, exclaimed: "My God! It's a woman!" Less bucolic observers never doubted that Lillie Hitchcock Coit was all woman—the part of her which was not pure quicksilver.

In "Larkmead" the mother and daughter reverted to the old days when they had been talented teacher and brilliant pupil; equals now but once more absorbed, in spite of their outdoor hours, in the world of the mind. Robert Louis Stevenson, who was living in the near-by mountains with his newly married wife and writing *The Silverado Squatters,* was their frequent visitor. He was not the first author who had been an intimate of the Hitchcock household; one of Dr. Hitchcock's closest friends had been that authentic humorist, Captain George Derby ("John Phoenix"), who had dedicated his "Phoenixiana" to his former physician at West Point. And Joaquin Miller, who had thanked God that Lillie had never tried to write, lived in her house now for weeks on end while she puzzled over his horrible scrawl, trying to put his manuscripts in shape for a printer to decipher. Once Joaquin went serenely to bed while Mrs. Coit and her mother struggled with one of his hen-track manuscripts. One phrase daunted them; the best they could make of it was "God's white tomatoes." Finally they woke Miller and asked for his help—and he could not read his own writing or remember his own poem! The next day they decided among them that the "tomatoes" must have been meant to be "tomorrows."

Dr. Hitchcock had left a third of his large estate to his daughter, with the request that when she died she would bequeath a sum to the University of California for annual medical lectures to be named for her parents. She did not wait, but made the gift at once. Through this connection with the university she met the famous geologist, Professor Joseph LeConte, also an unreconstructed Confederate, and one of the earliest advocates of evolution in America. When LeConte was exploring the Petrified Forest, at Calistoga, near Saint Helena, he made "Larkmead" his headquarters.

But San Francisco was too deeply entwined in Lillie Coit's heart to let her stay forever in exile. After a few years she ceased to live the year round at "Larkmead," and she and her mother took a suite at the Palace Hotel, built by her old friend Ralston shortly before his tragic death by drowning. There was no shooting and not much riding in the city, but there were older interests still—above all, Fire Company No. 5, whose "birthday" she had never once forgotten. Every phase of life had its healthy appeal for Lillie Coit. She had the fine palate for wine of a connoisseur, and the taste and zest for good food of an epicure. She loved to dance, and danced beautifully—a fellow debutante once remarked that when you saw all the men crowd to one end of the room and desert all the other girls, you knew Lillie Hitchcock had arrived at the ball. She smoked when women in America never touched cigarettes; she played poker like a man and rode like a cowboy. But unconventional as she was, she remained always the great lady, with no slightest whiff of scandal ever smoldering near her. Every afternoon for months she went alone to a men's club where no other woman had ever entered, went to the bedroom of an invalid friend who lived there, and read to him for several hours. Any other lady in society would have been ostracized for that; Mrs. Coit merely said: "He's lonely and he needs me"; and her explanation was accepted at once. Countless stories are told of her democracy, of her utter freedom from snobbishness, of her tactful consideration of her servants and her social inferiors. She had long been so authentically a part of San Francisco, a sort of city mascot, that when the new City Hall was built in 1872, two photographs of Lillie Hitchcock Coit were placed in the cornerstone. In 1906, when the City Hall was destroyed, they were found and given to the de Young Museum.

In all probability, if fate had not played her a sudden and nasty trick, Mrs. Coit would have remained in the glamorous city she loved to the end of her long life. The Palace Hotel was reduced to ruins in 1906, but it was rebuilt, and she would doubtless have continued to live in the new hotel, or have moved to one of the quieter and still more luxurious hotels built on Nob Hill after the fire. As she passed the half-century mark, though she was still active in body and young in mind—an inheritance from her youthful-spirited mother, who lived with her daughter until her death—her heart began to fail, and she knew she must be careful. No more dancing, no more riding, no more following Engine No. 5 to fires—though every October she still heard the toast to "our Lillie"; and she was the benefactress of every fireman who fell ill or died.

What happened, and drove Lillie Coit from her beloved San Francisco for twenty years, was a bit of raw melodrama. There was a needy Confederate veteran, a sort of Southern cousin, named Alexander B. Garnett. Because he was hard up, Mrs. Hitchcock and Mrs. Coit had employed him to collect their rents and look after their property during their frequent visits to Paris. On one of his collecting trips he had been sandbagged by a footpad, and though he seemed to recover, the blow on his head had affected his mind.

One day in 1904 Mrs. Coit was entertaining a caller in the sitting room of her suite at the Palace. He was Major J. W. McClung, son-in-law of that Dr. Beverly Cole who had been physician for the Vigilantes in the 1850's. The Coles and the McClungs were old friends of the Hitchcocks and the Coits.

Suddenly Garnett burst into the room, brandishing a pistol. Before either of them could rise, he had locked the door behind him. McClung, who knew Garnett well, tried to seize the pistol, and as they wrestled it went off and he collapsed into a chair, shot through the abdomen. Garnett aimed the pistol again at Mrs. Coit. Intrepid as always, she seized the maniac by the shoulders and cried: "Don't shoot! Remember how good my mother was to you, and how good I've tried to be!"

For a second he hesitated, and she could have escaped. But she could not desert the wounded man. She rushed to the closet where the telephone was, to call for the hotel detective, but Garnett seized it from her and tore the wires loose from the wall. Then, as Mrs. Coit leaned over McClung, trying to see how badly he was injured, the madman seemed all at once to come to himself. He went quietly for a doctor, and as quietly gave himself up.

Major McClung died the next day. Shaken and half-prostrated—though still sufficiently mistress of herself to explode scornfully, when a newspaper said the shooting had occurred in "the apartment of a Mrs. Coit," "*A* Mrs. Coit indeed!"—Mrs. Coit waited only long enough to testify at Garnett's trial, to see him convicted and sent to San Quentin. There his insanity became so obvious that he was transferred to an insane asylum in his native Virginia. Mrs. Coit had already fled to Europe.

She did not return until Garnett died, in 1924. She was always in terror that he would escape from the asylum and try to find her and kill her—though it never seems to have occurred to her that he could escape as easily to France as to California.

In 1872, in Saint Helena, Mrs. Coit had met a girl of eighteen named Floride Green. Lillie Hitchcock Coit never had a child, but Miss Green became her substitute daughter. She helped to soften Mrs. Coit's earliest exile, and for a year and eight months traveled about Europe with her. Her privately printed book of reminiscences reveals a staunch friendship rare between two women of different generations. It was Miss Green who cared for Mrs. Coit through all her dolorous last years, who was with her when she died, and to whom a large part of Mrs. Coit's estate of more than a million dollars was bequeathed. She died in 1936, but her niece recalls how she used to love to talk about "her dear friend Mrs. Coit."

The Lillie Hitchcock Coit who came back to San Francisco in 1924 was eighty-two years old. The city to which she came must have been almost unrecognizable, for she had left two years before 1906. She was already part of a legend. Her return was like a haunting. What George Derby had called "her famous sprightliness" was dead, but her spirit was still unbroken. And she still loved San Francisco. Hardly was she settled in the Fairmont Hotel—the Palace was too full of painful memories, her mother's death, the dreadful day when Garnett shot McClung — than she set about making inquiries whether she could not "buy Telegraph Hill to give to the city." She was told that this had already been done, in 1876, by "a group of prominent men." Since she could not buy it, she resolved to beautify it.

But anything more than could be done by bequest was soon beyond the powers of Lillie Coit. Just before Christmas she suffered a cerebral hemorrhage. For the four and a half years she survived, she was paralyzed and speechless. Nearly all that time she spent at Dante Hospital, where she died in July, 1929. But her mind seems to have remained clear, though her relatives had her declared incompetent and took over guardianship of her and her estate.

The formal notice of her death is a queer mixture of Southern convention and of that supreme insouciance to convention which always marked the dashing Lillie Hitchcock Coit: "Elizabeth Wyche Coit, aged 87, wife of the late Howard Coit, cousin of the Nathaniel Wyche Hunter family of Palestine, Texas, ... an Honorary Member Veteran Volunteer Fire Department No. 5."

And Company No. 5 came to her funeral. Men who had been Lillie Hitchcock's contemporaries in those dead romantic days of early San Francisco stood guard night and day in the funeral parlors, where she lay with her "5" in gold pinned to the lace above her heart. They marched in the funeral procession to Grace Cathedral, and three of the four living volunteer firemen of the company, as a special guard of honor, went before the pallbearers, and insisted on saying good-by to "our Lillie" before the funeral could proceed to Cypress Lawn Cemetery.

When her will was read, one third of her estate had been left to the San Francisco Board of Supervisors, "to expend the same in an appropriate manner for the purpose of adding to the beauty of said city which I have always loved."

The usual disputes ensued that seem inevitable when politicians have a lot of money to spend without definite directions. Quite early in the argument someone remembered Mrs. Coit's interest in Telegraph Hill, and so it was decided that something was to be built at its top. But what? Public feeling grew as heated as it did eight years later over Beniamino Bufano's giant statue of St. Francis.

Voices were heard loudly demanding a planetarium. Los Angeles had one; San Francisco did not: and what could be more appropriate as a memorial than a domed building on a high hill where men might view the stars? But then it was discovered that though there was money enough to build a planetarium, there was not enough to maintain it and support the necessary lecturer and his staff, and the city officials refused to appropriate the needed sum.

So in the end Arthur M. Brown, Jr., was commissioned

to build a cylindrical observation tower, whose summit is 540 feet above sea level. The top may be reached either by an elevator or by 245 winding steps. From it is a magnificent view of the bay, the bridges, and the whole of San Francisco. The tower is beautifully landscaped, surrounded by eucalyptus and cypress trees, and the neglected square around it, known as Pioneer Park, has been renovated in its honor. Inside the tower are murals by fifty-two artists done for the Civil Works Administration — the first government-sponsored art project anywhere in the United States. When the tower was opened in 1934 there was a brief flurry over a street scene where a newsboy was indubitably hawking a left-wing paper. But the title was hastily painted out and a conservative one painted in.

Coit Memorial Tower, its light stone pierced by narrow windows at the top for observation, was long an artistic storm center until habit dulled the shock of the first impact. It has been called "the smokestack" in derision; and the tall cylinder, visible from every hill in the city, is not pleasing to conventional aesthetes. Five thousand years from now, should it remain amid the ruins of San Francisco, seventieth-century archaeologists might be forgiven if they deduced that the barbarians of the Pre-Television Age were devotees of a phallic religion! But it provides the best—and almost the only—bird's-eye view of all the city on its score of startling hills; and for that reason it may be granted that it "adds to the beauty of said city" as its donor wished.

Old Engine No. 5 many years ago was sold to Carson City, Nevada, like an old horse with a few working years still in him. There after a while it was discarded as obsolete and antiquated. Some of Lillie Hitchock Coit's friends found it and bought it. It was given to the de Young Museum, where it stands at the end of a long hall, near her other memorials. When the Coit Tower was dedicated, on October 8, 1933, someone had a happy thought. Old No. 5 was trundled out from the museum in Golden Gate Park, and for the last time it was dragged up Telegraph Hill. It had always been the company's boast that No. 5 could make that hill, even in the days of bottomless mud, where other engines balked at the lower slopes.

And laid on the engine as it stood in the parkway before the tower were the Honorary Member's veteran's belt and black helmet. Two months later a sculptured memorial was unveiled in Washington Square.

Lillie Hitchcock Coit was the very spirit and essence of old San Francisco. If the dead could return, I do not think she would linger long by the white tower atop Telegraph Hill. There would be a faint misty light at the end of a museum corridor; and there a dauntless little figure would be standing, ready to follow Engine No. 5 wherever the fire bells called it.

CHAPTER VII

Chinese and Dynamite:
DENNIS KEARNEY and BURNETTE HASKELL

U P AND DOWN the Pacific Coast, San Francisco has always been known as a "labor town." The first unions in the Far West were organized in San Francisco, the first strikes called there. That is natural, since San Francisco was the first large industrial city on the Coast — for many years known simply as "the City." But the tradition has persisted, and even today San Francisco is commonly thought of as a "closed shop city," Los Angeles as an "open shop city" — even though neither characterization is 100 per cent accurate.

In the 1870's and 1880's, however, there could be no question of "the City's" being the center of labor activities and organization. And the name that dominated all other for the five years from 1877 to 1882 was that of a stocky, red mustached Irishman named Dennis Kearney. So closely was unionism in San Francisco identified with this ex-drayman turned agitator that it became known to the general public as "Kearneyism," and Kearney, with his sand-lot speeches and his constant, Catonian demand, "The Chinese must go!" became a figure of national interest. To this day one may occasionally meet San Franciscans who imagine that Kearny Street, one of the principal business thoroughfares, was named for the little Irish labor leader, instead of its true naming for General Philip Kearny of Civil War fame.

Dennis Kearney's celebrity—or notoriety—could not entirely eclipse the emergent figures of a few other spokesmen of the labor forces of the period—men like Frank Roney, General A. M. Winn, the young Andrew Furuseth, and Burnette G. Haskell. This man last named, as excitable and demagogic as Kearney himself, lacked the Irishman's power to draw the masses, but exceeded him in daring. Kearney was never afraid to talk about dynamite; Haskell loved to talk about it. Undoubtedly both of them would have balked at using it.

Dennis Kearney was born on the first of February, in 1847, in County Cork, the second of seven children of a poor family. At eleven he shipped as cabin boy in an American vessel, and sailed always under the United States flag. He first set foot on shore in San Francisco in 1867, as mate of the clipper *Shooting Star*. By the time he was twenty-one he had his master's certificate and was first officer of a coasting steamship. Two years later, in 1870, he married Mary Ann Leary, who became the mother of his four children.

In 1872, Kearney decided to quit the sea forever and settle down on dry land. San Francisco, where his family had awaited him between voyages, was his choice as a permanent home. In 1876 he was naturalized as an American citizen. With his savings from fourteen years at sea, he bought a draying business—a very good means to prosperity in the pre-motor-truck age—and he prospered from the beginning. Whatever else Kearney was, when he came to the labor movement he was not a pen-

Courtesy Society of California Pioneers.
Dennis Kearney during his sand-lot days.

niless have-not; and the only accusation he was ever known to resent keenly, of the many made against him, was that he had enriched himself at the workers' expense or juggled with their funds.

Kearney had had practically no education; he could at this period just barely read and write. With commendable ambition, he began to educate himself, though largely by annoying other people. He had joined the Draymen's and Teamsters' Union (practically all San Francisco unions, at this time, were autonomous and without national affiliations) and he bored the brothers at every union meeting by holding forth long-windedly on every extraneous subject under the sun, until he became a nuisance and members groaned when he rose to speak. He was a nuisance and a joke also at the Lyceum of Self-Culture, on Sundays. One of his perpetual tirades there denounced the volunteer riflemen who were, he said, "practising to shoot down workers." Many of his Lyceum speeches were directed against religion, and especially against the church in which he had been reared.

He was illogical and tiresome, his brogue was thick (he never lost it), he bellowed mightily; but he had a turn for the picturesque phrase, he was emotional, vigorous, and persistent. He was deliberately training himself to be a good public speaker. In the public library, meanwhile, he read Darwin and Spencer, shed the religious and political views of his boyhood, and prepared for a career beyond the draying business. He had already served on a committee from his union which presented a petition to United States Senator Sargent, and he had tasted blood.

Yet in spite of his diatribes against the riflemen, Kearney's chief subject in his Lyceum talks from the floor was the "shiftlessness and extravagance" of the working class. His mind seemed to shift from Kearney as employing drayman to Kearney as working drayman, and back again. But in either role, he offered Kearney as the prime example for workers: thrifty, completely sober—he loathed both alcohol and tobacco—and industrious. The bias in these early speeches was pro-employer, and also pro-Chinese. The man with whom is identified the struggle to drive the Chinese from California began by speaking as their advocate. And when, in the summer of 1877, an outdoor labor meeting in the sand lots near the City Hall was invaded by a group of fanatics who precipitated an anti-Chinese riot, Kearney was not among their leaders, but among their opponents.

The Chinese had begun to filter into California in the very early days of the gold rush. They were eventually driven from the mines, and naturally they drifted into every phase of industry. The cigarmaking business at one period was very largely in their hands, and the first union label known to history was used by white cigarmakers to differentiate their products from those of the Orientals. The Chinese worked for less than a white man could live on, and at hours and under conditions a white man could not endure. A strong working-class antagonism was inevitable against them and against the capitalists who found it profitable to employ them.

The riot started on the sand lots that July day in 1877 burned down half of Chinatown, and destroyed American-owned factories, chiefly cigar factories, hiring

Chinese. The regular authorities were powerless to cope with it. W. T. Coleman, who had led the second Vigilance Committee in 1855, came to the fore again and organized a "Pick Handle Brigade," which thus armed went after and subdued the rioters. One of the pick-handle operators was Dennis Kearney. His first really public appearance in San Francisco was as a friend and defender of the Chinese!

Just what caused his complete reversal of attitude between July and August, it is difficult to say. Undoubtedly he was shrewd enough to know which way the wind was blowing, and that his future lay, not with Coleman and his group, but with his fellow workingmen. Also, his firsthand experience may actually have caused a change of heart. Kearney's was a more complex nature than his contemporaries suspected. He was not all demagogue, though he was all emotionalist.

At all events, on August 22, 1877, the Workingmen's Trade and Labor Union was formed, with Kearney as secretary. This was a so-called "piece party," whose real purpose was to extract contributions from politicians—a rather common form of organization at the time. It had no political commitment; but it was definitely anti-Chinese. By the beginning of October the newborn organization was already lost in the Workingmen's Party of California.

This was very largely Kearney's own creation. There already existed a San Francisco branch of the Workingmen's Party of the United States, a Marxian party, an outgrowth of the recently deceased First International. (It is claimed that they had refused Kearney's application for membership.) It was one of their open-air meetings which was broken up by the July riots. The Workingmen's Party of California had no revolutionary tenets, and was in no way connected, except by an unfortunate accident of name, to the older group. However, the Workingmen's Party of the United States soon found itself outnumbered; its members defected in droves to the new party with its much more immediate demands, and its psychology so much more in accordance with that of the American worker; and before very long it was entirely absorbed in the Workingmen's Party of California, and ceased to exist as an independent entity.

Kearney was secretary of the new party, and a director of its organ, *The Open Letter*. He was also its chief spokesman, in meetings in halls and on the sand lots. The seeds of resentment of his dictatorial attitude were already sown, but it was nearly a year before they sprouted. For the time, the way was clear before him. And by now he had made himself, thanks to his long-suffering hearers, into a really effective orator of the rabble-rousing variety.

The original demands of the Workingmen's Party of California have in some instances a very modern ring. They included reduction of working hours, with subsequent periodical regulation; establishment of a State Bureau of Labor and Labor Statistics; strict accountability of city and state office holders; the cutting of official salaries to the wages of skilled labor; abolition of the national banks; assessment of property at its full value (there was certainly much chicanery and tax dodging among the holders of the huge California estates); creation by the Legislature of a Convention on Labor, to be held in San Francisco; and, of course, abrogation of the Burlingame Treaty with China, by which the Chinese continued to pour into the state.

The sand-lot meetings, which were the party's chief forum, were held on Sundays, when news is usually dull, and so they always got a "good press" on Mondays. As Viscount Bryce says, in his *American Commonwealth*, "the newspapers turned the Workingmen's Party into a force by representing it to have already become one." The *Chronicle* and the *Morning Call* were loudly for "the Sand-lot Party." Later, both papers deserted it; but the work of building the party up to its short-lived but very real power had by that time been done.

It was in his capacity as officer of the Workingmen's Party that Kearney delivered all the fiery speeches, intemperate and dangerous, which made his name a national byword, until *The Popular Science Monthly* was glad to publish an article (by Henry George) to explain to its respectable Eastern readers just what this dreadful Kearneyism really was. Kearney himself claimed, to Bryce and others, that the newspapers deliberately garbled his speeches, and put words in his mouth he had never dreamed of saying. Such a thing is scarcely unknown in newspaper annals; but in this instance it may be doubted. Kearney in his own right uttered just such peppery speeches as the newspapers quoted from the sand-lot meetings; they may have been colored and pointed up a little, but not very much. There is some evidence, however, that several of his earlier talks were written for him by one of the *Chronicle's* bright young men, with a view to Monday-morning circulation.

President J. G. Day of the Workingmen's Party resigned, alarmed by Kearney's speeches on behalf of the party, but Kearney succeeded him and continued his orations undeterred. A responsible labor man with a long view might well shudder at some phrases of Kearney's outline of his party's creed: "To unite the poor and the workingmen into one political party, to defend ourselves against the capitalists, to wrest the government from the rich and restore it to the people, to rid the country of cheap Chinese labor by any means, to destroy land monopoly, to tax the rich so as to make great wealth impossible, to elect only workingmen to office." Such a program was impossible without a revolution, and a revolution in the United States in 1877 was laughably impossible.

Henry George, in his article, pointed out that Kearney, "a man of strict temperance in all except speech," never directly incited to violence; there was always an "if." But since the "if" was seldom likely to be fulfilled, it is not strange that it sometimes disappeared in the public consciousness, and that what remained was some very incendiary talk. "Judge Lynch is the only judge we want." "Bullets will replace ballots; San Francisco will meet the fate of burning Moscow." "Bring guns to the sand-lots and form military companies; blow up the Pacific Mail docks [where the Chinese landed]." "The monopolists who make their money by employing cheap labor had better watch out; they have built themselves fine residences on Nob Hill and erected flagstaffs upon their roofs—let them take care that they have not erected their own gallows." "If the members of the Legislature ever step over the line of decency, then I say hemp, hemp, hemp, that is the battle-cry of freedom." "If any officer or leader in the workingmen's movement lags behind or proves recreant to his trust he should be hanged to the nearest lamp-post." "I want Stanford and the press to understand that if I give an order to hang Crocker, it will be done." "When the Chinese question is settled, we can discuss whether it would be better to hang, shoot, or cut the capitalists to pieces." "The city will be leveled to ashes and the ruins filled in with the roasted bodies."

Whether Kearney was always quoted fully and exactly or not, it is hardly surprising that during 1877 and 1878 he and his followers were repeatedly arrested "for using language having a tendency to cause a breach of peace"!

He never was convicted, never stayed in jail more than a few days, though once the militia was called out to prevent his rescue. At his first arrest, in November, 1877, he was the hero of a Thanksgiving Day parade of seven thousand marchers. The city supervisors passed the "Gibbs Gag Law" in a vain effort to curb Kearney. On each arrest he said he had been incorrectly reported and would be careful in the future to avoid the possibility of such misquotation. Yet the last of the fragments cited above is from a speech made as late as 1880.

At Kearney's arrest in January, 1878, the National Guard was called to protect the Pacific Mail docks, so real did the state consider the danger of their being dynamited; and the legislature passed the Murphy Riot Act, "to disperse riotous assemblages and arrest incendiary speakers." Workers sang songs about Kearney—

"So give three cheers for Kearney,
  For he's a solid man;
  He'll raise a grand big army,
  And drive out the Chinaman."

and—

"We must not forget Mr. Kearney, . . .
  To him alone honor is due."

It is no wonder that the rest of the country, hearing of these doings, pictured San Francisco as knee-deep in the blood of revolt.

To obtain a true perspective, it is necessary to shift the gaze a little. It is necessary to remember that all this was happening in San Francisco only a quarter century after the gold rush. The city that grew up overnight in 1849 was never mild and calm. It was used to rough ways and loud voices, and took them in its stride. It was extravagant in speech and action; it had a flair for drama; its ways were the ways of untamed men on the edges of civilization. It understood Dennis Kearney even while it tried vainly to put him under lock and key.

And the indubitable facts that the Workingmen's Party continued to grow both in numbers and influence, that it elected city and state officials in increasingly numerous instances, that it was a potent voice in the Constitutional Convention of 1878, all bear evidence that behind the smoke and fury of Dennis Kearney (accurately or inaccurately quoted) the voters at large, as well as the workers, recognized something substantial, forward-looking, and desirable. Kearney himself was squelched by his own party the following May, and never embodied it in his own excited personality again.

Burnette G. Haskell at the height of his career.

It was a time of economic depression, following the Jay Cooke panic of 1873. In January, 1878, Kearney led fifteen hundred unemployed men through the streets of San Francisco, demanding "bread or a place in the county jail." The legislature empowered the city to employ two thousand laborers for three months on "made work," but the supervisors callously ignored the action. It was under such circumstances that a convention was called in June to write a new state constitution.

The Workingmen's Party had fifty-one delegates to that convention, and it worked hand in hand with the Grange, which also was strongly represented. But soon after this time the story of the Workingmen's Party of California became dissociated from that of Dennis Kearney. In May the County Central Committee of the party met and formally accused Kearney of "disloyalty and personal dishonesty." There was certainly some trouble about the funds, and Kearney's heated protests of his integrity in later years sound suspicious. Nothing was ever definitely proved against him, though he was "more than suspected" of having sold out, of having compromised with the very forces he had attacked so intemperately. He was also charged with the use of indecent language, with being a "Caesar" and a dictator, with having no respect for the rights of others, and even with insanity. This last was mere hyperbole; nobody seriously considered Kearney insane. He still had his ardent disciples; he was finally forced out of the presidency after being re-elected in June, but a split in the party followed: and though its greatest days were still before it, its end also might now have been foreseen.

Kearney himself explained his gradual retirement from the party by saying (to Bryce): "I was poor, with a helpless family, and I went to work to provide for their support. . . . I stopped agitating after having shown the people their immense power, and how it could be used." He claimed he had never wished to be president, and had protested against his election. "I never received a dollar from public office or private parties for my services." Bryce apparently was not impressed; he called him "a demagogue of a common type, noisy and confident, but with neither political foresight nor constructive talent." However, it is hardly to be expected that even so liberal a British peer would feel very sympathetic with an Irish labor agitator. One thing is sure: Kearney's draying business, which he had turned over to a brother for management when he became actively engaged in the labor movement, had long ago been boycotted and had had to be sold at almost a complete loss. He really did not have a livelihood, and he really did have a wife and four children to support somehow.

He played no part in the constitutional convention, and he may not even have been in the state. In July it is known he was in Boston "to visit his aged mother." But the amazingly modern-sounding provisions incorporated in the constitution, and for the most part introduced by the Workingmen's Party delegates, were exactly the things which Kearney had urged them to demand and secure. They included prohibition of lobbying, limitation of the state debt, taxation of unimproved land (an echo of the emergent single tax), an income tax, regulation of public utilities, abolition of the fee system, an eight-hour working day, and a uni-cameral legislature—an idea still so new that only one state, Nebraska, has adopted it. Also, there were drastic anti-Chinese clauses: corporations were forbidden to employ Chinese; the Orientals were disfranchised, for-bidden employment on public works; and the coolie labor contracts under which they came to America were annulled. These contracts, copies of some of which still survive, did indeed provide conditions which made competition by white laborers impossible; in return for their fare from China and a dollar a day, the Chinese agreed to work at any task assigned to them from sun-rise to sunset, with an hour off for meals during the day.

At an election that November, the new constitution lost in every city of any size, including San Francisco, but it carried the state by 10,280. It went into effect on the Fourth of July of 1879. To the capitalists and big industrialists who by this time controlled and practically owned California — the "Big Four" and their railroad above all—it was unthinkable that so radical a document should be permitted to remain in force. All the bills of the first session of the Legislature following its adoption were declared unconstitutional, thanks to jokers care-fully inserted into them by obedient legislators; and the constitution itself was nullified, to a great extent, by subsequent legislation, though formally it is still in force in California. It was more than thirty years later before it was thoroughly and permanently overhauled and brought into line with progressive ideas.

The Workingmen's Party was still strong in 1879—stronger than it had ever been, though the strength proved to be hollow. At that election its candidates won one of the three Railroad Commissionerships and a number of Assembly seats. All this was undone completely by the following year. In 1879, San Francisco also had a Workingmen's Party mayor — a strange person, Dr. Isaac Kalloch, a Baptist minister who had once had the largest Chinese Sunday school in the city, but had turned violently anti-Chinese. The *Chronicle,* which had been the party's journalistic friend and nurse, having used it, now turned against it; any reporter who attended a meeting of the party was instantly dismissed. Kalloch, in his nondenominational, downtown Metropolitan Temple, attacked the paper, and in addition made scurrilous remarks concerning the mother of its publishers. Charles De Young, one of the two brothers publishing the *Chronicle,* then shot and badly injured the minister. Kalloch was elected mayor on the strength of this episode. The next April, Kalloch's son invaded De Young's office and shot him dead. In true San Francisco style, young Kalloch was acquitted.

The party could elect its candidates. But frequently they had merely ridden to power on its strength, and repudiated it as soon as they succeeded. One interesting example of this was a candidate to the legislature from Alameda County, a man named Bones. During his campaign Bones made his speeches with a rope tied around his neck, to symbolize his acceptance of Kearney's dictum that legislators who were untrue to their trust deserved to be hanged. As soon as he was elected, Bones went over to the other side. Presumably nobody ever mentioned rope thereafter in the house of this would-be victim of the hangman!

During the intensified anti-Chinese agitation in California in 1879 and 1880, Kearney was often out of the state. He made a nation-wide tour against the Burlingame Treaty, and he also spoke in New York on behalf of the Labor Party. For a while after the split in his own party it had seemed as if his influence had only been enhanced, but it was soon evident that those who remained with him were precisely the shifting and undependable portion of the movement. Though he was arrested for the last time in March, 1880, in June Kearney broke with the Workingmen's Party entirely and went East as a delegate to the Greenback Party convention; later he supported its candidate for president, General Weaver. (Before formation of the Workingmen's Party he had been a Republican, and immediately after becoming a citizen he had supported the candidacy of Hayes.) In consequence, he was formally expelled in July; but by this time this was a mere gesture. The Workingmen's Party lost the San Francisco election in 1880, and soon after it ceased to exist.

Kearney returned to draying. The sand lots saw him again, but now his speeches were mild and conciliatory. In 1881 he spoke for the Anti-Monopoly Party, in 1882 for the Democrats. He was no longer of value as a supporter to any candidate. In 1884 he retired from politics altogether, and set up as a real-estate, stock, and ticket broker. A few years later he ran an employment office. He seemed headed for a forgotten old age, though a fairly prosperous one, for some of his stock deals had turned out well. But early in the nineties an uncle died and left him a real fortune in real estate, principally in Fresno.

Kearney, the man who had talked about "shoddy aristocrats" and "thieving millionaires," who had advocated taxing unimproved land and wanted to "destroy all the rich hell-hounds in California," was a transformed man. In his labor-leader days he had dressed conspicuously in the rough, baggy clothes of a workingman, had passed his own humble hat at meetings for contributions. Wells Drury describes him as he was in 1899: "The canvas overalls and jumper had disappeared. Gone was the drayman's leather apron, fastened by copper rivets. . . . His powerful hands were no longer knotted and clenched, but white and soft. The chin no longer protruded, and the jaw had less of the appearance of aggressive prominence." He still had the broad head and flaring nostrils of the orator, still the bright blue eyes, the heavy shoulders, the perky ginger mustache; but all the effect was softened, glossed over, by the prosperous capitalist. "Watching the wheat game," he sighed to Drury, "is harder work than excluding the Chinese."

One thing, however, must be said for Kearney; right or wrong in his fight against Chinese labor, after his first flop he never changed his attitude again. To his last day he claimed proudly that he was more responsible than any other one man for exclusion of Chinese from America. Although the anti-Chinese provisions of the 1879 California constitution were declared unconstitutional by the United States Supreme Court, the Burlingame Treaty was abrogated in 1882. And certainly the agitation behind its abrogation was typified in the general mind by those reiterated words of Dennis Kearney: "The Chinese must go!" Today, with the Chinese residents of San Francisco regarded with pride and affection as the splendid citizens they are, it is hard for us to think back sixty years to the days when they were called "moon-eyed lepers." But it is true that coolie labor was a menace to American labor; and to that extent at least Dennis Kearney's crusade was not entirely wrong-headed.

In the disaster of 1906, Kearney's "beautiful home" in San Francisco was destroyed. He moved to Alameda, where he died at the end of April in 1907. He was only sixty; but he had been so long forgotten, and San Franciscans had so many other things to think of in the feverish year following the earthquake and fire, that the newspapers scarcely noted his death. Once he had filled the front pages every time he spoke.

Kearney was a common type of labor spokesman—a man who rises from the ranks. Burnette Haskell was another common type—the intellectual of the professional class who adopts the workers' cause as his own.

Haskell's heyday was about a decade after the time when Kearney was most in the public eye. The two men were diametrically opposite in almost every detail, except that both were agitators on behalf of labor, and that both were exceedingly violent in speech without carrying their speech into action.

Burnette G. Haskell was a "Native Son." He was born in June, 1857, in Sierra County, of pioneer parents. Restive and eccentric from the beginning, he sampled three colleges—the University of California, the University of Illinois, and Oberlin—but was graduated from none of them. It was hard for him to stay long in any one place. Somehow he was admitted to the bar in California in 1879, but practiced law very little, if at all. At some time in his youth, like so many other Americans of his era, he had learned the printing trade, and it was this which eventually drew him into the labor movement. His uncle had founded a weekly newspaper in San Francisco called *Truth*, and (doubtless after worried family conferences) he offered its editorship to his brilliant but unstable nephew.

In connection with his editorial-plus-reportorial duties on a one-man paper, Haskell attended the meetings of the Trades and Labor Assembly, one of the earliest of the labor union councils in California. This was in 1882, when Haskell was twenty-five. He was fired at once with a romantic devotion to the cause of the workers, and without consulting his uncle, the owner, impetuously offered to turn the paper over to the Assembly as its official organ. He, of course, would continue as editor. The offer was accepted; though in a few months, appalled by Haskell's headlong progress leftward, the conservative union members withdrew their official support.

Haskell plunged into intensive study of his new enthusiasm, and read everything he could find on the subject, until he was known as the best-read man in the California labor movement. Very soon he was calling himself a socialist, and very soon after that he announced himself as a communist-anarchist. A tall, slender, blond man, rather good-looking, with his bright eyes and fair mustache, he was soon a familiar figure at every gathering of workers. Like Kearney, he had a flair for moving, emotional oratory. But organizations already formed and functioning were too settled for Haskell; he could find no place for himself in them. Besides, his nature craved the romantically secret; mere trade-union organization was a humdrum affair.

He organized a group he called first the Invisible Republic, then the Illuminati, and finally the International Workingmen's Association. It was in essence a reorganization of the First International, which had been taken from London to New York and had expired in 1876. Although members of the old International Workingmen's Association (the First or Socialist International of Marx and Engels) formed the nucleus of Haskell's new group, in spirit it was much more akin to an organization with which it had no formal affiliation—Bakunin's International Working People's Association, the anarchist "Black International," which had a small San Francisco branch. Haskell, however, was more extravagantly unrealistic than Bakunin ever dreamed of being. His association was molded on the group system of some secret societies. There were nine in each group, each of whom was to form the nucleus of another group of nine, and so on; hence each member was known personally to only sixteen others. This was to avoid the possibility of mass betrayal. There were three grades of membership: red cards, students; white cards, organizers; blue cards, executives. All the members were known only by numbers, in an elaborate system which indicated to the initiated the exact affiliation of the

member. For example, N762 was the second member
of a group formed by the sixth member of another
group formed by the seventh member of an original
group in District N—the districts being geographical.
Actually, the greatest strength of the International
Workingmen's Association (Haskell's organization of
that name) was on the Pacific Coast and in the Rocky
Mountain States, and the greatest of all was in northern
and central California.

Truth became the official organ as soon as the association was established. It remained a weekly until 1884,
when for lack of funds it lapsed into monthly publication, and by July was merged with the Denver *Labor
Enquirer,* the association's organ in the Rocky Mountain
Division. During its two years or so as the mouthpiece
of the (new) International Workingmen's Association,
the paper under Haskell's editorship became increasingly
violent, sometimes to the point of absurdity. Under its
masthead, eventually, where other papers ran weather
reports or perhaps, in those days in the West, mining
stock quotations, *Truth* announced: "*Truth* is five cents
a copy and dynamite is forty cents a pound." Its motto
was: "War to the palace, peace to the cottage, death
to luxurious idleness!"

Haskell himself was division executive for the Pacific
Coast. The exact membership has never been known;
like some other societies, the association was always optimistic in its estimates. The nearest estimate is between
five and ten thousand. As dues were only ten cents a
month, any person sympathetic to the cause of extreme
radicalism could afford to join it. How many of them

accepted all the utterances of their division executive cannot be known; it may be suspected that the bulk of the membership was not among hard-headed working-men, but among the "intellectuals" and the "lunatic fringe" on the edge of labor. Haskell spoke of the as-sociation as "secret, mysterious, world-wide, quietly honeycombing society . . . the sole practical means of releasing the wealth-producers from the shackles of tyranny."

Society as a whole, however, remained distressingly free of honeycombing; and the only "practical" idea Haskell seemed to have was advocating the use of dyna-mite. He recommended that workers study chemistry, and he told Dr. Ira B. Cross (as that economist has stated in print) that he had manufactured bombs and hidden them in valises, with a view to blowing up the Hall of Records in San Francisco and so causing an in-extricable confusion in land titles. No attempt was ever made, so far as known, actually to dynamite this or any other public building. In a membership book of the association, Dr. Cross found, in Haskell's handwriting, the memorandum: "Seize Mint, Armories, Sub-Treas-ury, Custom House, Government Steamer [?], Alca-traz, Presidio, newspapers"—but when, how, or why all this was to be accomplished, and what was to be done next, was never revealed. The notation was probably made about 1883, when Haskell, beside himself with excitement, burst forth with: "Arm to the teeth! The Revolution is upon you!"

The Revolution did not materialize, and as might be expected of so highflown a temperament, Haskell gradually lost interest. The association lingered on until the late 1880's, when it was quietly dissolved. Haskell already had a new enthusiasm—a colony at Kaweah, near Visalia.

The Kaweah Co-operative Commonwealth, formally founded in 1886, was originally planned to carry out the ideas expressed by Edward Bellamy in *Looking Backward*. The disciples of Bellamy's theory, often spoken of as utopian socialism but really a sort of state socialism or an anticipation of contemporary totalitarianism, formed Nationalist Clubs, which spread all over the country. It was to exemplify this theory that Haskell, with another quick turn of adherence, established his co-operative colony in Tulare County, in the midst of a magnificent stand of Big Trees *(Sequoia gigantea)*.

The site of Kaweah Colony is now within Sequoia National Park. Haskell had named the Big Trees for prominent members of the First International. It would surprise tourists, for instance, to learn that the famous General Sherman tree once bore the name of Karl Marx!

The colony dragged along in a rather miserable existence for two or three years. Its members were in deadly earnest and worked hard, but the cards were stacked against them. Kaweah was doomed from the beginning by reason of its magnificent location, envied by private interests, and because in those preconservation days the trees were valued, not as scenery, but as timber. A group of Visalia lumbermen acquired a grove of the Big Trees to the north of Kaweah, and from this it was easy to get the state and the federal government to claim that the land had been filed on illegally by the colonists, who were also accused of destroying the sequoias. How much the latter allegation was worth was evidenced when, after Sequoia National Park had been reserved in 1890, and the army had been called on to disperse the colonists and all other claimants as well, these same lumbermen were widely accused of dynamiting Big Trees! *Sequoia gigantea,* the oldest and largest tree on earth, is not much good for timber, so the destruction was useless as well as vandalistic. Fortunately, before it was quite too late, many of the trees were saved by their inclusion in Sequoia National Park.

Until very recent years at least, two survivors of the Kaweah Colony still lived in California. But its dispersal was the end of Haskell's meteoric public career. Like Kearney, he was accused by some of his disgruntled followers of having sold them out, though the probability is that he was merely the erratic, unstable enthusiast he seemed to be. In any event, though he lived for nearly fifteen years more, it was in total obscurity. He was no longer prominent even on the lunatic fringe of the labor movement. He died in November, 1907, six and a half months after the death of Dennis Kearney. He was buried by the Sailors' Union of the Pacific, which, as the Coast Seamen's Union, he had helped Andrew Furuseth to found. Thirty-five years later, his son became clerk of the California Supreme Court.

Kearney and Haskell, so dissimilar in temperament and activities, both illustrate a phase of the working-class movement in the United States and in California which has now passed wholly into history.

CHAPTER VIII

Last of the Tolstoyans:
FREMONT OLDER

JOHN D. BARRY, editorial columnist on the San Francisco *Bulletin*, was passing the editor's office door. It was open, and he could see Fremont Older at his desk, and opposite to him an attractive middle-aged woman. As Older caught sight of Barry, he rose and called:

"John, come here a minute. I have to rush to catch my train, but I want you to meet Mrs. Searles [not the actual name]. You'll find her very interesting. She used to be a prostitute."

He snatched up his hat and hurried away, while Barry was left to succor the lady, who had promptly fainted!

That little episode was a sort of epitome of Fremont Older—his newspaperman's instinct for the sensational, his simple disregard of convention, his all-inclusive acceptance of his fellow human beings.

Shortly after the conviction of Tom Mooney, Older was standing at the bar of the Palace Hotel, when the district attorney, Charles M. Fickert, who had prosecuted the case, walked up to him, called him a vile name, and struck him to the floor. Fickert was much younger than Older, a hefty ex-football star (at Stanford his bulk and his lack of wit together had earned him the nickname of "Boob Fickert"), and still in good physical condition. Older picked himself up, and made no attempt to retaliate even in speech. Years later, when Fickert was down and out, he came to Older to "borrow" money, and got it; when he was ill and alone, deserted by all the followers of his successful years, the only person who came to see him, to offer sympathy and help, was Fremont Older.

Yet Older was no weak-kneed coward. When he was kidnapped and faced murder, he acted with the utmost calm. When he was hectored and badgered on the witness stand in the Billings supreme court hearing in 1930, he conducted himself with a cool dignity that wrung reluctant respect even from his hecklers. He had courage, and by that time he had something more—he had the pity and kindly aloofness of the Tolstoyan anarchist.

The Older of the last days, who said: "I have become a spectator in life," was a very different person from the fighting editor who confessed: "I was ruthless in my ambition . . . [I] might make people suffer, might wound or utterly ruin someone; that made no difference to me." He was very different from the boy who took Horace Greeley as his star and set his teeth into the determination to make a career for himself in spite of hell and high water.

Fremont Older's earliest environment could not have been more typically that of the orthodox American leader of his period. He was born in August, 1856, in a log cabin in a village appropriately called Freedom, near Appleton, Wisconsin. His father and his six uncles were all either killed in the Civil War or died in consequence of their war experiences. At ten he was a little drudge on a farm. It was there that he first heard of Greeley and resolved somehow to become a printer and eventually an editor. At twelve he spent a year in the preparatory department of Ripon College, which had been founded five years before his birth. He was unable to finance more schooling, and the next year found him a printer's devil on the Berlin, Wisconsin, *Courant*. His mother remarried and moved to California. By a devious track he began to follow her. He was a cabin boy on a Mississippi steamer; he worked as an apprentice printer on papers in Hudson, Wisconsin, and St. Paul; he searched in vain for jobs in New Orleans and St. Louis, and after a two-hundred-mile walk found himself back on his grandfather's farm in Egypt, Illinois. From there he went to an aunt in Wisconsin, who drove him away by her excessive religiosity. Then he found his first opportunity to become more than a printer; the editor of the Oconto, Wisconsin, *Free Press* was sent to jail for believing too thoroughly in the title of his paper, and during his sentence for libel, Older was editor. After a few months the editor was released, and the boy editor was demoted.

The beginning of 1873, when he was only sixteen, found him as partner in a run-down country hotel in Aurora, Illinois. His grandfather meanwhile had given up the hopeless struggle with a bankrupt farm and had followed his daughter-in-law to California. He found the money to send Older the fare on an immigrant train, and in the spring he arrived in the city with which he was ever after so closely identified that after he died

Bruce Bliven remarked: "To understand Fremont Older is to understand San Francisco."

He did not stay there long, however. After a few months as a typesetter on the *Morning Call*—his first association with the paper which was long afterwards to be so closely identified with him—he followed the bonanza rush to Virginia City, Nevada, where he set type for the *Enterprise*. Ten years before, a young fellow named Sam Clemens had been an unsatisfactory reporter for the same paper.

It was in Virginia City (Nevada being then as now a gamblers' paradise) that Older got once for all out of his system the itch for gambling which had seized him when, an unregarded cabin boy, he had watched with admiration the magnificent card sharps who infested the river boats. He gambled, he won heavily, he came back the next day and lost all his winnings, and he never risked a cent again. All that was left of that boyish hero worship was a lifelong flamboyance in dress, a cut of the mustache, a tilt of the hat, which could have made Fremont Older pass easily to the casual eye for an adventurer.

From Nevada he drifted, a journeyman printer, to Sonora, in the Mother Lode, then to Santa Barbara. In 1875, still only eighteen, he wandered back to San Francisco, where in spite of his youth he became foreman of the composing room of the *Daily Mail*. The *Daily Mail*, the shoestring enterprise of an Australian named Davison Dalziel, lived mostly on hope and daring. It ran to sensations and hoaxes; its chief reporter was the brilliant journalist Arthur McEwen, later one of the high-paid stars of the Hearst galaxy. (His son and grandson also became newspapermen.) The newspaper offices were in an ornately decorated room that had once been the parlor of a fashionable house of prostitution. Finally the paper died of acute alcoholism—on a hot summer day the entire staff partook so heavily of an epic punch spiked with champagne that the next edition never came out at all, and the nearly bankrupt paper gave up the ghost.

Older, just of age, reverted to his origin in the forests of northern Wisconsin. He went to Mendocino County, staked out a claim in the redwoods, and stayed as a hermit homesteader until the beginning of 1879. Then he sold his claim, came back to San Francisco, and used up all his money searching in vain for a job. He was very near starvation when, tramping hopelessly to the printers' hangout which served as an employment office, he met on the street a stranger who asked if Older knew where he could find a competent printer.

The man was R. G. Rowley, a San Mateo County attorney who was making it his mission to fight the strangle hold fixed on the state by the "Octopus," the Southern (formerly the Central) Pacific Railroad. To carry on his crusade he was establishing the Redwood City *Weekly Journal*. Older became Rowley's editor—in fact, he was practically the entire staff. It was his first battle with the "Octopus," some of whose long arms were later almost to crush the life out of him. The enemy drew first blood; Rowley was tricked into selling the paper, to find he had sold it to a concealed agent of the railroad. He took it back, but too late to save it.

And Fremont Older found himself business manager of
—the *Times-Gazette*, the Southern Pacific organ!

It was during this period that Older's brief first marriage occurred — a marriage of which he never spoke
and of which few knew. It was a mistake on both sides,
and was soon over. Its ending left him with even greater
incentive to free himself both of the connection with
the hated railroad and of his exile in a country town.
He found his way out through correspondence for the
San Francisco papers. One of them was the *Alta Californian*, which in 1884 gave him a chance as reporter.
From there he went again to the *Morning Call*, to the
editorial room this time, and it was on this paper that
he helped in the first crusade by a metropolitan newspaper against the intrenched privilege of the Southern
Pacific and its cohorts.

Older kept leaving and returning to the *Call* like a
comet with a short orbit. He escaped the next time by
becoming city editor of the *Post*. Robert A. Crothers, the
owner of the *Call*, drew him back as city editor there.
The next year the *Call* was sold. Older was out of a job
again. It was nearly a quarter century before once
more he became editor of the *Call*, and in between were
the years which made him famous.

Crothers' nephew, Loring Pickering, owned a mori-
bund paper called the *Bulletin*. He made Older editor-
in-chief, but with no contract. In less than a year Older
had brought the circulation from nine thousand to forty
thousand. These were the days of which he spoke, when
his ambition was ruthless and careless of others' suffering. He was a yellow journalist as early as Hearst or

Pulitzer; his headlines screeched in San Francisco while most headlines still murmured in New York. The most startling news, the shudder, the thrill, the sob, were what he wanted; he would skirt the edge of libel in search of a shock. He himself wrote little, but that little was vivid; for example, it was Fremont Older who invented and colloquialized the now common words, "higher-up," "mutt," and "gangster." His paper was a democracy of opportunity; it was perhaps the only one in the country where if a woman could get a story as well as a man, the woman was given the assignment. Women fitted more easily than men into some of his campaigns. But he liked his girl reporters to be pleasant to look at; no drab, mannish aspirants need apply.

Indeed, Older had an eye for beauty always. In 1893 he met and married Cora Miranda Baggerly, who was both pretty and intelligent, and Gertrude Atherton called them "quite the handsomest couple in San Francisco." Mrs. Older was more than an ornament; she moved into the *Bulletin* office and worked side by side with her husband; from their rooms in the old Palace Hotel they planned the crusades, the contests, the series, that made the paper talked about even by people who preferred to read it surreptitiously.

"Father confessor to a city," Older was also father of the "confession story." He ran autobiographical serials, sometimes under pseudonyms, by ex-convicts, reformed drunkards, rescued prostitutes. "I have never pretended to be an idealist," he said. His emotional response to the underdog was genuine, but it stirred and was stirred by his journalistic instincts. Picturesque people automatically roused him to sympathy and championship. Yet his outlook was always forward, his progress upward.

Because Older is so closely associated with the graft prosecutions which followed the catastrophe of 1906, it is not always realized that the beginning of his war against state and city corruption was in 1905. It was then that he trapped state senators with marked money they had taken as bribes from building and loan companies; it was then that he attempted in vain to elect a reform mayor of San Francisco. When his man, John Partridge, was defeated, the triumphant mob attacked the *Bulletin* office and came near to lynching Older. He marched out and walked through the angry crowd, unarmed, to his carriage; by sheer courage he awed the rioters, but he had sown a bitter crop of enemies. As his own paper said of him after his death: "He never persuaded, he pounded. . . . He never compromised, he won or lost. . . . He was loved and hated—there could be no middle ground."

The local graft which preceded and followed the earthquake and fire was tied up in the same bundle as the state graft stemming from the Southern Pacific and its allies, especially the big power corporations and their adjuncts, the street railways. Nowadays, when the Southern Pacific Company, chastened and respectable, is no longer the giant "Octopus" which openly bought and sold its newspapers and its legislators, it is hard to understand the situation which confronted Fremont Older in 1907, harder to untangle the strands of the woven maze. It was a period when, at the opening session of the state Assembly, every Assemblyman as a matter of course expected to find on his desk his free season pass with the compliments of the Southern Pacific. The *Bulletin* itself, until Older stopped it, received a subsidy of $250 a month. Corrupt labor unions — or their officials — were working hand in glove with the big bosses. It was not a condition peculiar to San Francisco or California. Lincoln Steffens had already publicized "the shame of the cities." Only, in California, where the "Big Four" had shrewdly built up their railroad empire, the source of power and of corruption alike was concentrated in one wellspring, and other corporations came hat in hand to enroll as vassals of the master *condottieri*.

It was this setup that Older, half journalist, half crusader, pledged himself to destroy singlehanded. The legal luminary of that day was Francis J. Heney, who had just prosecuted brilliantly the Oregon land-fraud cases. To bring him from Washington to San Francisco to confront the grafters would cost $100,000. Older got it half-and-half from two liberal capitalists, Rudolph Spreckels and ex-Mayor and Senator-to-be James Phelan. Those four—Older, Spreckels, Phelan, and Heney—were hated with an incandescent intensity by the hierarchy of privilege, from the lowest errand boy to the men at the very pinnacle. Older and his wife were ostracized: houses of those they had thought their friends were closed to them, Older was cold-shouldered at clubs, men moved away from him in restaurants. But the investigation went on.

"Front" for the San Francisco corruptionists was a lawyer named Abraham Ruef. Ruef's protection went as far as the state supreme court. When corrupt Mayor Eugene Schmitz discovered he accidentally had an honest district attorney—the late William H. Langdon, long the outstanding liberal in the California supreme court —he fired him and appointed Ruef in his place. Langdon went to Heney and offered to help prosecute the scoundrels whose unwilling associate he had been. A framed and phoney streetcar strike failed to turn public sentiment against the prosecutors. San Francisco, which twice before had shaken itself free from encircling crime and vice, was thoroughly aroused by now, though "the better element" still held itself carefully aloof from the four renegades and troublemakers. The board of supervisors was indicted *en masse;* it was rumored that its chairman, James Gallagher, was ready to talk. His house was dynamited, and he fled or was spirited away. The climax came when Heney was shot in open court, and lingered for weeks between life and death. A liberal young attorney named Hiram Johnson took his place.

Before this, Older had had his taste of personal attack. Always rash and indiscreet, he had already narrowly escaped a trap that might have ruined him and ended the graft prosecutions instantly. Two men representing themselves as disgruntled detectives discharged by the Pinkerton Agency almost persuaded him to let them crack the agency's safe to secure incriminating documents against the United Railroads, the streetcar company. He bethought himself just in time; undoubtedly the two, who were of course spies, would have implicated him in an attempted burglary.

Since that scheme had failed, another was tried. This

time Older deliberately put his head in the noose, by agreeing on an anonymous telephone call to visit an unknown address to receive a confession—though he did leave word that if he did not return in a half hour he was to be searched for. Near the house to which he had been directed, he was kidnapped on the street in broad daylight, hustled into a car, and forced into a train to Los Angeles. The two men who accompanied him kept him quiet by a persuasive revolver, and from their conversation he gathered that he was to be taken out into the mountains in southern California and killed. The merest chance saved his life; an attorney recognized him in the dining car, knew one of his captors as an agent of the attorney for the United Railroads, and sensed that something was wrong. He broke an important engagement of his own to get off the train at the next stop and telephone San Francisco. At Santa Barbara, Older was met and rescued by Franklin K. Lane, later Wilson's Secretary of the Interior. Since it was obvious that the plot was discovered, the two men were glad to let their prisoner go and make their own escape.

The net result of the difficult, dangerous, and long-drawn-out graft prosecutions was that just one man, the "mouthpiece," was thrown to the wolves. Abraham Ruef was given fourteen years in San Quentin. There were larger repercussions, of course — Hiram Johnson was catapulted into the governorship, and in the wave of progressive constitutional amendments which marked his incumbency the power of the Southern Pacific in California was broken. Also, when the election of a new

Fremont Older. The fighting editor in his great days.

district attorney was held, Charles Fickert was elected
on a labor ticket, pledged to prosecute the remaining
graft indictments. Instead, his first move was to have
them dismissed. A few years later he took on joyfully
the task of prosecuting for murder a left-wing labor
agitator named Mooney, who had incurred the enmity
of the Pacific Gas and Electric Company and the United
Railroads; the chief indictment dismissed by Fickert's
motion had been against Patrick Calhoun, the United
Railroads president. (Calhoun, grandson of John C.
Calhoun, lived until 1943, when he was killed by an
automobile in Pasadena, at the age of eighty-seven.)

It was with the end of the graft prosecutions, the
laboring of the mountain which brought forth the little
mouse of Ruef's imprisonment, that Fremont Older began to move from the turbulent storms of his youth to
the quiet eddies of his old age. He did not change all
at once: his greatest crusade was still before him. But
he himself realized that it was then that "from being a
savage fighter against wrong and injustice as I saw them
in the old days, I went clear over to the point where I
do not blame anyone for anything. . . . None of us is
pure black or white. Most of us are gray." Older had
just begun to be "respectable" again, just started to be
recognized on the street by the people who always ap-
prove of a movement when it shows signs of success,
when he astounded and disgusted those who had stood
by him all through the campaign by beginning an agitation for a pardon for Ruef. He himself had forced a
confession out of the cowering little lawyer by an appeal
to his religious sentiments and his love for his mother;

and now he was ashamed. Ruef had been only an agent of bigger and wickeder men; they went free, and Ruef was cooped up for fourteen years. Older went to see him; they became friends, and remained so as long as both were alive. But he could not force the outraged friends of virtue to reverse themselves so suddenly; Ruef served ten years of his term, and was then released for time served with good behavior.

Lincoln Steffens once wrote to Older: "You, who don't believe in human nature." It was a penetrating remark. Older was easily moved to compassion—as a boy he had shrunk from killing animals for food; and he was too sentimental ever to be a good cynic. But his faith was in the individual, not in the mass; he was incapable of joining in mass movements or organizations. (One wonders what he would have said of the Liberty ship *Fremont Older*, launched during World War II.) In 1913 he helped organize a twenty-four-hour protest meeting against capital punishment; but he never associated himself with organized groups working for abolition of the death penalty. His response was always that of an inverted egoist whose humanitarianism was half reaction, half self-identification. Gradually he was becoming what he called himself in later years—a philosophical anarchist, driven back by his extreme individualism to a sublimated and expurgated Christianity. "We are all red ants," he said, and yet: "I believe at all times man does the best he is capable of at the moment." He became acquainted with Clarence Darrow, both through his work and in person, and half-consciously modeled himself on the philosophy of that great pessimist. But he had a sentimentality that Darrow lacked, and which brought him nearer to Tolstoy than to Darrow. And to the very end he remained a shrewd and aggressive newspaper editor.

It was all these characteristics combined, plus others hidden deep in his subconsciousness, that made him the friend, the advocate, and the support of half the ex-convicts in California. He got and made jobs for them —often on his own paper; he kept them in his own home for months or years; he stood by them and took them back no matter how often they betrayed him or how badly they exploited him. Out of them all, only a very few always remained loyal to Older and actually abandoned crime forever. Chief of these was Jack Black, the burglar turned author who from his bitter experience wrote *You Can't Win*. Life in the end grew too much for Black, too; as he had threatened to do, he disappeared quietly and was never heard of again.

It was with one of his ex-convict protégés that Older went one day in 1914 to the ranch near Cupertino, Santa Clara County, which he had bought on an impulse. They had a portable house and a stove in the baggage car of the train, and by dinnertime the house was up and dinner was on the stove. This ranch, named "Woodhills," became the focus of Fremont Older's life. The rambling house he built there was wide open to all his incongruous miscellany of friends. His beloved dogs roamed the hills and, when they died, were buried on the estate with markers on their graves. No animal was ever allowed to be killed on "Woodhills," and it was a bird sanctuary.

For the last twenty years of his life Older was the most regular of commuters, always in his special seat on the four o'clock train to the Peninsula. From his many years of working on evening papers, he had grown accustomed to early rising. Often he excused himself from his guests and went to bed immediately after dinner; and usually he was up and about by five o'clock in the morning. His health was superb. "Till I was sixty," he said, "I felt that I was immortal."

It was when he was sixty that his last great fight began—a fight which outlasted him.

On July 22, 1916, a Preparedness Day parade in San Francisco was bombed. Ten persons were killed, forty-odd badly wounded. A radical labor agitator named Thomas J. Mooney was arrested and charged with murder. Four others were also arrested, including Mooney's wife and a young man named Warren K. Billings.

This is not the place for a history of the famous Mooney case. The point here is that at first, even before the arrests, Older was suspicious of Mooney. Their only previous contact had been during the trial of the Ford and Suhr case, arising from the Wheatland hop riots in 1913, when Mooney had written a letter to Older's old friend, Governor Hiram Johnson, coached in terms of unbridled invective. In general, Older, becoming more and more the "spectator," the philosophical anarchist viewing mankind with kindly contempt, was antipathetic to the left-wing-mass-action type represented by Mooney. Those who considered Older either a radical or a sob sister were unacquainted both with him and with the facts.

What brought Older into the Mooney defense was the gradual revelation of the suborning of perjury by the prosecution, and the accumulating proof that Mooney and Billings were victims of a frame-up by the very same forces which Older had begun to fight in 1905. No one better than he knew the antecedents of Fickert, or the identity of his associates and his masters. The photograph of Mooney and his wife on the Eilers Building roof, two miles but only two minutes from the explosion, helped to open Older's eyes still more; and when the Rigall letters were brought to him, with their clinching evidence that the chief prosecution witness, the "honest cattleman" Frank Oxman, had endeavored to secure the supporting testimony of a man who had at that time never even seen San Francisco, the fact of Mooney's and Billings' innocence cried aloud to heaven. Older was never one to ignore a challenge of that potency. He threw himself wholeheartedly into the war.

The columns of the *Bulletin* were open for pages upon pages of the Mooney case. Oxman's letters to Rigall were printed there; the entire Densmore report of the conversations overheard by dictaphone in Fickert's office, which makes up a good-sized pamphlet, first appeared in the *Bulletin;* Policeman Draper Hand's confession, made in Older's office (with Mayor—later Governor —James Rolph inveigled into being present, and running away in scarlet fury when he realized what he was being asked to listen to), was a *Bulletin* scoop.

Much of this was the achievement of a first-class newspaperman; Older kept the Mooney case in the news. When Judge Franklin Griffin, who tried Mooney, and the eleven living jurors came out for his pardon; when John MacDonald confessed and recanted and then confessed again; when Estelle Smith was caught in the maze of her hysterical, moronic contradictions, no one knew better than Fremont Older that this was front-page stuff. But Older the man was back of the defense every bit as much as was Older the editor. To the day of his death he kept on agitating for the release of Mooney and Billings.

It lost him his twenty-four-year-old job. As has been said, Older had no contract with Pickering, but was kept on at the owner's sufferance. He had made the paper, he had saved it from imminent death and built it up into a force in the community and a real money-maker, but he was merely its hired help. Pickering had been growing more and more disgruntled with Older's viewpoint and methods, and particularly with his involving the *Bulletin* so closely with the Mooney case. He adopted the small-spirited tactics of harassing Older in every mean and petty way, in the hope of forcing him to resign. But Older, whose purse and latchstring were always wide open, who always lived with the fine prodigality of a poor boy come at last on days of comfort, could not afford to resign. He was no longer young, with a future free to his grasp. He made no complaint; he endured in silence the most humiliating indignities.

Then Pickering ordered that the *Bulletin* was to drop the Mooney case. There was to be no more of Mooney in its pages.

Even that Older took—he had to, or leave. But he

cast about at last for a way out. And his rescuer was William Randolph Hearst, who offered him the editorship of his old paper—long ago bought by Hearst—the *Call*, now combined with the *Post*. "Come to the *Call*," said Hearst, "and bring the Mooney case with you." In 1918, Older said good-by to his associates—some of them colleagues since 1894—and moved his office around the corner. Eleven years later he had a sad triumph: the *Bulletin*, without his guiding influence, fell to pieces rapidly, and in 1929 it was merged with the *Call* as the *Call-Bulletin*.

It has been customary to pity Fremont Older for the seventeen years he spent as a Hearst employee. He has been spoken of as "Hearst's slave," as a sort of zombie pulled by strings from San Simeon, as a caged eagle beating at the bars. To Older himself, that was pure nonsense. He wrote categorically, in answer to an article in this vein by George P. West in the *Nation:* "My years as a Hearst editor have been the happiest years I have spent as a newspaper man." His persecution by Pickering still rankled. And he was more or less sympathetic to Hearst, whom he called "the most misunderstood man in America." The misconception has arisen in the minds of those who thought of Older as a radical, or even a liberal. He was neither. He was a fighting newspaperman who had grown tired of fighting; he belonged to the days when Hearst himself was thought of as a progressive, and economically and politically he had advanced little farther than had his employer.

The Mooney case was Older's last crusade. There were minor skirmishes, of course — for the most part shrewd journalistic circulation builders, but with a touch of Older's persisting love of the underdog. Even before he left the *Bulletin*, there was that amazing march of the prostitutes to the church of the young minister, Paul Jordan Smith, who had been foremost in advocating the closing of the Barbary Coast. Older engineered that, and it was an unforgettable drama, but practically it had no effect beyond allowing a few of the women to let off steam before they had to go back and pack up and find a refuge elsewhere. On the *Call*, Older continued this sort of humanitarian-sensational enterprise. Serial novels (stemming from the immortal *Chickie*, by Elinor Meherin), prize contests, pink outside pages— the *Bulletin* had been green—scareheads, and lots and lots of pictures, mostly legs: these were the hallmark of the *Call* and still are, with Older twelve years in his grave. But also, in Older's day, the editor's office was a confessional, an employment bureau, a loan office; everyone had access to him, and all day long a stream of visitors, mostly in trouble and needy, sat across from him at the desk scarred by careless cigarette butts, while Fremont Older leaned back in his swivel chair, his head against the wall, his ears and his hands open.

But by this time even he was beginning to realize that he was an old man. He had always been impatient of the burden of ill-health. When someone admired his commanding height, he said brusquely: "So much more carcass to carry around!" "Annie Laurie" told of a time when he still lived at the Palace Hotel and had not yet moved permanently to the ranch. He was very ill—he had long known that his heart was failing—and his doctor ordered him to stay in bed for several weeks, and then to have himself driven slowly, wrapped in a blanket, to the ranch for further convalescence. Two hours later he telephoned the doctor—from Cupertino. "I'm here," he announced. "I drove myself right down. I didn't bother about the blanket, but I didn't hurry—I didn't make over sixty or sixty-five all the way down!"

It was time to retire, to spend his last years among his beloved trees and animals at "Woodhills." Older played with the idea, but he could not make himself let go the harness. Often, sitting in his office, he felt so ill that he doubted whether he would last the night out. Then he used to write little notes of farewell to his closest friends on the staff and leave them on their desks. In the morning, feeling better, he would arrive before they did and carefully destroy all the messages. As his utmost concession, he gave up coming to the city on Saturdays and Sundays. On his seventy-eighth birthday, in 1934, he confessed that in spite of his pessimism, he was "glad to have stuck it out."

March 1, 1935, was a Friday. As Older left the office, he said to one of his editorial workers: "Well, do you think you'll see me Monday?" "I'll have to," was the blithe reply. "I have to get another look at that new green suit of yours."

Older chuckled as he made his way to his regular four-o'clock train—he still displayed in his dress a touch of the floridity he had once so admired in the Mississippi River gamblers. Indeed, the man who said Older "would have made a great cavalry general," impressed by his lanky height, his bristly mustache, his expressive hands with their constant gestures, never realized how much more he resembled that vanished figure of his youth. In appearance Older could have been anything—except a newspaper editor. A criminologist once noted how many of the "stigmata" of Lombroso he possessed, including his abnormally long ears. He was a living proof of the importance of environment; born and reared in a slum, he might very well have become a successful highwayman. The driving force to distinction was there, to take whatever avenue was opened to it. Perhaps it was a subconscious understanding of these universal potentialities that accounted for Older's deep interest in criminals and outcasts.

On Sunday, March 3, the Olders and their ward, Mary d'Antonio, drove to Sacramento to see a camellia show. Their chauffeur went with them, but Older liked to drive and took the wheel. He did not go into the show with the women; he had an editorial to finish, which he could write while they looked at the flowers. It is a curious fact that Older, who as so great an editor, was so very little of a writer. It was not until 1926 that he was persuaded to put down on paper some account of his own adventurous life; and his brief autobiography, centering almost entirely around the graft trials, first appeared in the columns of his newspaper. In his last years, however, he began to have the old man's itch for expression. He found interest in his daily column, made up of simple and discursive articles, reminiscences, and reflections. He was proud of it and jealous of its excellence. He would far rather sit in his car and write than waste a Sunday afternoon admiring camellias.

This column was on Montaigne, a lasting enthusiasm. Older, who pretended to be a cynic, a complete pessimist, betrayed himself by the fresh enthusiasms which seized him even in old age. Once he brought an editorial writer out of bed and down to his hotel suite at three o'clock in the morning—to read to him from some newly discovered author whom he could not wait to share! "Listen to this—this is the greatest book I ever read" was a phrase so often on his lips it became a by-word. The books, like the people who were "the finest I ever met," did not always stand the test of time; but Montaigne had never failed him. Now he was bringing to his readers the great Frenchman's "Thoughts on Death."

"He refused," wrote Older, "to be depressed by death, which is the inevitable end of us all."

Then Mrs. Older and Miss d'Antonio appeared, carrying white and red camellias for him to admire.

"If you had been a little longer," he said, "I would have been able to finish this."

But he took the wheel again from the chauffeur and started to drive toward Stockton. Suddenly "the inevitable end" was upon him. He was just able to stop the car at the side of the road.

He was rushed to a Stockton hospital, where he was pronounced "dead on arrival," of a heart attack. He had written his own obituary.

He was buried at "Woodhills" on Monday. It was a strange funeral. He had always detested black, and so none was in sight; Mrs. Older wore white. An odd mixture of mourners came to bid him farewell—newspapermen and writers, ex-convicts, state officials, prostitutes, priests. Francis Heney was there, and so was Abe Ruef. Henry Ohloff, the liberal rector of the Episcopal Church of St. Mary the Virgin, spoke the funeral address, and read Emerson's poem which Older had loved:

> "Goodbye, proud world, I'm going home,
> Thou'rt not my friend, and I'm not thine."

"Death is just something that happens," Older had said; and, to Clarence Darrow: "I wouldn't mind utter effacement if I could definitely get hold of any purpose back of life. But I can't, and as a result I bitterly resent having been brought into this conscious world."

There was no music; he had not cared for music. With his friends looking on, the silver casket was buried on the ranch, near the little graves of his dogs—Friendie, and Sister, and the rest. Later a boulder was placed over it.

On Tuesday, Father Leal, of Mission San Jose, said mass for him at St. Matthew's Church in San Mateo. "He was a member of that universal church of human kindness," said the priest.

The next day, Ash Wednesday, a man whom Older would have liked and who would have liked Older, died in Washington—the greater son of a great father, Oliver Wendell Holmes. The newspapers filled their front pages with other matters. The world moved on.

But on the four-o'clock Southern Pacific train down the Peninsula, a commuter, Horace Allen, laid a bunch of violets on the seat which had always been Fremont Older's. Nobody sat there that day.

CHAPTER IX

Charlatan or Dupe:
ALBERT ABRAMS

I N A LONG, dimly lighted room, with all red or orange objects excluded from it, a husky young man stripped to the waist stood, facing west, on two grounded metal plates. He held to his forehead an electrode which was connected with a series of rheostats. Before the young man sat a spectacled, white-bearded gentleman whose toupee concealed his complete baldness. Methodically he was percussing the young man's abdomen. Every little while he would call out numbers: "55, 13 ohms—42, 8 ohms," and so forth.

Dr. Albert Abrams was at work in his clinic of Electronic Medicine.

The young man was not the patient; he was merely the "subject," or "reagent," chosen for his perfect health. In the round box, the "dynamizer," connected with the electrode he held, there was a piece of filter paper, or blotter, on which were a few drops of blood, previously treated with a horseshoe magnet "to wipe out extraneous electronic emissions." It was the person from whom the blood had been taken whose disease was being diagnosed. Each disease had its number, and the ohmage indicated the degree to which it was present.

The theory on which the "Electronic Reactions of

Abrams" was based was that every illness has its exact number of electronic vibrations, made manifest through a dullness in some portion of the "subject's" abdomen, or a roughness of the skin if the touch system of diagnosis be used instead of the percussion sytem. The whole series—consisting of the dynamizer, a measuring rheostat, a strain-rate rheostat, a vibratory rheostat, and a rheostatic dynamizer—was known as a "biodynamometer." This was, so to speak, the diagnosing machine. The treatment machine was a box from which protruded several electrodes, which were placed by the patient at the appropriate portion of his body; this apparatus was known as an "oscilloclast." Dr. Haven Emerson, in a critical essay in *The Survey*, summed up the theory succinctly:

"[The claim is that] the basic components of the body are electrons, with vibratory motions and a definite radio-activity according to the conditions of the body in health and disease. Each disease has its specific rate. Produce the same vibratory rate by the use of drugs ('specific drugs possess a like vibratory rate as the diseases for which they are effective'), or by the use of Dr. Abrams' own invention, the oscilloclast, and you destroy the disease."

Sometimes, instead, the patient was rubbed with a salve whose color included the requisite number of vibrations.

An extension of the theory was Dr. Abrams' belief that the Occidental world is thoroughly syphilized. He used, indeed, to speak facetiously of "syphilization" as a synonym of "civilization," saying that nearly all white people by this time have a strain of congenital syphilis, which underlies all other diseases. Some of this, he thought, came from vaccination, which produced in man a strange thing called "bovine syphilis." As cows are not subject to syphilis, he must have known, though his patients did not, that this was pure nonsense. He was not, however, opposed to vaccination; only we must use a "desyphilized vaccine." Later, to spare people's feelings, congenital syphilis became known as "diminished resistance."

Another of his opinions was that all surgical operations, of whatever nature, are inevitably followed by cancer.

The biodynamometer did more than merely diagnose disease. From a few drops of blood or saliva, from the handwriting of a signature or a few lines written on paper, even from a photograph, definite "areas of dullness" on the "subject's" abdomen, accurate to an inch, would tell the patient's racial or national descent, his religious affiliation to the very denomination, and his degree of love, fear, or deceit!

In its heyday, from about 1918 to 1924, the Abrams' system attracted some three thousand medical disciples, all of whom paid large fees for a course of instruction either in Abrams' own clinic in San Francisco or in one of the twelve schools of Electronic Medicine founded subsequently. Each of these pupils was obliged to lease an oscilloclast, at $200 or $250 down and a perpetual rent of five dollars a month. The machines were not for sale, and the lessee had to sign a contract never to open the sealed box. The actual cost of manufacturing the oscilloclast was about thirty dollars. Similar arrangements were made in leasing the diagnosing machine, the biodynamometer.

Among these physicians who adopted the Abrams' system the American Medical Association found the names of many quacks on record in its files—adherents of strange cults, faith healers, men who had been convicted of using the mails to defraud, at least one "medical astrologer." There were some chiropractors, and more than half of the total number were osteopaths. But very many were regular physicians, though usually from colleges of poor standing and hailing for the most part from obscure towns in the Middle West.

Electronic Medicine for a few years had a national reputation—even an international one, since its first recognition came from England and England provided the only prominent names of medical adherents. (In Trafalgar Square in London, an electric sign once flashed the message of Electronic Medicine to the ailing world.) It was of sufficient importance to justify the *Scientific American* in undertaking a yearlong, careful investigation, at the end of which its committee reported:

"This committee finds that the claims advanced on behalf of the E.R.A. (Electronic Reactions of Abrams), and of electronic practice in general, are not substantiated; and it is our belief that they have no basis in fact. In our opinion the so-called electronic treatments are without value."

The committee was made up in equal parts of distinguished medical men and of men trained in electrical engineering and in physics.

Indubitably many persons were "cured" by Electronic Medicine. Nature, given time, frequently does her own healing; moreover, innumerable afflictions, though quite real, are *subjectively* real, and arise, not from functional disorder, but from neuroses. The cure is equally subjective. Each of these cures might be matched by a just as impressive failure. After Dr. Abrams' death, the system, which his chief assistant had announced his disciples would "carry on unflaggingly," gradually declined, until now it is practically nonexistent.

This is the history of all charlantry. But this special instance is of wider interest, largely because of the unusual man who fathered it. Albert Abrams possessed a complex and contradictory nature. It is not at all certain that he was aware of the essential quackery of his system—at least, not all of the time. The *Scientific American* itself, in a preliminary report, remarked: "It may be, although it now seems rather doubtful, that Dr. Abrams did come across some mysterious characteristic of the human body, and that in a crude, blundering sort of way due to insufficient scientific training and lack of precision apparatus, he was unable to master what he had discovered."

In the first place, Abrams' personal history is not that of a quack. Few physicians have been better trained. He was born in San Francisco in December, 1863, and after preparatory training went abroad. He received his M.D. degree from the University of Heidelberg in 1882. At that time no better medical education was possible. And he was a brilliant student. From 1893 to 1898 he was professor of pathology and director of the medical

clinic of Cooper Medical College, which is now a part
of the Stanford University Medical School. He was
president of the Emanuel Polyclinic, and consulting
physician at the French and Mount Zion Hospitals,
both institutions of high standing. He had been president of the San Francisco Medico-Chirurgical Society,
and vice-president of the California State Medical Society. He was a Fellow of the Royal Microscopical Society, of London. In 1897 he demonstrated the value
of the X ray in diagnosing cardiac disease. He worked
on the discovery of heart and lung reflexes by use of
the fluoroscope.

He was rated by his colleagues as an unusually talented
diagnostician. This ability he never lost, even in the
days when he claimed to do his diagnosing by electronic
vibrations. He never lost, either, his shrewd knowledge
of humanity. On one occasion a young German came
to consult him. Without touching the biodynamometer (if the patient were present, he himself could take
the place of the "subject"), Abrams told him instantly
what was wrong with him. He was asked afterwards
how he had done it. He chuckled.

"I was graduated from Heidelberg," he said. "I recognized at once, from the dueling scars on the young
man's face, that he came from Heidelberg too. Knowing the wild life led by wealthy young students there,
and watching the embarrassed, shamefaced expression
with which the young man came to me, and his reluctance to talk about his symptoms, it was easy to tell him
what ailed him!"

Possessor of a Master of Arts degree from an Oregon

college, Abrams was interested always in cultural as well as in medical subjects. The reception hall of his clinic on Sacramento Street in San Francisco bore evidence of his status as an art collector with a special flair for the Orient. The tapestries, the huge brass figure of a Chinese god, the dark wood Chinese lanterns, the ebony furniture heavily carved in dragon shapes were all authentic pieces. He loved to surround himself with beautiful things; in his house in the Sea Cliff district, which he used little after the death of his second wife, he had a fine pipe organ, besides a workable telescope mounted on the roof. He possessed a large library and he read widely.

And his writing—he was always articulate—reflected his varied interests. Many of his books were technical (and quite orthodox) medical works—*Synopsis of Morbid Renal Secretions, Manual of Clinical Diagnosis, Diseases of the Heart*, and so forth; but others were in a lighter mode. *Transactions of the Antiseptic Club*, published in 1896, was a series of humorous sketches in a medical vein. *Scattered Leaves of a Physician's Diary* was rather ill-naturedly described by Dr. Morris Fishbein as "a sort of medical *belles-lettres* considered quite clever in its day." These books *are* clever, even today; and his early medical works were useful and quite sound.

This is not the education and background of a quack. And there was no financial reason why Dr. Abrams should be induced to leave "the straight and narrow path" of medical orthodoxy. He had been married twice, and both his wives had died, each leaving him a fortune. He was a successful and prosperous physician,

with a right to expect a still brighter future in his profession. The change came about 1909, in that rather
upset and disorganized period of human life known as
middle age. His very open-mindedness and receptivity
to new ideas betrayed him. From an unbiased investigation of two rapidly growing schools of healing—osteo-
pathy and chiropractic—he was led further than either
to a system of his own evolving called "Spondylotherapy": "every organ has governing nerve centers in the
spinal cord which when stimulated by manipulation of
the vertebrae can be made to contract or dilate," thus
affecting the diseased organ. His two books on the subject were condemned by the *Journal of the American
Medical Association*, and thenceforth Albert Abrams
was a pariah in orthodox medical circles.

From the "system of visceral nerve reflexes," it was
an easy approach to the gradual development of the
Electronic Reaction theory. This in turn was constantly
being elaborated while Abrams lived; in his last conscious hours he worried over a new machine, a "radio"
which was to supplement the biodynamometer. Though
this "radio" was said by his assistant to be "in a state of
completeness," it was never demonstrated thereafter.

The most interesting thing about Dr. Abrams was his
own psychology. Others have duplicated the furore he
aroused by his methods of diagnosis and cure; fortunes
have been made many times, and much notoriety attained, under similar circumstances. But seldom has so
complicated and self-contradictory a personality stood
behind the facade. Was he, as Paul deKruif called him,
"a magician who believed in his own magic," or was he

cynically aware that mankind loves to be fooled and cynically willing to accommodate it?

The third solution, that the E.R.A. constituted a genuine system of healing, must by this time, when it has practically ceased to exist, be ruled out of court. The *Scientific American* investigation was thorough and exhaustive, and the system failed in every test. Indeed, Dr. Abrams did not like the word "test"; he preferred to speak of "demonstrations." If the results did not tally with those secured by ordinary clinical diagnosis, so much the worse for the latter, for the electronic diagnoses were, by definition, always right!—in itself a revelation of his mental attitude. Dr. Robert A. Millikan, one of the very greatest contemporary physicists, inspected the Abrams' apparatus and said it "did not rest upon any scientific foundation whatever." He pointed out that actual electronic vibrations are billions of times higher in frequency than any used in the Electronic Reactions of Abrams. Several times essential wires in the apparatus were cut without the operator's knowledge, and the machine kept on diagnosing just the same; in one instance constituent parts had actually been removed from the box. Paper, including filter paper, is a nonconductor of electricity, and the specimen to be diagnosed was always placed on paper. Frank Rieber, of the Roentgen Appliance Corporation, dissected an oscilloclast and said: "No current appreciable to the most delicate galvanometer passes from the oscilloclast to the patient." Dr. Abrams always got around this by saying that he was dealing, not with electric, but with electronic, vibrations — a distinction too subtle for the physicist. One of his pioneer disciples, testing bottles of pure germ culture, got nearly every one wrong. He blamed the failures on a red edge to the labels on the bottles! (This man claimed to have "cleared" Typhoid Mary, the famous typhoid carrier, who died recently after many years' detention on Welfare Island, New York — still uncleared.) The *Scientific American* remarked on "the grave discrepancy between the crudity of the apparatus and the extreme refinement of the results claimed from its use," and pointed out that Dr. Abrams' insistence that undue skepticism in investigation hindered the process was analogous to the similar claim familiar to those who have investigated fraudulent psychic mediums.

So, was Albert Abrams a charlatan, or a fanatically convinced dupe? The answer seems to be that he was both. Sometimes he was one, and sometimes he was the other.

The man who manufactured the earliest of the oscilloclasts once said that when he asked Dr. Abrams for the exact arrangement of the wires inside the sealed box, he was told it did not matter! When Abrams himself tried to arrange the attachments of the wires, he made elementary mistakes which, someone has remarked, "would have flunked a high school student of physics." The whole thing was described by an engineer as "a poorly wired set of coils of German silver compacted into simple masses, with open stretches."

When Abrams was invited to hold clinics in Boston and New York, he never definitely accepted, though he never declined. Dr. Benzion Liber, a noted physician

Dr. Albert Abrams demonstrating one of his contraptions.

who attended demonstrations held by Abrams' disciples, stated flatly that he "failed to hear what it was claimed must be heard, and failed to see what it was claimed must be seen." Abrams' attitude always was, "the diagnosis of the medical doctor *cannot* tally with ours, as he is wrong." The insistence that the oscilloclasts be left sealed by their lessees is a sufficiently suspicious circumstance.

On one occasion a woman was brought into the clinic on a stretcher. She claimed not to have slept for an incredible number of days and nights, and to be in a critical condition in consequence. Abrams, the old-time diagnostician, recognized this neurotic syndrome at once. Without recourse to the biodynamometer, he placed the lady on a couch in one of the booths where patients sat holding the electrodes to their afflicted regions, put a metal plate on her head, and told her firmly that an hour of treatment would end her insomnia. In considerably less than an hour, the patient fell sound asleep. She walked out several hours later, refreshed by her nap, and cheerfully sure she was cured. Abrams smiled, and, waving his hands expressively, remarked to the bystanders: "It's all in the mind!"

During the great influenza epidemic of 1918, he said that the only cure was to go to bed, stay there, and drink plenty of whiskey. When his secretary complained of a headache, he did not give her the proper number of vibrations on the oscilloclast, but told her to take some aspirin. And in his last illness, from bronchopneumonia, although his two physicians were both disciples of the electronic method, they were also regular doctors of medicine, and gave him the orthodox treatment for the disease.

All this points to deliberate charlatanism. But there is an equally impressive array of data on the other side. Here is an instance in point:

At one time the chief assistant in Abrams' clinic and school was a little, elderly woman of Danish birth, who almost deserves a chapter herself, except that she was so pathetic a creature it is kinder not to mention her name. The name itself may not have been hers; the given name was Scandinavian, but masculine, not feminine, and the last name was French. Rumor said that in New Zealand, where she had lived before coming to San Francisco, she had worked in some capacity for a physician, and that at his death she had stolen his certificate and adopted his name. She had certainly had some medical training somewhere, but it had strange gaps in it. She was also an accomplished pianist, of the heavy-handed variety, with brilliant technique but no feeling; and she claimed, perhaps with truth, to have been a pupil of the famous Leschetizky. She was an invert, and she secured permission from the Board of Supervisors to wear men's clothing. One of her great friends was a drugless healer with a theory of therapy by colored lights. He was very tall and spare, but the little doctor, who admired him greatly, imitated his attire to the last detail. It used to be most ludicrous to see them on a street together, with more than a foot's difference in height, but with identical suits and hats, the hats cocked at the same angle, identical overcoats carried with the same gesture over the same arm.

Later Dr. Abrams dismissed her, and she set up for herself as an electronic doctor. Several years after his death, she was found dead in her dingy office. Her practice had dwindled to nothing, and she had actually starved to death, too proud to let anyone know her straits. The coroner's verdict was malnutrition. The manager of the shabby hotel where she had rented a tiny room for several years was astonished to discover that she was a woman.

One day while she was still Dr. Abrams' first assistant, he came down to the clinic in the morning and discovered one of the oscilloclasts missing from its accustomed place. He had a burglary and larceny policy with one of the big insurance companies, and he called up and reported his loss. When the claim adjuster called on him, Abrams said at once: "I want you to arrest Dr. ——" (the little old lady). The adjuster explained that if any warrants were to be sworn to, the claimant must do the swearing, since insurance companies take no chances on suits for false arrest. That considerably sobered Dr. Abrams' excitement, and the adjuster then asked why this particular person was suspected.

"Because," said Abrams, "I took the biodynamometer at once to the place where the oscilloclast always stood, and it gave a Danish vibration!"

A short time later, it was discovered that a boy who had been hired to help around the clinic had taken the machine home, out of curiosity to open it and see what made it work. The boy was Irish.

But here Dr. Abrams quite sincerely believed that his diagnosing machine was capable of registering the "vibrations of nationality" of the person last in a given place! And here is further evidence of his self-duping:

His admirers called Dr. Abrams "a physicist, as well as a medically trained man." As a matter of fact, he was abysmally ignorant of physics. One day a startling idea occurred to him. He would place a silver half-dollar in the vibration of gold, and see it turn to gold!

The acquaintance to whom he communicated this project was amazed. As it happened, he was a writer on scientific topics, and thoroughly familiar with physical theory. On inquiry, he found that Abrams had never even heard of Mendeleev's Table of the Periodic Law, the foundation stone of modern physics, which arranges all the elements by their atomic weights and shows their relations. Abrams could not understand when he was told how far, atomically, silver is removed from gold, or that the nearest element to gold is mercury. He remained unmoved even when reminded that a half-dollar is far from pure silver, and unless sterilized would also be covered with various microbes, each with its own "vibration." He insisted obstinately on trying the experiment.

After about four hours he could no longer contain himself. By this time, he felt, some evidence must be forthcoming. It was just dusk. He hurried into the clinic, took the coin away from the oscilloclast, and exclaimed excitedly: "It's working! It has a distinctly yellow tinge."

The other man looked around, and noticed that the walls of the clinic were yellowish in color. "Bring it into the other room," he suggested quietly. In the next room, Abrams' face fell. The walls there were a dead white. "You're right," he said sadly. "It hasn't changed at all."

Such episodes as this indicate not so much self-deception as actual aberration. And that may very well have been the case. Certainly his later writings were confused, rambling, and sometimes incoherent, in direct contrast to his earlier crisp and lucid style.

The *Scientific American* listed some examples of the grandiloquent names Abrams gave his apparatus:

A resistance box was a "reflexophone"; a magnet, a "depolarizer"; a slide-wire rheostat with two electrodes, a "biodynamometer," and the electrodes themselves were "distal and proximal." An arrangement of spark coils, turning coils, variable condenser, electrodes, and connecting wires was a "sphygmobiometer"; a current interrupter connected with a lighting circuit was an "oscilloclast"; simple marks made by a muscular movement of the "subject" were "gyrograms" or "pathograms."

This is the bombastic phraseology of the charlatan; but it is characteristic also of mental derangement.

Abrams was an excitable, quick-tempered, impulsive man, full of contradictory characteristics. He was generous and stingy, kindly and harsh, optimistic and depressed, scrupulous and unscrupulous.

An interesting story comes from his childhood—a story told by himself. His mother kept in her pantry a sugar bowl which was always full of change, used for meeting small tradesmen's bills and the like. When Albert was ten or twelve, one day, overcome by the urgency of some boyish need, he took two dollars from this sugar bowl and spent it. Immediately he was seized by remorse, though no one discovered the loss or up-braided him. He must find a way to replace the money, and after several sleepless nights he worked one out. Every morning he got up at three o'clock and sneaked out of the house. He went to the commission district and scaled fish for a wholesaler. After three hours he ran back home and was safe in bed in time to get up for breakfast and school. It took him a week of this grueling labor to earn back the two dollars he had stolen.

Several years later he confessed the whole thing to his brother. The brother laughed. "Why," he said, "you were a chump to pay that back. The rest of us used to take money out of that sugar bowl whenever we wanted it. We all did that for years."

Yet this is the boy who grew up into a man who claimed to have made a medical discovery of world import, and instead of giving it to the world, as is the custom with scientific discoveries, sold it at the highest rates he could obtain.

Cases were brought to his attention where his incorrect diagnosis had caused untold misery; but he never seemed to care. There were some pitiful stories in that clinic; he himself complained that too many people came to him only in desperation, after they had been given up by everyone else. One woman spent the last money she had for treatment by Abrams; when it did her no good, and her money was gone, she found she had cancer, no longer operable. Abrams knew about that case, as about many others, but remarked merely that the later diagnosis was mistaken. Nevertheless, the patient died after months of agony. Dr. Henry Harris says, in *California's Medical Story,* that "it was not uncommon in the free clinics of San Francisco to see patients with incurable diseases . . . left moneyless and hopeless after their electronic treatments." He relates also that "at the orphanage where Abrams had served when a young practitioner, the children had feared his rough, almost brutal handling."

Yet in other cases he was kindness and gentleness themselves. The recipients of his mercy must, however, be worshiping believers; he could not stand contradiction and flew into violent rages at the slightest opposition. And even believers did not always fare well at his hands.

One day there came to the clinic a tubercular boy who had tramped all the way from the Mother Lode country, in northern California, to be treated by Abrams as his last hope. When he found the boy was penniless, Abrams absolutely refused to give him a diagnosis or even one treatment. It was his secretary who reached into her own pocket and paid for the boy's care until he could return home. Yet that same day, leaving the clinic, Abrams saw a blind beggar trying to cross the street. He ran after him, helped him safely to the other side, and folded a dollar in the beggar's hand.

And, to carry the contradiction further, when he died he left his entire fortune, between three and five million dollars, to establish a hospital of Electronic Medicine "where the poor could be treated without charge"!

Memories of Abrams are always of an agitated, talkative little figure, striding about the room, gesturing, smoking incessantly the cigarettes which he cut in half and kept in boxes. (The object of this was to enable him to take a few quick puffs when his work would not allow him time for a real smoke.) He was always full of great plans and soaring projects. Yet in his last newspaper interview, given to Evelyn Wells a few days before his fatal illness, he was very gloomy.

"I've had enough," he said. "Life is something one can get enough of, like anything else. I have a contempt for the man who wants to go on after he is through. I am through. I've worked hard. I've been unappreciated. They make fun of me in the newspapers. That's all right. Some day people will know just what it is I have done. I've claimed to do nothing I cannot do."

This lament, in which any psychiatrist would recognize familiar elements, contrasts strongly with his assistant's statement: "He died fighting. He tried not to show how deeply he was wounded by the constant and bitter attacks made against him by the orthodox medical men, but the attacks undermined his strength."

It is undoubtedly true that he fell an easy prey to pneumonia because his resistance was weakened by anxiety. He was about to leave for Arkansas, where one of his followers, Dr. Mary Lecoque, was to be tried for using the mails to defraud. She had diagnosed disease in a specimen which turned out to be not human, but chicken blood—a trick played more than once on Dr. Abrams himself, with the same unfortunate falling into the trap. After that he intended to go to Ohio, where Electronic Medicine was under heavy fire, and from there to New York and London. His assistant said he had had a breakdown from worry in October, 1923, and had been forced to cancel the trip; but he wrote the *Scientific American* Committee a week before his death, which occurred on January 13, 1924, planning to meet them in New York, "after Arkansas and Ohio," in the spring. Dr. Lecoque, incidentally, was acquitted.

After Abrams' death, stories were circulated to the effect that, by electronic diagnosis, he had predicted the time he would die—"by examining his own blood and making tests of its energy output." The story grew by repetition until it became a detailed prophecy to his staff: "I shall go in the first month of next year, some time in the first half of the month." He claimed to be able to tell by his machine how long any given person would live.

It is quite possible that Abrams, who was growing increasingly more melancholy, more than once prophesied his imminent end. In 1921 he told Upton Sinclair, whom he had converted to his theory, that he (Abrams) would die in three years. As a trained diagnostician he undoubtedly knew that his physical mechanism was breaking down under the strain he put upon it. But that his prediction was by no means so clear-cut and specific is shown by a rather amusing episode which took place in 1920.

In his Sea Cliff house, besides the organ and the telescope, he had a roulette wheel. In an idle moment, he suggested to an acquaintance that each of them spin it "and see how many years they would live." Considerably surprised at this highly unscientific suggestion, the other man nevertheless agreeably spun the wheel. The number it stopped at does not matter, except that it was incorrect as a prediction of his remaining years. Then Abrams spun. The wheel stopped at Zero. He laughed uncomfortably. "That doesn't count," he said. "I'll try it again." Again Zero. This time he turned pale. "Once more," he said. It came to Double Zero. He was so upset that he insisted on leaving the house at once. (Actually, he lived for more than three years longer.)

Albert Abrams, at his death, had gone a long way from the brilliant young physician who came back to his native city from Heidelberg in 1882. "Spondylotherapy" had been his first medical aberration; by 1912 he was claiming to have cured appendicitis "by pressing on the eleventh dorsal vertebra and cleansing the appendix of foreign matter." He was outlawed by his orthodox colleagues, and at first his new system, as he developed it, grew slowly. Through numerous publications, and the establishment of schools outside his own clinic, it spread gradually until Abrams' name was familiar wherever English was spoken. He claimed to have cured both Calles and his enemy de la Huerta in Mexico, and to have been consulted—by whom he did not say— during Lenin's last illness! In 1922 Judge Thomas Graham of San Francisco admitted as evidence of paternity in an alimony suit an electronic analysis (a very different thing from the matching of blood types common in such cases) showing that the defendant was father of the plaintiff's child. But a year later the tide was already turning; test cases were beginning to arise; and even if Abrams had lived, the system, like other healing fads without scientific basis, would inevitably have declined as it arose.

The Blanche and Jeanne Abrams College of Electronic Medicine, with a hospital included, had been started before Abrams died. A ten-story building was already in course of construction at Sutter and Hyde Streets, one block from the St. Francis Hospital, one of San Francisco's finest. It was to be a memorial to Abrams' two dead wives, Jeanne Rath and Blanche Schwabacher. But after his death, when it was found that he had left everything he possessed to the college and hospital, his relatives contested the will. After long litigation a settlement was reached; but the unfinished building was converted to other uses. The college was never founded, and the project has long ago been dropped. A few obscure healers still employ the Electronic Reactions of Abrams as part of their method of therapy. Otherwise, the grandiose theory, which once drew its thousands of physicians and hundreds of thousands of patients, which enlisted the most enthusiastic support and turned a whole magazine—*Pearson's*, under Alexander Markey—into its virtual organ of propaganda, is dead.

But it would be a pity if Albert Abrams, too, should be completely forgotten. He was one of the most amazing phenomena to come out of a city which is prolific of prodigies.

The "Christ Angel":
ELLA MAY CLEMMONS

SAN FRANCISCO'S famous Chinatown, the most populous in America, is limited in extent—two blocks east and west from Kearny Street to Stockton Street, half a dozen or so blocks north and south, from Bush Street to Columbus Avenue, where the Italian district begins. Within these narrow confines, though she was born in Oakland and died in Alameda, was spent most of the colorful, pathetic life of a strange woman whose death was as troubling and mysterious as her career had been.

One Christmas week in the 1870's a little girl in Oakland was taken by young friends to an "entertainment" at the Congregational Church. The star performers were two sisters, children of about her own age. "I was one of seven," she said, looking back over sixty years. "My mother had no time to curl my hair or dress me up. I remember how bitterly I envied those two pretty little girls, with their blond curls and their frilled dresses. Most of all I remember the ribbon bracelets they wore, with little bows on them—one blue, one pink."

It is the first discoverable glimpse of Ella and Viola Dayan, who were to become Ella May Clemmons and Katherine Gould.

The Dayan girls' stepfather, whose name they used, was a bookkeeper for the Southern Pacific Railroad. Their own father's name was Clemmons. After Ella May died, a claim was made that the name should be spelled "Clemens," and that they were nieces of Mark Twain. That has never been authenticated, and is rather unlikely.

Ella May's early days are obscure. At some time in the 1880's the family moved to Palo Alto, but this was probably after she had been married, very young, to Charles Overacker, County Recorder of Alameda County. They were soon separated, and apparently were finally divorced.

Meanwhile Viola, who preferred her middle name of Katherine, was beginning her glamorous years as an actress. She appeared first on the stage of Maguire's San Francisco Opera House, in Shakespearean plays. She was beautiful, to Ella May's mere blonde prettiness, and she seems to have had some talent. It was in these earliest theatrical years that the name of William F. Cody ("Buffalo Bill") first appears in connection with hers. Soon—allegedly with his help—she was ready for a world tour. Her sister Ella, free by this time from her husband, went along as chaperone. The two sisters were together, and inseparable, until 1897, when they quarreled and Ella May returned alone to San Francisco.

The next year Katherine married Howard Gould, son of Jay Gould and heir to all his millions, which he jeopardized by the match. He escaped the disinheritance he had risked, and Mrs. Gould retired from the stage. The couple spent much of their time on their yacht, the

Niagara, making several world cruises in it when among the guests were Kaiser Wilhelm II of Germany and Czar Nicholas II of Russia. Fatality hung over all that safe, gay company.

Katherine was still at outs with her sister, and refused to communicate with her. No one knows the cause of their rupture, but judging from Ella May's later development it may have arisen from her disapproval of her sister's "worldly ways." She was growing very puritanical.

Meanwhile, back in San Francisco, Ella May Clemmons had begun her long years of service in Chinatown. She was still a Congregationalist, and under these auspices she opened a sort of mission kindergarten for Chinese children, which she called the "Little House of Gold." She spent herself and all she had in devotion to the Chinese, just emerging from the period when they had been the hunted and hated *bêtes noires* of the competing white workers. They were grateful, and they rewarded her with the title she bore proudly all her life, "the Christ Angel of Chinatown."

At five o'clock on the morning of April 18, 1906, San Francisco was rocked and ruined by the greatest earthquake of its history, the destruction being completed by the fire which followed. All of Chinatown was in the midst of the catastrophe; it was wiped out, and the "Little House of Gold" with it. Katherine Gould did not even inquire if her sister were dead or in need, though from Europe she cabled help to her mother in Palo Alto —which, though untouched by fire, was equally devastated by the tremor. (The geological fault line which slipped extended a great distance both north and south of San Francisco.)

Ella May Clemmons, penniless, went with other refugees to live in a relief tent in the Presidio. On her canvas wall were pinned two objects: a crucifix (though she had not yet formally become a Roman Catholic), and a clipping from a newspaper, a picture of the sister who had repudiated her.

Because of her friendship for and experience with the Chinese, when rehabilitation began she was put in charge of Chinese relief. To her tent came men, women, and children, bereaved, bewildered, and destitute, and she arranged for their feeding, care, and rehousing. Among them one day was a tall, well-set-up Chinese, of about her own age, named Wong Sun Yue. When Chinatown was rebuilt and the Presidio camp was emptied, Ella May Clemmons went back to live among her friends. A short time later, she and Wong Sun Yue were married by Oriental rites in a joss house. Later their marriage was confirmed by a Methodist ceremony.

This marriage was by American law no marriage at all, for Wong had a wife in China. Ten years after, when it was all over, Ella May asserted that it had been a marriage in name only; that she had discovered Wong was a victim of the opium habit, and had married him to watch over him and cure him of it. "I put my soul in pawn with God," she said, "to be given back to me only when my mission was accomplished. . . . There never were any marital relations." And after her separation she added: "God had released me, my soul was again my own." But there was plenty of testimony to the effect that she was deeply in love with Wong, and that no question arose during the time they lived together that they were husband and wife in every sense of the word. Moreover, around the curio shop which they opened together on Grant Avenue, there played two Eurasian children, a boy and a girl. Later she said these children were adopted, though obviously they were half-white. Both grew up; the boy was graduated from an Eastern university, the girl married a Chinese and moved away from San Francisco. The advertising card used by Ella May Clemmons for this curio shop shows a lack of delicacy. One side, adorned with a picture of the couple, both in Chinese costume, reads: "Call Chinatown and have a cup of tea with us. Mr. and Mrs. Wong Sun Yue Clemens [*sic*]. Mrs. Howard Gould's Sister." On the other side, a Chinese and a Japanese maiden are portrayed, as "China and Japan Serving Tea," while a placard near by reads: "Pompeii of America. Our original refugee house, showing relics of the Great Fire."

If Mrs. Gould had quarreled with her sister previously, it may be imagined how she felt about having a Chinese brother-in-law. This time their mother, Mrs. Dayan, also was outraged; she was not reconciled to her daughter until she lay on her deathbed in 1911. But two years before that, Katherine Gould had herself become involved in notoriety when she and her husband separated. In the ensuing suit she was charged with undue association with "Buffalo Bill," then a man of sixty-three, and with Dustin Farnum, the actor. She was legally exonerated, and was awarded a separation maintenance of $36,000 a year; the couple were not divorced.

Katherine was free now, however, and the ordeal through which she had passed perhaps made her remember the devoted sister of the days before the rupture. She offered Ella May a large amount of money if she would leave her husband, but Ella May flatly refused. For seven years Mrs. Gould struggled to break the marriage, and she finally succeeded by what has been claimed as a deliberate plot to separate Wong and his wife, but which may have been an inevitable accident.

Ella May had become an ardent disciple of Dr. Maria Montessori's method of child training. In 1916, she, Wong, Katherine Gould, and two Chinese girl protégées sailed for China. In Pekin (now Peiping) they established, with Mrs. Gould's money, a school based on the Montessori method, and called the "House of Childhood." It seems almost certain that Wong and Ella May, at least, expected to remain at its head for the rest of their lives; Wong had made no legal provision for his return to America.

But before long, for some reason unknown—perhaps, as has been alleged, as part of a scheme planned in advance—Katherine Gould quarreled once more with her sister, withdrew her support of the school, and departed. Without her money the school soon failed. Next, the two girls they had brought from San Francisco fell ill of smallpox. Ella May nursed them until they recovered, and then she too left, taking the girls with her. Wong remained. He was reunited with his first wife, and Ella May Clemmons never saw him again. It was on her return to San Francisco that she made the statement about "putting her soul in pawn," and she added as her only other explanation: "Our protégées were marked down for rich merchants to make slaves of, so I brought them with me and gave him back to his Chinese wife."

She opened a tea room and curio shop again, this time on Stockton Street near Jackson, and ran it alone until 1926. Once more she became "the Christ Angel," blessed by the poor of Chinatown. She was converted to the Catholic faith, and became well known to the Paulist Fathers who conduct Old St. Mary's Church—one of the oldest Catholic churches in San Francisco, once the cathedral of the diocese, whose white congregation must come to worship now in the very heart of Chinatown, across the street from Bufano's statue of Sun Yat Sen. Beneath its brick tower, where the solemn words stand over the arched doorway, under the clock: "My son, observe the time, and flee from evil," Ella May Clemmons, once Mrs. Wong, passed almost daily. She had always been devout; now she was fanatically pious. She walked the streets of Chinatown with a huge crucifix hung around her neck; she wrote out prayers and gave them to her friends.

She was, in fact, becoming increasingly eccentric. At times she sold newspapers on a street corner or served as a waitress in restaurants. She dressed in loose robes in semi-Oriental style. She ran after fads and shopped around for cures, for by this time her health had broken. Orlando Miller, a swindler who later went to prison for defrauding hundreds of small investors by fake stock schemes, got a good piece of Ella May Clemmons' savings. She was a disciple of Dr. Albert Abrams and his Electronic Medicine. She was an enthusiast for "psycho-

Ella May Clemmons in Chinese dress, with her sister, Katherine Gould.

logical lecturers" and the prey of any quack. Yet though she was erratic, she was decidedly never insane or incompetent. All this time she was also conducting her shop efficiently and working regularly in the philanthropic activities of the Chinese Catholic Mission conducted by Old St. Mary's. Every city has thousands like her—middle-aged women with no ties, pathetically trying to fill their empty lives, half-educated graspers after "culture." What chiefly differentiated her from the rest of them was her feeling for and closeness to the Chinese people.

The pretty little blonde had grown very stout now, and her silky hair was grey. She still had her beautiful, well-kept hands, and no matter how she neglected her dress she still had a natural pride which sent her to have her hair cut and waved and her nails manicured. But she was ill, very ill, and none of the healing cults she patronized could help her.

In 1926 she gave up her shop and went to live alone in an apartment on Stockton Street just on the edge of Chinatown. She filled the rooms with the choicest of her Oriental furniture and decorations, including a beautiful carved teakwood bed which later was called into evidence before the grand jury. Gradually she became a recluse, though for several years a few old friends were allowed to penetrate to her secluded rooms. She lived frugally, and every day she might be seen, an old-fashioned market basket in her hand, going to buy the day's supplies for her lonely meals.

In those last ten years of her life, only two things of importance happened to her, and both were fatal.

In 1928, the mysterious illness from which she suffered flared up sharply and she underwent some kind of seizure, probably uremic in nature, for her sight was failing. She went for treatment, nobody knows by whose recommendation, to a drugless practitioner named Hjalmar Groneman.

In December, 1930, in Lynchburg, Virginia, Katherine Gould died. There are conflicting statements as to just how much she left to the sister with whom she had never again been entirely reconciled. There was certainly an $11,000 trust fund, which was to be paid to Miss Clemmons at the rate of $250 a month. At the time of her death this was down to three thousand dollars. But apparently there was another much larger legacy, mostly in real estate, estimates of which have varied from $40,000 to $80,000.

When Mrs. Gould, in a last gesture of sisterly affection over the years of dissension, bequeathed to Ella May Clemmons whatever she did bequeath her, unwittingly she signed her sister's death warrant. The warrant was not served for five years more, but served it was. The account of what happened is all drawn from court records and from uncontroverted stories in the San Francisco *News*.

Miss Clemmons fell completely and slavishly under Groneman's influence. Whatever he said was gospel, whatever he did was law. For a long time he forbade her to drink any liquids; she suffered, but she obeyed. Then he gave her an entirely liquid diet, at the same time ordering her to walk five miles and to swim daily. This was only a few months before her death. She collapsed, but when a doctor was called by her landlady, she sent him away—and refused to pay him, saying she had no money of her own, all her money was being taken care of by "Doctor" Groneman. The practitioner's conviction in 1932, carrying a thirty-day suspended sentence, for prescribing medicine without a license and for calling himself "Doctor" without adding "of Chiropractic"—and his subsequent trial and censure by the Board of Chiropractors as well—made no difference to her. This forceful man with startlingly white skin, deep-sunken eyes, and high square forehead under a completely bald head, had become for her the center of her world and the god of her adoration.

After 1930, when her sister's legacy was made, her doom was sealed. Bits of telltale information leaked out —the five thousand dollars she told someone she had given Groneman to bring his yacht (a thirty-five-foot power cruiser) down from Seattle; the old friend who was forbidden to call on her again because "the doctor" thought her a bad influence; the terrible dirt and disorder in her neglected apartment, full of its antique Chinese furniture and with anatomical charts on the bedroom walls; her direct words to Dr. Cox, the medical man she turned away, that "Dr. Groneman is next to God." Every day she cooked dietary meals for Groneman's patients, then put on her old-fashioned cape and hat and carried them around in her market basket. After a while she was too ill to be of such mundane service. Her fate closed in on her.

At the end of summer, in 1935, Ella May Clemmons said to one of the last of her old friends whom she was permitted to see: "I am planning a long trip. I may go to Paris to study medicine. Wherever it is, I am going far away."

"Won't you have an address you can give me?" she was asked.

"No, I shan't be able to have any visitors, because I'm going too far away."

She did.

An order was left in the post office for her mail to be forwarded to Groneman's office. When people telephoned him about Miss Clemmons, he said she was ill and in a sanitarium in Palo Alto. Letters and (later) Christmas presents could be sent to him, and he would see she got them. She could not see anyone, he added; she had cancer, and was very sensitive about having anyone visit her in her present condition. She was getting along well. Everyone knew, he reminded inquirers, that she had a horror of publicity after all that she had suffered from it in the past. Yes, thank you, she was doing very nicely—as late as the beginning of 1936.

It was in the middle of January that an enterprising reporter on the San Francisco *News* broke the story.

Bit by bit, in the month that followed, first the newspaper, then public officials and the courts uncovered the lurid and amazing tale.

After her collapse in the apartment house lobby on September 7, and her turning away of Dr. Cox, Miss Clemmons never left her rooms, unaided, again. Groneman established a blonde young woman as nurse. Once the landlady caught her going over Miss Clemmons' papers. She said she was merely tidying the room.

This young woman was Charlotte Enberg, described as an artist. She was not a nurse, and knew nothing about nursing. Miss Clemmons must have been unconscious or semiconscious when she was brought in to her apartment, for it was stated that, a few years before, she had found Miss Enberg on Groneman's yacht and had quarreled with her violently. Miss Clemmons seems to have known that Groneman was married and had a grown son; his wife had died in 1932. But she certainly never knew that Groneman and Miss Enberg, by their open confession before the grand jury, had lived together for several years in an apartment in the Mission District which they rented as Mr. and Mrs. Enberg.

It was to this apartment that all the Chinese furniture in Ella May Clemmons' home was delivered by a storage company in October, by Groneman's orders. It had been removed from the Stockton Street house, also by his orders, on September 14. Four days before that, Groneman and Ella May Clemmons had been married.

At the time common-law marriage was abolished in California, a law was passed, to protect the feelings of people who might have been living under the common law for many years and might have grown children, permitting the marriage, without a license, by any ordained minister, of an adult couple with no legal impediments otherwise who testify that they have been living together as husband and wife. It was under this law that the marriage took place. It was performed, though Miss Clemmons was still a Catholic, by a Protestant minister. The only witness was Charlotte Enberg.

In all probability the marriage was invalid. Miss Enberg herself swore before the grand jury that Groneman had never lived in the apartment on Stockton Street, and that for the period he claimed to have cohabited with Ella May Clemmons—varying, according to stories told the minister and others, from one to three and a half years—he had actually been living with her, instead. Miss Clemmons was during all this period a very ill woman, whether she actually had cancer or not. She was besides a puritanical woman, who had long outlived any passionate impulses of her youth. Just what her age was, no one, including Groneman, really knew. In her will dated 1931, she said she was fifty-five; her death certificate, four years later, made her nearly fifty-nine. But in 1935 she told a friend she was seventy-four, and that is in all probability the correct figure, judging from the age of living people who were her contemporaries in girlhood. Curled hair and well-kept fingernails were not the only vanities retained to the end by the pathetic woman who was once the pretty little blonde girl in Oakland.

Finally, it was brought out that Groneman actually *could* not have lived in the apartment on Stockton Street, since the only bed besides the single one on which the sick woman lay was the ornate Chinese period piece, which had no mattress.

Legal or not, the ceremony took place. It must have been a weird scene, under the electric lights, amid the Oriental carvings and hangings: the sympathetic minister, who thought an erring couple were "doing the right thing" before the invalid's approaching end—the bride, already a dying woman, rousing herself from semicoma to murmur her responses, then falling into a stupor with a high fever—the only witness the hard-faced girl who was the bridegroom's mistress.

One wonders just how conscious Miss Clemmons was, all through this. The week before, she had received extreme unction from Father George Johnson of Old St. Mary's.

This was September 10. On September 14 the furniture was carted away. The apartment had already been empty for several days when the landlady, hearing no sound from it, used a passkey and found it stripped. She had somehow missed seeing the moving van.

On the very day of the marriage, it was brought out by subsequent inquiry, Groneman had rented an apartment in Alameda, telling the owner of the house in which it was situated that his wife had had a nervous breakdown and that he wanted a quiet place for her to stay in. The morning after the marriage, before daylight, he ordered an ambulance. He told the driver to park a block and a half away and to turn out his headlights. The driver and his assistant were then taken to Miss Clemmons' Stockton Street apartment, where the electricity had been turned off and they had to use flashlights to see. She was placed on a stretcher and carried to the ambulance. They reached the Alameda address before six o'clock in the morning.

For a week Miss Clemmons — or Mrs. Groneman, if she was Mrs. Groneman—lay there. Most of the time she was alone. Miss Enberg had been installed again as "nurse," but she left the sick woman frequently. Groneman came in the evenings, after office hours in the city.

The landlady, naturally curious, listened often, but heard nothing from the mysterious tenants. Once, however, she was startled by a deep groan, followed by the slamming of a door. "Miss Clemmons was allowed only liquid food; she was hungry and cried all the time," Charlotte Enberg callously told the grand jury. Once she met the landlady at the front door and remarked: "My patient is unconscious." She did not see anything unusual about leaving an unconscious patient alone in the apartment.

By September 18 even Groneman could see that Ella May Clemmons was about to die. He had to think about a death certificate, and he had to act fast.

That night he sent for a physician, who saw at a glance that the case was hopeless, and ordered her sent to a hospital. She was taken to the Alameda Sanitarium, where Groneman gave a false address in San Francisco, the machine shop of an acquaintance, and described himself as a "mechanic."

The next day Ella May Clemmons died, without regaining consciousness. Groneman went straight from her deathbed to the apartment he had rented in Alameda, and tried in vain to get a refund on the rent before moving out. The physician was about to leave for Omaha, and did leave, returning much later. Before he went, he signed the death certificate, the cause of death being given as cholecystitis, jaundice, and uremia. But —the certificate was dated September 20, instead of the correct date of September 19 (apparently because the law requires that the physician signing a death certificate must have been in attendance at least twenty-four hours); and on information from Groneman it stated that the deceased had been a resident of Alameda for seven months instead of for the actual nine days. She was buried in Hayward, Alameda County.

While friends were calling up and being told that Miss Clemmons was "getting along nicely" at an unnamed sanitarium on the Peninsula, her ungrieving widower (who told the grand jury later that he had never loved her, that he married her "only because she wanted it") had appeared in a lawyer's office with a will dated February 16, 1931, making him sole heir. He stated, falsely, that they had been married for a year; and when he filed the will it bore a codicil in the form of an affidavit saying that he was the testator's husband and that she was "a legal resident of Alameda." Her own attorney said she told him she made another will in 1935, but it was never found. However, in all probability it also left her entire estate to Groneman.

This was the state of affairs when the *News*, put on the trail by suspicious acquaintances of the dead woman, ferreted out the whole unsavory story.

Both Groneman and Miss Enberg were subpoenaed to appear before the grand jury, and both told as little as they could. Miss Enberg, in fact, was threatened with contempt proceedings before she could be induced to talk at all. The "doctor" was less muddled and more cynical. He had not called a real physician earlier, he said, or sent Miss Clemmons to a hospital, because he "didn't think it necessary." Nevertheless his own diagnosis was cancer of the gall bladder; and she had had a hemorrhage the night before she died. He had sold her furniture (and

apparently also some valuable jewelry, never found),
because "she was my wife and I was settling her estate."
She had given him $75 a month for several years, because
he "never charged her for his services." His whole attitude was that the entire matter was nobody's business
but his own, and that the grand jury was being imperti-
nent in inquiring into it.

In February, 1936, Hjalmar Groneman was indicted
on charges of manslaughter and criminal negligence.
Charlotte Enberg missed by one vote an indictment for
manslaughter and conspiracy.

Immediately Groneman and Miss Enberg took out an
application for a marriage license. By California law
they had to wait three days before being able to marry.
This was a serious situation for the prosecution, since
the state law also provides that a wife cannot testify
against her husband, and Miss Enberg was the only important witness. Groneman went out of his way to remark superfluously to a newspaper reporter that he
didn't love Miss Enberg either, but was just marrying
her because her reputation had been injured by the reve-
lations before the grand jury.

The day the two could legally have been married, they
announced that they had changed their minds, and had
decided to postpone the wedding until after Groneman's
trial, so that he would not be accused of having married
merely to prevent Miss Enberg's testimony. The prosecution breathed a sigh of relief. The authorities should
have known "Doctor" Groneman better than that.

He retained State Senator Walter McGovern as attorney, and was arraigned before Judge Frank T. Deasy,

where he pleaded not guilty and was released on one thousand dollars' bail. For some unexplained reason he was not fingerprinted.

Immediately afterwards, before date had been set for his trial, Charlotte Enberg disappeared.

While efforts were being made to trace her, a move to have Miss Clemmon's body exhumed was made and then dropped. There had been no autopsy.

Search went on intensively for Miss Enberg, but she was never found. Alive or dead, under whatever name, she had simply dropped from sight. And she has stayed there ever since.

In December, 1936, the principal witness being un-available, and in all likelihood permanently unavailable, the case against Groneman was dismissed.

He had closed his San Francisco office, but he no longer needed to practise his profession. The will was valid, and he was executor and sole heir.

Six years later, through an investigation for assessment of Groneman's yacht, the *Rendezvous*, it was discovered that he had gone to Tibet. Later he was reported to be driving a truck on the Burma Road. The last direct news from "Doctor" Groneman came when he requested a woman who had been acting as his business agent to sail the yacht to Singapore. She refused. That was in 1941. Where Groneman is now—or where Miss Enberg is—is anybody's guess. If he survived the war, he is prob-ably still living comfortably somewhere on a large share of the Gould millions which so fatally descended to "the Christ Angel of Chinatown."

CHAPTER XI

Gentleman Jim:
JAMES J. CORBETT

FOR FIVE years, from 1892 to 1897, a native San Franciscan was heavyweight champion of the world. He was the first champion under the Marquis of Queensbury rules, "the father of scientific boxing," "the most scientific boxer who ever lived in any class," "the mathematician of the ring," "the most powerful single influence in giving the fight game a touch of respectability." To the late Norman Selby (Kid McCoy), who worshipped him and lost his entire savings on him in the Fitzsimmons fight, he was the man who had "pounded John L. Sullivan into insensibility, stood up to Peter Jackson for sixty-one rounds, and in three rounds whipped Charlie Mitchell, champion of England." W. O. McGeehan, the sports writer, said of him that "on his record he was the greatest of his time, and since his time is regarded as the greatest time of the prize ring, he must be at the end saluted as the greatest of the American heavyweight dynasty." He found prize fighting an affair of slugging between two bruisers, outlawed in every state except Louisiana; he left it a scientific sport whose major exhibitions call forth international radio broadcasts and front-page newspaper stories.

His name was James Joseph Corbett. He was one of the nine children of a livery-stable owner on Hayes Street, San Francisco, where, in the flat over the stable, he was born in September 1, 1866.

All the Corbetts were sports minded. Jim's heart as a boy was set more on baseball than on anything else; he was a major-league prospect till he split a finger. Joe Corbett was for a long time pitcher for the Baltimore Orioles. Harry and Tom Corbett were boxing authorities, the latter state boxing commissioner. And once, when Jim was a boy, his father and mother made a trip to the training quarters of the great John L. Sullivan himself, and at supper that night Mrs. Patrick Corbett told with trembling awe how "HE shook hands with us." Jim sat wide-eyed, his food forgotten. Someday he might behold the hero himself. He did—in an exhibition bout with "Professor" Robinson, thereafter known as "Peek-a-boo" because he took a count of nine in every round, trying to escape the terrible Sullivan, who yelled: "Whatcher doin' — playin' peek-a-boo?" But Corbett was eighteen before he gave up baseball and wrestling and took to boxing seriously.

Patrick Corbett made up his mind that one of his boys at least should have a good education, in spite of the six-thousand-dollar mortgage on the livery stable. He sent Jim to parochial school and then to the preparatory department of Sacred Heart College. Jim was a fair to average student; he wrote a good, angular hand, he had some mathematical ability, he was a bad speller but he read a lot, including the whole of Shakespeare. After school he sold newspapers downtown, one of his colleagues and his special chum being William A. Brady, later one of America's best-known theatrical managers. Brady was three years Corbett's senior, but as they grew older they "went with" sisters, and were more inseparable than ever. They were the usual tough, upright, devout, gregarious Irish-American lads of the lower middle class of whom San Francisco was full, especially "south of the slot." In addition, they both had more than the usual amount of brains. They were likeable boys; Jim had a quick temper in those days, but most of the time he was genial and friendly. He had been a frail child— which may have been why his father picked him to receive more schooling than the rest — but by rigorous exercise he had built himself into a husky youth in perfect physical trim.

When he was fifteen he quit school. The stable wasn't doing so well, and besides the mortgage there were other debts. Nine children cost a lot to clothe and feed, even when they brought in their newsboy pennies. Jim got a job as runner, or messenger, for the Wells-Fargo Bank. He did well, and he was gradually promoted until when he left the bank he was assistant paying teller.

He joined the Olympic Club, the oldest athletic club in the United States, and began to take regular boxing lessons from the instructor, Walter Watson, a hard-bitten Englishman with a punched-in nose. Watson could smell a coming champion from afar, no matter what had happened to his nose. He had his eye on Corbett from the first.

There was at that time a pest who loudly proclaimed himself as "club champion," and bullied every mem-

ber he could into letting himself be slugged. Watson had
to swallow the boasts because he was only the paid instructor; but he quietly set about training one of the
junior members to put a quietus on the braggart once
and for all. He picked Jim Corbett. In a few months
Watson judged the boy to be ready to take the man on.
He was. It was a short battle. The "club champion"
hit the floor hard in the very first round. He never put
on gloves in the Olympic Club again.

Corbett at this time had reached his full height of six
feet one and a half inches. His weight gradually increased until he passed through the welterweight, mid-
dleweight, and light heavyweight classes to reach full
heavyweight status at 187 pounds. His chief difficulty
was his hands. They were delicate, as had been proved in
his baseball-playing days; they could not possibly stand
the punishment which the power behind his blows could
have given them. People who said Jim Corbett was not
a hard hitter were completely mistaken. He could deliver a mighty blow, but in self-preservation he had to
save it up until it would do some good. Those weak
hands were Jim Corbett's boxing instructors. Because
of them he learned to box scientifically, to feint, to bob,
to weave, to spar—above all, to use his mind—to wear
his opponent down until he had him where he wanted
and could deliver the final punch. As Paul Gallico remarked, Corbett invented shadowboxing; he feinted
with his arms, his legs, his head, and he "could feint with
his eyebrows." The average pugilist of his day, even
the champions, near-champions, and ex-champions
whom he met, depended on brute strength; Corbett,

though he had and could use the strength, depended on his mental superiority.

They started at the Olympic Club calling him "Pompadour Jim" and "Gentleman Jim" in derision, because he was a bank clerk before he succeeded Watson as instructor, because he liked to associate with the business and professional men, the amateurs who made up the membership of the club, because (though he was no teetotaler) he was more at home in a French restaurant than in a barroom. He took up the gibe and flaunted it. To the end of his days, he loved to be called "Gentleman Jim." He modeled himself deliberately on the idea of the gentleman-pugilist, much as Gene Tunney was to do after him. In fact, Tunney's career is in many ways a parallel of Corbett's except that Tunney aspired even higher, socially, and that he retired from the championship, while Corbett held on to it until he was beaten.

Until 1890, Corbett, who still had no thought of turning professional boxer, was instructor at the Olympic Club, with D. C. Van Court, another Hayes Valley boy, as his assistant. He took on, in exhibition bouts, any of the club members or any stars of other athletic clubs in the Bay District. Once he broke the nose of John D. Spreckels, the sugar magnate. Years later he said that Jack Kitchen, afterwards Coast heavyweight champion but then an amateur with the old Acme Club in Oakland, was "the hardest man to hit" he had ever faced. But the decisive fight of this period, the fight or rather series of fights that first gave him more than strictly local renown, was with Joe Choynski, in 1889.

There was bad blood between Corbett and Choynski.

There was more truth than ballyhoo in the announce-
ment of the impending fight as "Labor vs. Capital,
Golden Gate Avenue vs. Hayes Street, Professional vs.
Amateur, Jew vs. Gentile, California Club vs. Olympic
Club."

It must be remembered that prize fighting then, like
cock fighting now, was an outlawed sport. Corbett and
Choynski met first on May 30, 1889, in a barn near San
Rafael, Marin County. The sheriff arrived in the fourth
round and broke up the fight. On June 5 the rivals met
again, this time on a barge anchored outside Benicia, in
Southampton Bay. Among Choynski's seconds were
Nat Goodwin and the earlier Jack Dempsey, "the Non-
pareil." Choynski wore ribbed driving gloves, Corbett
three-ounce mits; he had broken his right thumb in the
previous encounter and had to have some padding on it.
During this fight his delicate hands betrayed him again,
and he broke all the left-hand knuckles. Unable, because of the pain, to deliver a straight left, by necessity
he invented the left hook, which was consciously used
then for the first time. The fight lasted twenty-eight
hard rounds. In the twenty-eighth, Choynski took the
count of ten. But both participants were so exhausted
they had to be carried off the barge. A month later
Corbett beat Choynski again, this time in round four.
He had proved himself capable of knocking out a professional; he began seriously to think of turning professional himself. He was justified; in later years he called
the Benicia fight one of the toughest he had in his entire
career.

He left the Olympic Club instructorship, as he had

left the teller's cage, and set about preparing for his new career. Already, in the back of his mind, was the idea of challenging the heavyweight champion, the mighty, the redoubtable John L. Sullivan, whose huge paw Jim Corbett's father and mother had once been allowed humbly to shake. He studied the methods, the strengths, the weaknesses, of other fighters; and he studied their minds as closely as he did their bodies.

In July, 1889, in the last bare-knuckle bout in America, Sullivan had knocked out Jake Kilrain in the seventy-fifth round. In February, 1890, at New Orleans, Jim Corbett knocked out Kilrain in the sixth. Next he took on Peter Jackson, the giant Negro whom Sullivan had refused to fight, drawing the color line. In May, 1891, Corbett fought him for sixty-one rounds. The referee then stopped the fight. Jackson was helpless, and unable to take any more punishment.

Back in San Francisco, the great "Jawn L." appeared on one of the exhibition tours which were his custom after he became champion. Here was Corbett's golden opportunity. Sullivan was persuaded, on a purely non-commercial basis, to box four rounds, in the Grand Opera House, for the benefit of the Olympic Club, with the club's ex-instructor, "Gentleman Jim" Corbett. Amused and contemptuous, Sullivan agreed, but he would not waste energy by stripping for such a show. Besides, there would be ladies present. So both participants appeared in full-dress suits, taking off their top hats, coats, and vests for the match. Sullivan was supremely confident, as always. All he had to do was to let loose his unbeatable punch. Only—Corbett was never there to punch. He held Sullivan off for the scheduled four rounds. At the end he whispered to his second: "I feel sure that I can beat Sullivan if I ever have a chance to meet him, because I can hit him and he can't hit me." After the bout, Sullivan and his pals adjourned to the nearest barroom. Corbett, tipping the wink to a friend, relaxed on — ice cream and strawberries!

A few months later, in a Chicago saloon, Corbett heard Sullivan boast, "I can lick any —— in the world." Politely, Corbett contradicted him. Sullivan laughed. Corbett said nothing more and bided his time.

He was then en route to New York, where his old friend, William A. Brady, had invited him to appear on the stage. He was to spar in a concert-hall scene in the melodrama, *After Dark,* which Brady was then producing. Corbett's first experience as an actor was brief. Brady decided instead to become Jim's fight manager, and in his name to challenge Sullivan for the heavyweight title. He put up $2,500 as an initial payment on the $10,000 required, and the match was arranged for September 7, 1892, in New Orleans.

Jim had been using his head, and by this time he had Sullivan very well sized up. He knew his temper, his self-confidence, his domineering spirit. He knew that Sullivan (or his press agent—the phrase was a bit beyond the champion's vocabulary) was calling Jim "a bombastic bluffer." He deliberately played up to the situation. In New Orleans, during his training period, he dressed like the fashionable "dude" of the period, fancy clothes, little cane, and all. He encouraged Sullivan to think he had a walkover. "I studied," he said, "to dominate Sullivan instead of his bullying me."

Sullivan wanted Corbett in his corner first, so that he could appear as the climax and receive the roars of the crowd. Corbett courteously and modestly said that as the challenger it would not be fitting for him to precede the champion. Sullivan bellowed his insistence. Very well, Corbett agreed. He entered the hall with a very light round of applause; no one knew him in New Orleans. But as he reached the ring, he turned to an utter stranger, held out his hands, and cried: "Why, what are *you* doing here? It's fine to see you!" He engaged the bewildered man in conversation until Sullivan, who had already entered, had no choice but to climb in the ring and go to his corner. The process of enraging the bull had started. For Jim Corbett in the ring was the nearest thing to a matador which this country has ever seen.

D. C. Van Court, who succeeded Corbett as instructor at the Olympic Club, remarks in his book, *The Making of Champions in California*, that "in a twenty-round fight Jim Corbett could easily defeat any heavyweight champion that ever lived." However, he ranks Corbett behind both Jim Jeffries and Sullivan because he was not so strong as either. In the championship match with Sullivan, Corbett did not need twenty rounds, though the fight went to the twenty-first. In the third round he broke Sullivan's nose—the equivalent of the picador's thrust in a bullfight. He feinted, he sparred, he weaved —and Sullivan had no answer except the straightforward rush on an antagonist who was never there. "Come

out and fight, you!" he yelled to Corbett—but Corbett
wasn't ready. "I delayed hitting him," he said afterwards, "and then I *hit*." The knockout came in the
twenty-first round by a left hook, the strategy Corbett
had learned by necessity in the barge fight with
Choynski.

As the great, the unbeatable "Jawn L." lay on the
sawdust, "Gentleman Jim" pronounced his obituary.
"The old pitcher has gone to the well once too often,"
he said.

In the Olympic Club, where they had been watching
anxiously the stereopticon slides cast on the screen giving the progress of the fight as it was reported by telegraph, there was high carnival after the final triumphant
flash. In Patrick Corbett's livery stable, there was open
house all night and plenty of free beer. Good reason for
that—for the fight was for "winner take all," and Jim
had collected $25,000 plus a side bet of $10,000, and
the very next morning he wired his father enough to
pay off the mortgage and all his debts.

But elsewhere, even in San Francisco, there was no
rejoicing. The odds had been six to one; most of the
fight fans in the country were wiped out. In many cases
people refused to believe the news, and would not pay
their bets until the fact had been confirmed, a few days
later, by the *Police Gazette*.

Besides, Sullivan had been the fight followers' idol.
Far from being admired, Corbett found himself abused
and reproached for having taken from the pugilistic
scene this colorful and satisfying figure who had been
supreme for ten years. "We do not want gentlemanly

fighters," said the New York *World*, the next day. "We
want a fighter to be nothing on this earth but a fighter."
It was several years, almost time for him to face losing
the championship he had won, before "Gentleman Jim"
was really popular. We have seen the same phenomenon
ourselves in regard to Dempsey and Tunney; but no
prize fighter of today has ever occupied the almost
legendary position of John L. Sullivan in his great days.
It was impressive, not just a vaudeville joke, to be invited
in that era to "shake the hand that shook the hand of
John L. Sullivan."

As for Corbett, he remained for the time under
Brady's management, and for several years he alternated
between exhibition bouts and acting. As an actor, it
seems to be agreed that he was a good boxer. In general, his plays had something to do with boxing—the
best of them was Shaw's *Cashel Byron's Profession*, a
play made from a novel about a gentleman prize fighter.
There was also one called *Gentleman Jack*, which was
openly a *drame à clef*. Also there were melodramas, in
the style of the one in which he had first appeared, *After
Dark: or, Neither Wife, Maid, nor Widow, The Naval
Cadet, The Adventurer*.

Alternating with these, Corbett boxed all comers of
sufficient rank, and prepared to defend his title when it
should be challenged. He returned frequently to San
Francisco, and always to the Olympic Club. Once when
he was there, a truculent Irish warehouseman who had
never forgiven the trouncing of Sullivan offered to put
up his fists to the heavyweight champion. Corbett
agreed with a smile. The warehouseman never got a

chance to touch Jim. He was kept so busy protecting his face and body from feints, that finally with a wild swing he knocked himself cold!

Sometime during this period Corbett consented to box four rounds with a young Scottish laborer who fancied himself as a pugilist. The youngster proved his mettle; he had to be good to face Corbett even so long. Later on, the young man lost his leg in an accident, and perforce turned, first house painter, and ultimately a portrait and landscape painter of great talent, though all his life he was essentially a self-taught workingman. He died recently, a lately "discovered" artist. His name was John Kane.

But between 1892 and 1897 Corbett also fought several matches with professional pugilists of standing. Among them were Charlie Mitchell, the English champion; Peter Courtney; and Sailor Tom Sharkey, all well-known names in their day and even now. The first two of these contenders he beat, the third he fought to a draw in an exhibition bout in Mechanics' Pavilion, San Francisco.

A champion prize fighter by tradition (though there have been many exceptions) is expected to go soft from easy living and the usual excesses. Corbett remained "Gentleman Jim," a title he prized as highly as he did his championship belt. No scandal ever touched his name. In 1886 he had married the girl with whom he had "gone" in San Francisco while Brady "went with" her sister. She was Olive Lake, who had gone on the stage. In 1895 she secured a divorce from him, and a month later, at Asbury Park, New Jersey, he married

Jessie Taylor, of Omaha. They remained a devoted, though childless, couple all the rest of his life. In spite of his divorce and his remarriage to a Protestant, Corbett was always a devout and practicing Catholic.

Without being a spendthrift, he was a free spender, as people are likely to be who have been used to financial restrictions in youth and then discover a seeming gold mine. But he did not waste his money, as Sullivan had done, standing drinks to yes-men in saloons. A fashionable restaurant and the company of "bankers, statesmen, and sportsmen" were more to his taste, a taste formed in the Wells-Fargo Bank and the Olympic Club.

But he was emphatically never a snob. When he came home, as he did often, to San Francisco, his headquarters was his parents' home over the livery stable. He was amiable to the old friends of the family who flocked to see him, and took meekly his brother's scoldings if he could not remember everybody's name. And though he was more often seen in the Palace or the St. Francis Hotel than in the Irish section south of Market Street, he never snubbed an acquaintance of the old Hayes Valley days. Once he was leaving the St. Francis with a group of Nob Hill acquaintances when a sprinkling cart passed by, and the old man who drove it pulled up his horses and called: "Jim!" "Pat!" responded Corbett enthusiastically; and for ten minutes they held up traffic on Powell Street while the champion gossiped with the watering-cart driver.

One of San Francisco's pet lunatics in those days was an imbecile nicknamed "Oofty Goofty," who made his living by letting people punch and kick him, since he was largely insensible to pain. Once, however, John L. Sullivan had struck him with a billiard cue, and seriously injured him. Oofty Goofty hated Sullivan after that, and when Corbett knocked out Sullivan, Oofty Goofty decided that Corbett was his "agent" and had acted by his orders to avenge him. Whenever Corbett was in town, Oofty Goofty tagged him as much as he could, his faithful shadow.

It was on one of his visits to San Francisco that Corbett, with a sparring partner, put on a private bout for Lillie Hitchcock Coit in her rooms at the Palace Hotel, so that Mrs. Coit might see the great boxer perform, without attending a prize fight.

Once in a while, at the Olympic Club, Corbett tried his old hobby of wrestling. George Mehling, the wrestling instructor, a short, barrel-shaped man, he had once derided as a "German sausage." Mehling got Corbett down with a scissors hold, unable to escape from the mat, and demanded that he take it back. Pinned inexorably, the world's heavyweight champion was forced to apologize humbly before the little German let him loose!

The showdown and the final challenge to "Gentleman Jim's" championship came in 1897 when he was booked to meet Bob ("Ruby Rob") Fitzsimmons, at Carson City, Nevada, on March 17. It was Saint Patrick's Day, but for once the patron saint of the Irish deserted and favored the Sassenach!

Corbett's sparring partner at the training camp in Carson City was James J. Jeffries, who was later first to take the title and then prevent Corbett's regaining it.

By the time Corbett met Fitzsimmons, although no one ever had exactly the place in the fight fans' hearts once held by John L. Sullivan, "Gentleman Jim" was a popular favorite. "Ruby Rob," with his red hair and freckles and aggressive jaw, was a throwback to the "strong boy" tradition as opposed to the clever boxer. And Corbett, genial as he was in private life, a good fellow, a raconteur, with a touch of pardonable and likeable vanity, in the ring became transformed. "Disdainful," "cold," and "merciless" were the terms applied to him as a fighter. The matador baiting the bull recurs to one's mind. Sometimes it was more like a cat playing with a mouse—or a lion playing with a human victim.

Once more flashes of the progress of a championship fight were thrown on the screen in San Francisco, but this time not merely at the Olympic Club, but in front of every newspaper office, where crowds gathered who remembered fervently (most of them had bet their shirts on the outcome) that Corbett was "one of ours," a Hayes Valley boy.

The fight lasted for fourteen rounds. Perhaps it can be recalled most vividly in the reminiscence of a distinguished man who was then a very young shipping clerk in the basement of a wholesale shoe company near the old *Chronicle* building. The young man, though he had never seen (and never did see) a prize fight, had an uncanny facility for "calling" them, based on a scientific study of the conditions and the participants. He never bet on them, for he had a feeling that if he were personally involved his judgment would be weakened.

But every employee of the shoe company had been reluctantly persuaded, by the young man's reputation as a "picker," to put his hard-earned money on Fitzsimmons.

"As the fight went on," he said, "one man after another would rush down to me in the basement, and exclaim: 'Are you sure you're right? The flash at the *Chronicle* says Corbett's having everything his own way.' 'Fitzsimmons will win,' I would answer. At the end of the thirteenth round one fellow ran down almost in tears. 'It's all up!' he cried. 'The flash says Fitz is staggering all around the ring, covered with blood. You'd better not be here when Corbett knocks him out and every one of us has lost our money because we listened to you!' 'Go upstairs and don't worry,' I said. 'Fitzsimmons will win.' He left sadly. In a minute he was back. He threw his arms around my neck. 'There were only two words on the screen,' he cried jubilantly— 'Fitz wins!' "

Fitzsimmons had knocked Corbett out by a solar-plexus blow, his own invention, and used for the first time. As W. J. Doherty remarks in his book, *In the Days of the Giants,* up to the very instant of the knockout, Corbett would undoubtedly have won on points.

After the defeat by Fitzsimmons, Corbett made several futile attempts at a comeback. He left Brady's management for that of George Considine, though he returned later to Brady, who was also managing Jeffries. He opened a restaurant in New York, on Broadway between Thirty-third and Thirty-fourth Streets, and for about a year it was a great success; then he was obliged to neglect it because of his other interests, and it failed. He appeared in vaudeville, on both the Keith-Orpheum and Pantages circuits, giving sparring exhibitions and playing in sketches built around boxing. (In 1941, he himself became the subject of a motion picture.)

Jeffries became champion in 1899 by beating Fitzsimmons in eleven rounds. Corbett, returned to Brady's management, fought his former sparring partner twice —at Coney Island in 1900 and in San Francisco in 1903, Corbett's last fight. The 1900 fight went to twenty-three rounds, and for the first sixteen things looked bad for Jeffries, but he rallied and knocked out Corbett (by Corbett's own invention, the left hook) in the twenty-third. Corbett by this time was thirty-three, which is old age for a fighter. But Van Court says that if it had been twenty rounds, Corbett would have taken the decision.

Three months later he met and defeated Kid McCoy, who had never resented the loss of all he had on the Fitzsimmons fight, but who throughout his own tragic later career continued his youthful hero worship of "Gentleman Jim." There were some grumblings about this fight, some talk of "fake," based apparently on nothing but the fact that Corbett was supposed by now to have the habit of failure. Corbett's indignant denial ended summarily the only accusation of the sort ever brought against him.

In 1903, in the Mechanics' Pavilion in San Francisco, where he had fought Sharkey to a draw, Corbett was knocked out in the tenth round by Jeffries. Jeffries was two years from retirement, seven years from the unlucky day when he emerged to be beaten by Jack Johnson at

James J. Corbett. Ex-champion and vaudeville actor.

Reno. It was Corbett's last professional match. The fight grossed $62,000, then a world's record.

He returned to the stage, to vaudeville, to the lecture platform, and in later years he appeared also before the microphone. With his fine physique, his infectious smile, and his bright blue eyes, he was more popular on the stage than was justified by any acting ability he had. As early as 1905, he anticipated Orson Welles by advocating Shakespeare in modern dress, though he never (perhaps fortunately) got the chance he wanted to play "an up-to-date 'Hamlet.' "

A series of newspaper articles under his name gained him the undeserved reputation — him whom Doherty had called "the greatest judge of boxing and boxers"— of being "the man who never picked a winner." Finally, in self-defense, Corbett was obliged to acknowledge that the articles were ghost-written, and that it was his "ghost" who insisted on making (invariably wrong) predictions. However, it is probable that he himself wrote his autobiography, *The Roar of the Crowd*— though George P. Putnam claimed it was written by R. G. Anderson.

For more than a quarter century, all the years left to him, Corbett and his wife lived quietly at Bayside Queens, New York, in a small stucco house overlooking Littleneck Bay. He commuted often to Manhattan, and was never missing from the Polo Grounds when the Giants played there, for he was a faithful rooter. He was a member both of the Friars and of the Lambs Clubs. At the latter club, when he applied for membership, he received more endorsements than any other man in the club's history. Unaccustomed to saving money, as the years passed on he had to think of his financial future. At one time he contemplated opening a health farm, but abandoned the idea. In the end, what with writing, lecturing, and careful investment unharmed by the debacle of 1929, he managed to leave an estate of about twenty thousand dollars. He was not without social consciousness, either. In 1930, at the beginning of the depression, he was chairman of the special Emergency Employment Committee of the Borough of Queens. Two years later, purely as a hobby and a public service, he promoted amateur boxing matches at Jamaica.

Always very young in appearance—he never received a mark on his face in the ring — Corbett slipped into approaching old age without realizing it. What brought him up short in his middle sixties was fatal illness. Jim Corbett never knew what his disease was. By a kindly conspiracy his wife and his physician, Dr. G. Willard Dickey, kept from him the truth that he was suffering from carcinoma of the liver. Dr. Dickey told him— and even told the newspapers, since Corbett was an indefatigable newspaper reader — that the trouble was heart disease. It was not until after his death that the revelation was made.

He had been critically ill since January, 1933, and he had the last rites of his church at the beginning of February; but so extraordinary was his vitality that he not only remained conscious but actually insisted on leaving his bed on February 16. Then he lapsed into a coma. On the 18th he died, in his wife's arms as he had wished, and so quietly that she did not even know that he was dead. He had refused to have a nurse, and only two old friends, John and Dennis Kelleher, were with her.

A long list of honorary pallbearers, from Corbett's friends among sportsmen, actors, politicians, and businessmen, was drawn up, but in the end there were so many that none at all was asked to serve. The brother and three sisters who survived him were unable to go to New York from San Francisco. But his funeral, in a pouring rain, called out two thousand persons who came to say good-by to "Gentleman Jim." It was held from St. Malachy's, the "Actor's Church," in Manhattan, by his own long-ago request, for he had often worshiped there. For the two days before the funeral, Bayside had had to provide special traffic officers to handle the crowds who came, in limousines and broken-down jallopies and even on foot, to look at him for the last time, as he lay, first in bed in his old rose-colored dressing gown, emaciated and weighing only 140 pounds, his rosary wound around his left hand, and later in state in his bronze coffin. He was buried in a crypt he had bought in Cypress Hills, a nonsectarian cemetery, so that his non-Catholic wife could, when her time came, lie beside him.

"The inventor of shadow-boxing," Paul Gallico called him. "Feinting was a lost art after him." Others spoke of his "almost fabulous career" as a boxer, recited again how he raised prize fighting from the sport of bruisers and plug uglies to a science and an art. In May, 1933, friends planted a memorial tree for him in Crocheron Park, New York. There is no visible memorial to him in his birthplace. (They tell a story of Tony Galento, the heavyweight who trains on beer, that when he visited the Olympic Club and was shown a picture of Corbett, he asked blankly: "Who's he?" "Aw, you know," answered his manager, Joe Jacobs. "He used to be manager of this here club!") But no San Franciscan has ever forgotten "Gentleman Jim" Corbett, the Hayes Valley boy, the bank clerk, the Olympic Club instructor, who became "the most competent and graceful heavyweight pugilist who ever drew on the gloves."

Literally and figuratively, he had lived up to his own advice. Someone once asked him, says Milton Bacon, what a man must do to become champion. "Fight one more round," answered "Gentleman Jim."

CHAPTER XII

Laureate of Bohemia:
GEORGE STERLING

IT WAS like a unicorn dying . . . or one of those sinewy and eternal children of Pan," Idwal Jones wrote when George Sterling, on a November day, swallowed poison and slipped away from his "cool gray city of love." One does not write or feel so of ordinary men. Whatever George Sterling was or was not, he was not ordinary. To quote Jones again, he "became while still in the flesh half-fabulous."

The night before he died, Robinson Jeffers, in his stone tower near Carmel, dreamed that he and Sterling were in the "stone twilight" of an ancient church. The day was fading, and Jeffers rose and departed. But Sterling would not go. He was still there in the shadows when Jeffers left—and awoke.

That same evening Ethel Turner, the novelist, who with her husband had kept house for Sterling in Carmel after he and his wife were separated, was in a Chinese restaurant in San Francisco with friends. Someone in the party idly started telling fortunes in the tea leaves. All she could see in Mrs. Turner's cup was "a ghostly Dante-esque figure leaning over a cross." Mrs. Turner laughed. "The only person I know who looks like Dante," she said, "is George Sterling." The seer tried once more, but could find only the same portent of death. After the next day, she would never read a fortune in a teacup again.

There is something old-fashioned in all this, something romantic and *fin-de-siècle,* which fits its subject well. George Sterling, to California and above all to San Francisco, was The Poet, a holdover from the days when, as Robert Cortes Holliday puts it, "a poet was popularly expected to be a picturesque figure." His personality, his appearance, and his poetry all belonged together; and about all of them was a faint haze of long ago and far away. Those who knew him loved him, and with cause; but it is difficult, in the harder and more complex age which has come upon us even in the few years since his death, to describe him so that to eyes that did not know him he will not seem slightly ridiculous.

No one writes or reads today his kind of poetry—noble, sonorous, richly colored, but also platitudinous and bombastic. His work is as dead as that of Stephen Phillips or Ernest Dowson, with both of whom he had much in common. Perhaps, if we ever attain again a period of calm between storms, this sort of rolling, dignified imagery, by Tennyson out of Keats, will have its day once more. There are mines of beauty in it as well as shreds of fustian. Today those who still cherish it do so with a nostalgic twinge. The man and his writing together belong to a past that is still remembered. Sterling was as much a part of San Francisco as the ferryboats or the cable cars. But the ferryboats are gone, and the cable cars may go soon too. His world was dying around him before he left it.

Every attribute of the traditional poet was Sterling's except one—conceit. He was the most modest man who ever lived. He carried his pockets full of poems and gave them away to anyone who asked. He left as much unpublished as published, and doubtless as much again was lost. He refused lucrative offers from Eastern publishers because he wanted the San Francisco imprint on his books and was grateful to A. M. Robertson, who had first placed it there. He submitted himself like a little boy to the crippling criticism of Ambrose Bierce; he let Jack London give him lessons in authorship; in his last years he tried humbly and vainly to write like Robinson Jeffers. It was fortunate for him (though not for his work) that he had this engaging quality. No man with an ounce of vanity could have withstood the adulation he received, the comparisons with Shakespeare and Coleridge and Poe, with Shelley and Euripides. He stood up well, too, under the personal worship, the women who came to pick up the shavings from his chopping block in Carmel, the pilgrims who journeyed to sit at his feet as once he had gone to sit at Joaquin Miller's, the almost visible laurel set upon his brow by a self-conscious Bohemia of which he was the undisputed king.

Modesty, loyalty to the point of fanaticism, and a generosity as wide as the sky were his salient characteristics; but with them he combined an uneasy nature, subnormal in energy, whipped to stimulus only by alcohol or sex, seclusive and claustrophobic. This Lord of Bohemia was essentially introverted; he was happiest and best and most himself tramping the hills and woods and seashore in his Lincoln green clothes. As ardent a swimmer as Swinburne, a keen hunter and fisherman in spite of a reputation which accredited him with reluctance to "crush even a spider," he was the legitimate descendant of his grandfather, the old whaling captain of Sag Harbor. He was also, unhappily for him, the legitimate descendant of the neurotic physician who was his father.

George Sterling was born in Sag Harbor, Long Island, New York, at the end of 1869. Next door lived Julian Hawthorne, whose children played with the nine little Sterlings. George was an ordinary, normal small boy, leaving memories of a "pirate flag" posted in the steeple of the Presbyterian Church, and similar pranks. He was sent to the public schools and the public high school. He was a good, diligent student with streaks of laziness, and no one suspected him of any particular literary talent.

When he was seventeen, his father was converted from the Episcopal to the Roman Catholic Church, and brought his family into the new faith with him. Like many converts, he became a zealot. He determined that one of his three sons must be a priest. George, the eldest, was experimented on first. He was sent to St. Charles College, near Ellicott City, Maryland, conducted by the Sulpician Fathers. He remained there three years.

The professor of English at this college chanced to be a fine and undeservedly forgotten poet, John Banister Tabb. It is tempting to think that Father Tabb would recognize and encourage the budding genius of the boy from Sag Harbor, would train and develop his reading and his style. It is a temptation to which several eminent critics have succumbed. Unluckily the facts are quite to the contrary. Tabb was also a convert from Episcopalianism, but there any resemblance between him and Sterling ceased. He was a Virginian, a Confederate veteran who had served time in a Federal prison, a close friend of Sidney Lanier, and an admirer of Poe. He was a classicist, a lyrist with an almost Greek touch, and also a satirist with an earthy, almost Swiftian approach. The only American poet whom he suggests in the least is Emily Dickinson.

Sterling dutifully admired Father Tabb, but Tabb might as well have been writing in another language so far as any influence he could have on the boy might go. Moreover, by the account of a classmate who was very close to Tabb, lived with him afterwards and was almost his adopted son, Sterling was not even a favorite of Tabb's. The school was populated mostly by hearty, tough Irish boys, or second-generation Irish, from New York. They did not care for the few stiff, starched lads from another environment whom they called "English" or "Episcopalian" or "High Church," in derision. And Tabb shared their distaste. Like the English metaphysical poets of the seventeenth century, he was intent on reality, even though it were an inner reality; and bourgeois conventionality seemed to him unreal.

There is an amusing instance of the extent to which Sterling was out of touch with his companions. A quarter of a century later he remarked to this same classmate, William McDevitt, that in his three years at St. Charles he had never heard a profane or obscene word! "If that is so," remarked McDevitt, "it means only that you never played ball with the boys or were really one with them." Sterling himself, though he had the most picturesque and inimitable vocabulary of vituperation, was highly squeamish about ordinary smut or profanity. He had indeed that nice-Nelliness which is often characteristic of the Don Juan type. (Bierce, who was no Don Juan, was even more fastidious; at the Bohemian Grove in Sonoma County he was shocked even by Sterling's remarkably decent bathing suit!)

At all events, Sterling got nothing much in the way of literary impulse at St. Charles, and seems not even to have had any literary aspirations. His was a very slow development as a poet. The chief thing he appears to have learned from Tabb was to enjoy eating nasturtiums! He was not graduated from the college, which was for most of its pupils a steppingstone to the theological seminary. By this time his father knew George would never be a priest. In fact, George's Catholicism had been something less than skin deep, and he very speedily became the pagan he remained for the rest of his life. Dr. Sterling tried the process on his second son, Wickham, equally without success; the third son, James, did actually achieve ordination, but died soon after. Just how far George's education went is no longer ascertainable, but he told someone afterwards he had never read a line of Latin poetry. R. L. Burgess noted long afterwards that "his knowledge of all the poets was that of a lover, not a student." Outside of astronomy, which he did know well in an amateur way, his acquaintance with science was negligible. He was a devout adherent of Dr. Abrams and his Electronic Reactions.

Since he had no bent for any profession, the only thing left to do with him was to put him in business. In 1890 his father shipped him off to Oakland to work in the office of his mother's brother, Frank C. Havens, who was laying the foundations of a fortune in California real estate. Reluctantly, and compelled only by poverty, George Sterling was a clerk in his uncle's office for the next fifteen years. It was during those years—part of the time literally while commuting by ferry between San Francisco and Oakland—that he began to write poetry. Once the psychic dam was burst, the flood came in full spate. The final impulse was given by Ambrose Bierce, whom Sterling met in 1892. But it was five years more before he wrote very much.

Though there were periods of alienation, and Bierce's last letter to Sterling was an angry one, he was the greatest single influence in the younger man's life through all his formative years as a writer. Bierce, with his strange twisted need for domination, his tortured misanthropy, his rigid limitations of style, was bad and bitter medicine in some ways. But in others he was good, for where at last he was convinced he gave generously of praise, and Sterling was always one to do better under encouragement. "You grow great so rapidly that I shall not much longer dare to touch your work"—that was heartening to a poet still three years from his first volume. "You shall be the poet of the skies, the prophet of the suns," wrote Bierce when *The Testimony of the Suns* came out in its first small edition in 1903.

Bierce's was a jealous nature, and he demanded that his disciples have no other gods before him. He did not

mind Sterling's friendship with Herman Scheffauer, another promising poet (who later, crushed by World War
I and its aftermath, killed himself by poison while
New York *Times* correspondent in Berlin), because
Scheffauer was also a Bierce worshiper. But he resented
fiercely Sterling's new and close intimacy with Jack
London. Bierce and London met only once, and the
meeting was not a success. Bierce was especially antag-
onistic because Sterling, with his quick reliance on other
people's viewpoints, had immediately announced himself a socialist, since London was one. As a matter of
fact, London's own socialism (though he joined the
party, as it is not certain that Sterling ever did) was
hardly orthodox, and Sterling's was little more than a
vague humanitarianism, and was dropped at its first real
test.

Even this, however, was too much for Bierce, who was
violently anti-labor. Some of the sentences in his letters
to Sterling sound as if they came from Hitler or Musso-
lini. "Let the 'poor' alone—they are oppressed by nobody but God. Nobody hates them, nobody despises.
'The rich' love them a deal better than they love one
another. . . . I would not live in a state under union labor
rule. There is still one place where the honest American
laboring man is not permitted to cut throats and strip
bodies of women at his own sweet will. That is the District of Columbia. . . . I note that at the late election
[1912] California damned herself to a still lower degra-
dation and is now unfit for a white man to live in.
Initiative, referendum, recall, employers' liability,
woman suffrage—yah!" And then this openly Hitlerian

remark: "I yearn for the strong-handed Dictator who will swat you all on the mouths."

Bierce's constant effort was to keep Sterling securely locked in an ivory tower. Because other influences were around Sterling, the effort was not altogether successful; other voices stole in at the barred windows—voices belonging to Jack London, to Upton Sinclair, to Austin Lewis. But to a great extent Bierce did force Sterling's talent into a narrow channel, where the only escape from grandiose romanticism was into light verse and the facetiousness of such things as "The Abalone Song." Sterling, as has been said, refused to take his muse as a responsibility; he boasted that he could "rhyme to order and do it well." In consequence he seldom reached real fulfillment of his indubitable powers. He acknowledged in after years that "Ambrose Bierce laid a hand of ice on my youthful enthusiasm," but he remained "a Bierce fanatic," as H. L. Mencken called him, to the end.

Perhaps he knew his own lyrical and wayward nature best, so far as concerned him as a writer. As a man he never understood himself so well. If he had, he would never have married, as he did marry, the beautiful statuesque Caroline Rand out of his uncle's office in 1896. George Sterling could neither make any woman happy, nor himself be happy with any woman. As Mary Austin says, "he made a kind of life-philosophy of his dependence upon women. . . . He was never able to enter into the psychic life of any woman." Sara Bard Field notes that "the feminine side of his nature was not nourished by the love relation. It fed, rather, on friendships with men." And Charmian London remarks acutely of his relation to his wife: "He was not her man; he was no one's man—not even his own man." Like so many extreme varietists, he was unconsciously slightly epicene in temperament; the woman was not born who could hold and satisfy all of his roving nature. Throughout his marriage there was one "episode" after another, until the scandalous one that broke it. And through all the rest of his years, there were always several women at one time, each of whom sincerely believed that she alone held his heart. He did not intend to deceive them; he simply could not help the tender, ingratiating adoration with which he melted the hardest spirit. The bevy of women (aside from his six sisters) who wept through his funeral, one unfeeling commentator dubbed "the committee." When he died, at least one woman firmly thought she was engaged to marry him; and another woman unfortunately allowed a public statement to appear that certain of his poems were written to her, were the fruits of a long and hopeless love of her—the very same poems which other women cherished under the same delusion. At his death it was discovered that he had for a quarter of a century paid rent on a small locked room in the historic Montgomery Block, into and out of which he would flit secretively. The papers announced that doubtless it was full of manuscripts, that perhaps the greatest of his work would now be found. It was empty. An old friend acknowledged that it had been merely the place he had used for rendezvous.

All this in another man would have spelled caddishness; but not in Sterling. To him all things were permitted, because his utmost dalliance was inextricably

tied up with generosity, tenderness, and a lasting loyalty
that might drop a lover but never lost a friend. And as
in his sex life he was judged even by Babbitts as a man
privileged and apart, so too in his alcoholic habits. Mary
Austin thought that "for Sterling alcohol was the apparatus by which all his energies were stepped up to the
creative level. . . . He was ridden by restless impotencies
of energy, which only by sharp exaggeration of sensation
would find their natural outlet in creative expression."
This is a penetrating observation, much keener than
Upton Sinclair's idea of Sterling as the helpless victim
of evil companions and of the "place of satyrs," which
was the harmless, rather tepid Bohemian Club where he
lived from 1915 to his death. He drank steadily even in
his Carmel days, when he had swimming and walking
and wood chopping to provide other energy outlets. In
later years, he went for long periods without drinking;
then his dread of failing power came upon him, or the
tangle and burden of life became too oppressive, and he
found relief in liquor. Alcohol was a true poison to him;
he was one of the persons who should never have touched
it, for it never brought him the happy relaxation which
it brings to the genuine moderate social drinker. It was
only then that he ever became quarrelsome or surly, especially if his privacy were violated, or his hidden claus-
trophobia impinged upon. Once in Oakland with Austin
Lewis during some popular fiesta, the crowd in the
street so irritated him that he lowered his head like a
goat and butted his way through the throng. Again, at
a dinner when he mistakenly thought someone had made
a slighting allusion to a friend ("I am on my knees to

that man!" he had just exclaimed with his customary romantic exaggeration), he drew a useful-looking knife and announced that he would be glad to employ it on the supposed maligner. But, in general, even at the end of a long bout, Sterling was still Sterling—ill and exhausted, ashamed of silly exploits avidly seized on by the newspapers—wading in the Golden Gate Park lakes by moonlight for water lilies, and poetic gestures of that variety—but still integrally his sad and lovable self.

Between *The Testimony of the Suns* in 1903 and *The Wine of Wizardry* in 1909, Sterling published no volume. All this time he was chafing in bondage to his uncle's office; part of it he lived in Piedmont, where he made money for the first time, by investing in and selling residential lots through and with Havens. He and Jack London—"Greek" and "Wolf" to each other—and other close friends tramped the hills above Oakland, came back to his fireplace to talk the night away over gallons of red wine. Whenever money ran short, his aunt, Mrs. Havens (who, incidentally, was also his sister-in-law), unobtrusively supplied the lack. And it was she who saw how unbearable a business existence was becoming for him, and found him a way out by advancing the money for him to buy land and build a house on the Monterey Peninsula.

Sterling was not the first writer or artist to settle in what became Carmel, but he drew others after him until before long there was an actual colony—now only a hollow copy of its first carefree, simple being—of which he was the heart. Mary Austin, James M. Hopper, Albert Bender, Herbert Heron, John K. Turner

George Sterling when he was king of San Francisco's Bohemia.

and his first wife Ethel, sometimes Jack London and Upton Sinclair, were the inner circle. The sisters, Alice MacGowan and Grace MacGowan Cooke, were there, and often the beautiful, doomed Nora May French. It was in Sterling's house that Nora May French took poison and died, in 1907. "Our little sister left music and memories behind her," wrote Sterling of his fellow poet. He had no part in her unhappiness or her death, though scandal as usual was busy with his name. But her suicide haunted him, and every year on its anniversary, in his fated November, he visited the spot on Point Lobos where her ashes had been strewn.

But that house held happy memories, too, many more than it held of sorrowful ones. Its center and soul was the long living room, lined with books, covered with paintings by Charles Rollo Peters, Xavier Martinez, and other California artists of that early twentieth-century Bohemian group, and dominated by the huge fireplace, on whose mantel stood seashells brought by Jack London from the South Seas. Near the house stood a shack which Sterling used as a studio, and the barbecue oven which was the scene of innumerable clam and mussel bakes. Hard by it stood a pine grove, on whose trees Sterling had fixed the skulls of horses and cattle that he had picked up on the hills around. Robinson Jeffers, when first he came to Carmel, chanced on this grove and felt for a weird moment that he was in the presence of some ancient sacrificial rite.

Worn out by too frequent forgiving of too many escapades, Carrie Sterling left abruptly in 1912. But the thread was not yet broken; she returned for a few

months more. Then an affair of scandalous proportions
became the prey of every wagging tongue, and she left
again and forever. Sterling wrote a satirical song dedicated to "The Old Cats of Carmel," "bached it" for a
while disconsolately in his shack, then asked the Turners
to live in the house, cook for him, and hush the demanding voices of its memories. In a year he could no longer
endure Carmel even by this compromise. He went to
New York, his first time East since he went West in
1890, and the last time he saw Ambrose Bierce.

By this time Sterling had published two more volumes,
The House of Orchids in 1911 and *Beyond the Breakers*
in 1914. Until 1923 all his work came out under San
Francisco imprints, usually Robertson's. His reputation,
however, was now more than local, thanks to Bierce's
insistence that the *Cosmopolitan* (then pre-Hearst)
publish "Wine of Wizardry." The poem, with its
grandiloquent imagery, its glowing purple patches, created a minor sensation and insured an audience for better work, though Sterling's national fame never came
within miles of his unique celebrity in the city he loved
and serenaded.

He was called back from a second visit to New York,
where, says Upton Sinclair austerely, he was "reveling"
in Greenwich Village, by a shocking tragedy. Carrie
Sterling, no longer in her first youth, untrained in management of business affairs, had tried hard to establish
herself in a new and independent life. Her ventures
failed, her life grew disorientated. She had a natural turn
toward melancholy, and she changed gradually from the
radiant Juno of Carmel to a brooding woman her friends

no longer knew. One day in August of 1918 she asked a friend to have dinner with her. When Miss Stone arrived, she found the house in Piedmont swept and garnished, a note saying, "I am unhappy. Call the doctor," and her hostess, carefully dressed and exquisitely groomed, lying on her bed—a suicide by poison.

The shadow of that act never lifted altogether from her divorced husband's heart. He was not to blame, or not all to blame—her own temperament and the buffets of fortune had as much to do with Carrie Sterling's suicide as had the disillusionment of her marriage. But he mourned her more dead than he had regretted her alive. After that he carried with him always a little vial of the same swift poison Nora May French had taken. He told people about it, but ostensibly it was for some dreadful emergency — for being caught helpless in a burning building, for example. He dreaded pain as all supersensitives do; James Hopper well called him "compact of exquisite nerves, agonizingly sensitive." In general it was small things that he dreaded more than great, and more than once he wrote welcomes to death; yet he told Ethel Turner that often at night he lay awake and thought with panic horror of dying. It was as if his hedonism, his joy in living, floated on the surface of an unsuspected abyss of darkness.

Ever since the 1906 earthquake and fire (which he lamented missing, as one would grieve not to have been with one's beloved through some terrible accident), Sterling had occupied occasionally a cottage in Harry Laffler's "compound" on Telegraph Hill, built of wood salvaged from the disaster. Laffler had been editor of

the *Argonaut,* and was one of Sterling's earliest "dis-
coverers." It was to this cottage, still full of his books
and belongings years after he had left it forever, that he
went on his first return to San Francisco in 1915. Soon
he moved to the Bohemian Club, where an anonymous
friend paid for his room during all the rest of his life. He
had joined the club in 1903—Bierce, nervous over "the
danger of the drink habit," had finally given his blessing
to Sterling's membership, thinking it safe for "one of
your age and well grounded in sobriety." He had written two Grove plays for the club's famous "High Jinks";
the club's officials felt, and showed that they felt, that
he conferred a distinction on them by consenting to
live there; and very soon he occupied precisely the same
position in his new environment as he had occupied in
Carmel—he was the accepted and lauded "High Pan-
jandrum," to quote Bierce once more.

Irresponsible in some ways, Peter Pannish to the point
of irritation, George Sterling may have been; but he
was never lax in money matters. If a friend paid for his
lodging, if other friends saw to it that he was not in
want, he gave full value in return. A poem laid in a
friend's hand might not seem to some an exact equivalent
for a bill paid; but to Sterling and to the friend (and
there were dozens of such in San Francisco) the debt was
all in Sterling's favor. He was San Francisco's trouba-
dour, and San Francisco through its more cultured men
of wealth acknowledged and recompensed him for his
song. He gave freely of himself, his time, his talent—
had done so ever since he licked the rough edges off Jack
London's early work, or was left with *The Sea Wolf* to

edit and see through the press while its author wandered off to Japan. It was his custom to borrow money for the needs of other writers and Bohemians who did not have the advantage of wealthy relatives or acquaintances: then when the money was returned, as like as not Sterling would feel that some other necessitous fellow artist needed it far more than did the original prosperous lender, so off it would go on another charitable journey. And nine times out of ten, the man from whom it had first been borrowed, if he ever thought of it again, was quite content to play Maecenas at second hand.

After 1918, Sterling seldom went much farther from San Francisco than the Bohemian Grove, though he did visit Yosemite and write an ode to it which contains some of his most magnificent passages. He was the natural person to be asked to write an ode to the 1915 Panama-Pacific Exposition, and another poem, "The Evanescent City," in 1916 when the fairy buildings of the exposition ended their temporary existence. World War I shook him out of the last vestiges of his un-Marxian socialism. An English acquaintance paid him twenty-five dollars apiece for poems full of the most burning invective against the Germans, some of which were collected in 1917 as *The Binding of the Beast*. Herman Scheffauer, who had once been his friend, wrote him bitterly, but no echo of past affiliation shook Sterling's confidence in the righteousness of the war. With its end he returned to his ivory tower, from which came dramatic poems, "Lilith," "Rosamund," and "Truth." In 1923, for the first time, an Eastern publisher brought out his *Selected Poems*. But he felt the East increasingly as another world from his, and preferred, as life grew colder, to sun himself in his local fame.

As early as 1912, Sterling had felt that his power was waning. He feared that he might have to return to the drudgery of his uncle's office, and he cast about for ways to avoid it. As it turned out, he never did go back; but neither did he ever give up the hope of finding some short cut to prosperity without dependence on his friends and admirers. With remarkable naïveté, he, who labored so diligently over his poems, decided that any-one could dash off stories and sell them. In general (though such serious prose work as his book on Jeffers is well done) his prose was quite inferior to his verse. Later on, in the *Overland Monthly*, he had a regular column which at times reads like the very poorest of Bierce's uneven "Prattle." Even some of Bierce's vin-dictiveness creeps into it, as if by infection. He despised all magazine fiction, and never learned the lesson that no one can write successfully for an audience with which he is not in sympathy. He even tried to write motion-picture scripts, unbelievably amateur; from somewhere he had gained the idea that he could easily sell a script for $50,000. And once at least he tried his hand at writ-ing jazz songs!—he who, though not unmusical as some thought, had only what Homer Henley called "a shy, furtive sort of passion" for melody. He could not en-dure concerts, any more than he could endure seeing a play—his unacknowledged claustrophobia forbade; but he could and did lose himself for hours in listening to music. That music, however, was Beethoven, not jazz.

The only kind of stories for which George Sterling

showed the least flair were fantasies, and of these he wrote very few. Perhaps the best was one which he sold for a hundred dollars to Jack London, who in his last years ran a sort of fiction factory and bought plots everywhere. This, however, was not a bare plot but a completed story, and a little gem. It was too slight and too short for London, who was paid by the word, and he expanded and ruined it until it was a prolix manuscript for which he received ten times what he had paid for it. (This episode, incidentally, is given by Irving Stone as an example of London's generosity!) Then he forced Sterling to listen while he read aloud what he had made of the poet's delicate fancy, saying, "I want to show you how to write a saleable story." Perhaps it is no wonder that Sterling had contempt for the magazines and for magazine fiction.

For more than ten years Sterling remained the heart and ruler of San Francisco's Bohemia—and not of that rather meretricious Bohemia, as much businessman's as artist's, which made up the celebrated club where he lived, but of the true Bohemia of Telegraph Hill in predepression days. His slender, square-shouldered figure, which seemed taller than it was, his profile like Dante's, with the lock of gray hair falling over his high forehead, his gray "tragic and hopeless" eyes, his "wailing Yankee voice," were everywhere, the center of every gathering. He sat in Coppa's or Bigin's, drinking his vile mixture of whiskey and warm water and sugar; he walked the San Francisco streets at night with his "stealthy tread" and loved to vanish suddenly from his friends into the fog; he produced from stuffed pockets newly written poems which he gave away with the simplicity of a child. Until London's death he was the most constant intimate of the ranch at Glen Ellen, with its innocently rowdy parties where people laughed and sang and played practical jokes, and where Sterling could give vent to the sharp wit which is the obverse aspect of all the deeply melancholy.

People told anecdotes about him, some of them fictitious but many of them true—how he had hated his only long trip, to Hawaii after his marriage, and said that books were enough travel for him; how he was a bad winner and a bad loser at cards, and so cross after a game that London refused to let him play any more in his house; how he loathed horses, which he considered stupid and frightening animals; how proud he was of his prowess in outwalking and outswimming younger men (though the breast stroke was the only one he knew); how he adored San Francisco with a parochial fervor:

> "At the end of our streets is sunrise;
> At the end of our streets are spars;
> At the end of our streets is sunset;
> At the end of our streets are stars."

"An invincible, believing child, full of passion and kindness and pity," said James Rorty, remembering him from those years. "The faun-type of man," said Mary Austin. "Incurable romanticist and indefatigable Bohemian," said Carey McWilliams. They all meant the same thing.

He was not well in those years. He used to speak of a pain "like a pencil boring into him," which may have been gastric ulcers or something worse. He drank to relieve it, and drinking increased it. His mind dwelt more and more on death. He and London, as Irving Stone relates, "had always agreed they would never sit up with a corpse; when their work was done, their life spent, they would bow themselves out." He had written of his longing to

> "put by the guerdon of the breath
>   As one grown weary in a twilight land,"

he had written of "the eternal Peace," where "the happy dead hear not at all."

And there was more. Jeffers said truly that Sterling "refused the experience of old age." Almost literally, his life had been made up of "wine, woman, and song." Now he could not drink without pain and a hideous long recovery; he was eating the ashen bread which is the fare of all Don Juans grown old—the lovely young, on whom his heart was still set, now smiled and evaded him instead of turning in quick surrender, found him no longer irresistible, but slightly ludicrous or, what was worse, venerable; and though he was too generous a critic of his own as well as of others work, he was uneasily aware that his best poems were behind him, that he was becoming a tradition instead of a force. It needed only some relatively slight incident to precipitate the compound.

That incident was innocently supplied by H. L. Mencken. They were a queer pair of friends—the apostle of forthright common sense and no nonsense about it, and the peddler of what Mencken must have considered beautiful flapdoodle. Mencken understood Sterling so little that he thought he was happy! But he did recognize him as "one of the last of the free artists," and Sterling was the chief attraction which led him to San Francisco in the autumn of 1926.

Pieced together from gossip and contemporary report, this seems to be the approximate story:

Mencken was traveling west in the company of Joseph Hergesheimer. In Los Angeles Hergesheimer, who was a keen chess-player, became involved in a series of games with a young lady, who was beating him; piqued, he refused to leave until he had conquered. Meanwhile, this being the era of the "experiment noble in purpose," Sterling had been collecting from friends bottles of pre-prohibition liquor and the products of wangled doctors' prescriptions for Mencken's entertainment. Two bottles of whiskey had been given him—the only pay he would accept—for a "Saga of the Pony Express," forty quatrains long, contributed to a children's magazine edited by a friend. Sterling had been "on the wagon" for some time, and until the date first announced for Mencken's arrival he resisted touching one of these bottles. But there was a streak of real childishness in his nature, and he was petulantly jealous of Hergesheimer. He kept calling up Gouverneur Morris and complaining that Mencken was staying too long with Hergesheimer when he should be in San Francisco with him. He began consoling himself from the hospitable store he was saving to entertain his friend.

Still Mencken delayed. And one by one all the bottles were emptied. Sterling was left with no supply of liquor for Mencken, no money to buy more, and no way to secure more without the mortification of confessing to the friends who had provided the first lot. He sat in his room in the Bohemian Club, drank, and brooded. Soon he was very ill—worse than he had ever been before. He was obliged to take to his bed. His fellow club members, used to episodes of this kind and not realizing how much more serious this one was, looked in on him once in a while, but no one called a doctor.

Worse was to come. The club was planning a dinner for Mencken, at which of course Sterling was to be toastmaster. By the time Mencken really arrived, he was totally unable to serve. Mencken, with Morris and Thomas Beer, came to see him, and they were shocked by his appearance, though he rallied and they had an evening of lively talk. Mencken tried to persuade the club officials to send for a medical man: "That isn't a hangover," he said. "He's really ill." They laughed— they had seen George Sterling through too many sprees. But of course it was impossible for him, still bedridden, to preside at the dinner. By ill chance they substituted another writer whom Sterling, with his occasional rare hatreds, actively disliked. Sterling lay in his room, and in an agony of humiliation, imagined the scene downstairs.

The evening after the dinner, November 16, Mencken came to call, but found the door locked and the transom dark, so he went away. The next morning the room valet opened the door with his passkey. Sterling was apparently asleep, so he closed the door softly again. At noon he became alarmed and called the manager.

The room was full of charred bits of paper—poems and letters. A few scraps could be read:

"I walked with phantoms that ye knew not of,"

and

"Deeper into the darkness can I peer
Than most, yet find the darkness still beyond."

On the bed lay George Sterling, dead.

All those years Sterling had carried the little vial of the instantaneous poison from which Nora May French had died. When the time came to use it, he knew all would be over in one sharp moment. A well-authenticated story goes that a woman, in an impulse of mistaken helpfulness, had, unknown to him, decided to save him from himself when that time should come. She had taken the poison from the bottle, and filled it with baking soda. As soon as he tasted it, he knew the truth. But he had outwitted her—he had a further supply. The odor of bitter almonds filled the room.

The first reports were that George Sterling had died in his sleep from heart failure. An autopsy soon revealed the facts. To San Franciscans, it was as if Golden Gate Park had fallen into the sea.

Even without the autopsy, there would have been plenty of evidence of suicide — the torn and charred papers, the half hints dropped to friends, the visits, made a few days before, to Austin Lewis and Ethel Turner. To each of them he confided books and manuscripts, asking them, without explanation, to keep these for him. Both noted his illness and his depression. In

Mrs. Turner's hands he left the manuscript of his last
published writing—the preface to a new edition of
Bierce's In the Midst of Life—and it was she who later
delivered it to the publisher. She had typed it for him
in the first place; he asked her often to type his poems
as well, saying that he wanted to have her do it because
she too was a poet.

George Sterling would not have liked his funeral. It
should have been a simple ceremony on the wild sea
cliffs near Carmel, where Mary Austin had remarked
the "perfect suitability" between him and the environment. Instead, he who had been for so many years not
even an agnostic, but a pure pagan, was by the desire of
his six sisters given an Episcopalian funeral, as a compromise with the Catholicism he had abandoned. The felici-
tous phrases of the Episcopal burial service would have
moved him, and the thunderstorm that stopped just as
the funeral began—but not the dean's impassioned sermon, or the women (some of them quite unknown to
him) who wept and knelt and crossed themselves. The
Bohemian Club conducted the rites, with organ selec-
tions by Uda Waldrop and violin solos by Rudy Sieger.
To those who knew him, it did not seem to be George
Sterling lying there, with rouge on his white cheeks and
a spray of heliotrope in his clasped hands—Sterling, of
whom Jeffers had written: "The instinct of his life was
for action."

There had even been talk of his lying in state in the
City Hall, but this was vetoed by his family. Haig
Patigian took his death mask, with the intention of mak-
ing a bronze bust which he does not seem ever to have

made (though the mask has been cast in bronze, and is now owned by Rudolph Blaettler); and then Sterling was cremated. But his ashes were not scattered on Point Sur or Point Lobos as he would have wanted them to be, but placed conventionally in an Oakland columbarium.

The only memorial to Sterling in the city he so adored is a bench at the top of Russian Hill, near a city reservoir. The president of a water company years ago erected the bench and in 1928 a group of his friends set up a plaque to the poet's memory. There has been talk of renaming the plot of green around it, now Lombard Park, for Sterling, but this has never been done.

Nearly fifteen years have passed now since George Sterling died, and the world of poetry has long since passed him by. It is doubtful if today, even in San Francisco, he could find a publisher. As far back as 1916, Harriet Monroe, though granting that he was "capable of lyric rapture," in an article in *Poetry* censured his dealing in "things of tinsel and fustian, the frippery of a by-gone fashion." Louis Untermeyer has had little good to say of him: "Sterling's rhetoric is high-pitched, strepitant, unrestrained . . . flamboyant . . . full of oratorical trumpets . . . brassy declamations . . . glittering and archaic vocabulary . . . clouds of polysyllabic adjectives . . . a mixture of familiar cadence and cliché." Carey McWilliams noted how "his poetry and character came in time to reveal the strain of an insupportable exertion after the elusive phrase, the delectable experience." R. L. Burgess deprecated his "grandiose booming style with a touch of rococo."

And Miss Monroe again, in an obituary notice in *Poetry,* said justly that he was "on too facile terms . . . with his muse and with life in general; he never quite got the best out of either."

Yet when all this is granted, there remains a poet. Not a poet of our era, perhaps, but equally perhaps one who, when properly pruned and culled, may have something to say to immortality. He told young Audrey Wurdemann in 1926 that he wished he could write "a perfect poem about a single leaf of a tree." He never did even that. But there are lyrics and sonnets that cannot be forgotten; there are memorable lines: "the seaward print of unreturning feet"; "the star-usurping battlements of night";

> "Seas that flash on alien eyes
> The riven sunlight of Altair";

and that final tribute of all tributes to Beauty:

> "We know that we shall seek her till we die,
> And find her not at all, the fair and far."

There are many, many others. Each will select his own.

For a while, after George Sterling's death, a story spread that he who had been so long a legend was now a phantom—that his wraith had been seen haunting the third-floor corridor of the Bohemian Club. The tale died as such tales do; no reputable psychic investigator has yet reported seeing Sterling's veritable ghost! But in another sense, he does indeed haunt the Bohemian Club. He haunts San Francisco. He haunts the hearts of his friends.